AN UNCHARTED DESERT ISLE

Rick Fernandez

authorHOUSE®

AuthorHouse™
1663 Liberty Drive
Bloomington, IN 47403
www.authorhouse.com
Phone: 1-800-839-8640

First published by AuthorHouse 11/23/2009

ISBN: 978-1-4343-3738-2 (sc)
ISBN: 978-1-4343-6032-8 (hc)

Library of Congress Control Number: 2007907025

Printed in the United States of America
Bloomington, Indiana

This book is printed on acid-free paper.

In the fall of 1971, I suffered a massive head injury, and contrary to what most would believe, it has turned out to be one of the best events in my life. Anything that happens in your life can be turned into whatever you want it to be. Thinking that my experiences just might be beneficial to others, I thought I had better put my thoughts to print before they faded away. I wrote this book in about three and a half years. It took me close to a year and a half to collect all the notes that I needed to fill the pages, and it took me two more years to organize and have it typed. I was working two separate jobs (forty-five hours a week) at the time, but even that did not stop me from sending out the message that was burning a hole in my brain.

After I had finished putting my thoughts on paper, it took me a few more years before I found a publisher who would put me into print. Actually, I did not have this book published as books normally get published. I self-published the book, and I'm glad I went that route. It cost me a bit more than it would have if I had gone the conventional way, but it was a lot quicker.

After I had sent the completed manuscript to the publisher, who would put my work into print, he suggested I have a person look it over and make some suggestions in places where my writing could be better understood. I followed his advice, and I am glad I did. With my injury, I had made several repetitions that I was unaware that I had made. There were quite a few other locations in the writing that I needed to clarify. However, as I reviewed this person's suggestions more and more, I determined that if I cleaned it up too much, the reader wouldn't grasp the authenticity of the book.

I changed the book in places where it simply would not be understood by the casual reader, if I had let it stand as is. But, in other places where an error was made, and the average reader could understand my intent, I left it as is. I want the reader to understand, a head injury doesn't necessarily have to stop a person. For me, it opened many doors.

I dedicate this book to my mother, Nati, and to my father, Al
Without whose help, love and understanding, I could have
done nothing.

Abelardo Fernandez
Nov. 6, 1913 - May 21, 2001

Surley goodness and mercy

shall follow me all the days

of my life, and I will dwell

in the house of the Lord

forever.

Psalm 23:6

THIS IS MY FATHER A FEW MONTHS
BEFORE WWII BROKE OUT. HE WAS
AN ENLISTED MAN IN THE COAST
GUARD.

PRIVATE 1ST CLASS
LADY KILLER, U.S.
ARMY

(the only "military action"
this guy ever saw)

I was watching a *Gilligan's Island* rerun the other day, and I was amazed at how much the cruise situation mirrors my own. In 1971, at age eighteen, I suffered a head injury, as a result of an equally serious car accident. After the collision, I remained in a coma for the following sixty-seven days. In various ways, my rehabilitation replicated a good number of the antics seen on that television series.

The evening of my fateful venture through the streets of East Los Angeles can be analogized to that fateful three-hour tour taken aboard the *Minnow*. Just as there were seven persons on that deserted island, with seven distinct personalities, I too had to deal with a myriad of different persons and services to bring me this far. Everyone on the island was looking out for one another. It seemed as if everyone in the United States was looking out for me.

It seems as if my disability never stops giving back to me. Disability begs to be used. I thank my lucky stars that I was not too disabled to use it. Learning the use of others and things in a proficient manner was key.

Just as Ginger had aspirations to become a great star, I had similar longings to discover what I was searching for. It seemed as if every dire situation the castaways confronted was alleviated by a prop found on that deserted isle. The same was and is still true with me. I discovered a multitude of methods to face my disabilities head on.

It was amazing. As in the *Gilligan's Island* series, methods to overcome each situation that presented itself fell into my lap. With this severe head injury would come props that would surface, seemingly out of nowhere. Disability brought out a part of me I never knew existed until I was forced to use it.

The crew and passengers aboard the *Minnow* were dressed similar to the way they were on the mainland. Their clothes never wore out. I relate that to all the services and money I received; they were also long lasting. It is fairly remarkable. I can mirror the years prior to my accident to that three-hour cruise, and I can analogize my disability to life on that no-man's land.

Over the years, this head injury has rendered me with an enthralling experience. It has been the time in my life in which I have felt most in control. In that time, I made a grand 180-degree turnaround back to the person I was before my accident—however, with a lot of changes for the better.

Before my accident, my only thoughts of the disabled were those of unwarranted fear. It is probably not too much unlike you if you are not a disabled person.

Awkwardly enough, I found much good in disability. In fact, I found more good with it than I found without it. Perhaps, that is because I was not looking for anything good before my accident. There is virtually no way to lose when you have a positive thought pattern throughout your disability. You get back as much as you put in to it.

Even the little experience I had prior to my accident paid off a fairly large dividend throughout my rehabilitation period. With the onset of my disability, I have found myself. I have found who I truly am. This injury has been my saving grace.

I am much more than I ever thought. I have learned how to use people, though not in the negative way that it sounds. Everyone wins when a person rehabilitates to their fullest extent. I manipulated my disability to its best end. In fact, it has been an enjoyable experience.

I've had to give up a lot through this rehabilitation. But if I had to, I sense I would be able to give up more. The trick was to learn what was expendable. I feel, at this point, better than I ever have.

Disability is neither an end in itself nor is it rehabilitation. They are both a process.

To me, brain damage has been a wonderful thing. It taught me so much more than if I would have never acquired this disability. My disability separated me from many of the factors that would have brought me down. Ironically, disability has introduced me to the real me. I was more disabled before my head injury. Let me repeat that. I was more disabled before my head injury. Disability gave me the elusive goal of making myself whole once more. It is fun and rewarding to thwart something as powerful as a severe head injury.

There is good for everyone through proper rehabilitations. I don't waste time in grief. What's gone is gone. I work on things that I find productive. In the same vein, this country should spend more time and money rearing its children rather than squandering it on relics of the past. This head injury has rendered the ability to turn, what most people would seem to feel as a misfortune, into something that can eventually work in one's favor.

I could have driven to my doctor's office, but to reduce pollution, save fuel and get some exercise, I decided I would walk the mile-long distance. I simply needed her to clarify a prescription. I walked a mile or so to her office, and on the way back, the urgent need to urinate grew and grew.

Having had a bladder infection when I was released from the hospital years ago, and knowing that if I didn't relieve myself in a hurry, I realized I could easily incur another infection. While attending, and also graduating from, universities about fifteen years ago, I had to make sure to tell the instructor of each class, longer than one and half hours, of my problem. My bladder is very small, and having to rise during the middle of any class to use the restroom was a common thing.

In more than thirty years of disability, I have witnessed scores of other disabled persons, and I have not seen any who have tried as hard to rehabilitate as me. If I were to have an acquaintance or loved one with a disability, I only wish they would try as hard as I have to rehabilitate as well. But, unfortunately, the majority of other people I have met with head injuries did not put forth half the effort I did.

I had a choice to make that day. I could have held it and continued to walk that half-mile distance to my apartment, I could have urinated on my pants and continued walking, or I could have made the choice I did. What would you have done?

The lady who stopped at the curbside to gawk at me was breaking the law. The bus stop was an equal distance from either the traffic signal in back of her or the one in front. She had no business stopping where she did.

It cost money to have me arrested, booked, and thrown in jail. Who do you think pays for all this? When I went to court, I got the name of this person, and in a future book I will publicize her name so you can thank her for doing her civic duty.

The day I was arrested, I was wearing my "Puerto Rico … me encanta" T-shirt, and it just so happened that the officer who arrested me was also a Puerto Rican. When he told me, it instantly brought back an old saying that my mother has always used: "Puerto Riquenos son como aros blanco … son donde queran." "Puerto Ricans are like white rice … they're everywhere." This simply states the availability of "ocean tigers" and white rice. I could see in his face, it strained him to have to bust me. But, at the time, there were a few other officers there, so off I went. Yes. There were a couple motorcycle cops and a paddy wagon present to ensure my capture. Ironically, on the way to the station, we talked about the island like old buddies. I had vacationed there in 1976, and I told him if I would have been born there, I never would have left—it is an incredibly beautiful place. When we got to the station, he merely opened the back door and stepped back. He did not place his hand on my head, as you see cops do for other criminals, as they rise from the back seat of the black-and-white. I could sense, by the look on his face and the vibes he was sending, this was something he did not want to do.

During my interrogation, at the Sunnyvale station, I was not hostile, angry, or any other emotional state that would be out of the norm. They had me strip down to my birthday suit and handed me what looked like something a clown would wear—only it was solid green. I could sense that they wanted to get me for something. The young lady who was asking me questions asked me if I liked little boys, who was my girlfriend, when was my last sexual experience, and other questions in that genre. For an instant, it was as if she questioned my virility.

You can imagine how I felt when first talking to this young, very attractive, plain-clothed female officer. She told me that I had been seen masturbating, and I had been turning to face the school while I did this. After the first moment of anger blew away, I realized what she was doing. What she wanted was for me to blow my cool, but I remained collected.

The young lady asked me, "What kind of girls do you like?"

Very diplomatically, I said, "A pretty young lady like you would do just fine."

The reason I did not tell the truth about simply relieving myself was simple fear and shame. The female detective even offered to let me slide, momentarily, but I refused to admit guilt. Very acceptingly, she told me it would merely be like a traffic ticket offense if I would simply admit to it.

What now crosses my mind is that *Seinfeld* comedy program that airs daily on reruns. If you have not seen the episode, it is where Jerry is in an underground parking facility and desperately needs to take a leak. He can't find the car he came in, and after he and the other cast members of the show did much searching, he went and relieved himself in a corner of the lot. Unfortunately for him, the guard was within eyeshot of him and placed him in custody. It was a very funny show—quite unlike mine.

After about thirty-five hours at the Sunnyvale jail, the young female police officer once again asked me to admit guilt; however, wanting to appear as if I were tough, I stupidly responded "No." She quickly left my cell, and I only had to wait a few minutes before I was transported in a patrol car to the Santa Clara County jail. There were twelve other gentlemen in my cell at the Santa Clara County station. This was quite unlike the clean, empty cell I was placed in at Sunnyvale. The cell was very small, with two benches facing each other and a toilet with a three-foot-high separation from the rest of the cell for privacy. The toilet, which I only used a couple times to take a leak, was so filthy I wouldn't let my dog sit on that germ-ridden spot designed to relieve oneself.

I would have to assume that I was as clean as a whistle, so, while at the Sunnyvale station, the female cop asked me if she could go to my apartment for a simple inspection. This was before I was taken to the Santa Clara jail. She told me, "I'm going to take another police officer with me," which I told her was fine with me. They took the key from my property and went to inspect it.

I quickly rummaged through my mind and realized my spotless apartment would not turn up anything incriminating. So I told her, "Sure, go ahead." However, I told her that I have one photo of a beautiful young woman at the top of my calendar, in a bathing suit, that would turn a couple heads.

With a serious look on her face, she retorted, "That's all right, I have a couple of little brothers also."

I was upbeat the entire time I was in custody. This was even when I was in that filthy holding cell at the Santa Clara jail. The majority were sleeping it off. I just kept my mouth shut, shut my eyes for a while, and spoke very little to my fellow residents. I was in the drunk tank, and persons would come and leave once their five hours were up. This was not done by the clock—I spent six and a half hours in that small room separated from freedom by a large glass door—not bars.

After I was released, I had to call a cab for a ride home. The ride cost me around twenty-six dollars. I paid the woman driver, gave her a few extra bucks, and had her drop me off as close to my apartment door as she could. I was still dressed in my clown suit, and I did not want anyone at the complex to see me. The Sunnyvale jail kept my clothes to have them inspected at the lab.

When I entered the apartment, it appeared as if a tornado had hit it. My apartment was trashed, and they didn't even bother to clean it up. However, I knew they had a job to do. I cleaned up the apartment, which took close to an hour and then jumped into the shower.

My father passed away a couple of years ago, and I'm very happy that he did not have to witness any of this nonsense. I know it would have hurt him more than it was an inconvenience for me. He would not be able to handle the shame and exasperation this would incur. My mother is living down south, and I do not believe I have to worry about her getting wind of this.

I worked at a convalescent hospital as a nurse's aide, after graduating from two universities, earning a little more than minimum wage. I changed soiled diapers, stripped urine-soaked beds, I bathed, dressed, fed, and, most importantly, I socialized with the frailest patients. I once had a very weak and mentally incoherent lady spit in my face as I was turning her to avoid her getting a bed sore, but I realized she didn't know what she was doing. I even had an elderly stroke victim put all his force, on the side that was not weakened by the stroke, as I tried to transfer him to his bed, and he punched me right in the nose. I was holding him in midair, I did all I could to place him softly on his bed, and I did a very good job. I have close to eleven years working with Senior citizens, as well as disabled persons, on top of hundreds of volunteer hours before I began working, and I hope to continue in this field.

I had a bladder infection while I was in the hospital as a patient in 1971–1972, and I learned that that is not a fun thing to have. You incur bladder infections by failing to relieve yourself as need be, and after you are blessed with this little sickness, it burns like hell whenever you urinate. Realizing it was about a half hour before I'd reach my apartment, I tried to be as discrete as possible; however, that bus stop bench was not as shielding as I thought it would be. I now recall the lady passing by the bench in a car, very slowly. I had thought that no one could see me behind the bench. Apparently, she thought it morally correct to have me thrown in the slammer.

It was a new experience for me, but, as things happen, eventually everything turned out all right for me. We'll see what happened when I faced the judge. Now that I think about it, I should have simply admitted guilt, accepted the ticket, and went on my way, as that young, very pretty officer instructed me to. Live and learn!

It is now a couple months since those ominous days I was incarcerated, and a most fitting analogy came to mind. Imagine yourself at a meeting with very important persons from your business in attendance. You are having lunch at this meeting, and everything seems to be going fine. You are invited to eat with these persons because they notice what a positive difference you have been making in the company. You are in line for a big promotion. However, something you ate, earlier in the day, is not sitting well in your stomach; you then, uncontrollably, expel a large quantity of gas from your large intestine. Fortunately for you, it cannot be traced. However, no one can dispute the ominous sound or smell. You are seated at a large circular table. Do you raise your hand and say, "That was me?" Better yet, let's have all you persons out there, who have ever urinated in a public pool, where persons are in direct contact and some accidently swallow the liquid they are in, also spend a few days in jail. This is the only way we can curtail this lawless behavior.

Shortly after my release, I was required to appear in court for a hearing. I remained all morning in court, that day, for the judge to listen to my plea. I was the last person called, or one of the last, to be read the charges against me. I was overdressed for the event. The majority of other "criminals," about ten or fifteen, came in street clothes. I stood there in my shirt and tie, had the judge look me over, and then read the charge.

Now that I reflect on it, I'm very glad that the majority of other persons had already left when I was read the charge. Since the bus stop bench was about fifty yards from the school (the children were all in class, and there was no one out in the field), and I was in front of the bench, with the back of the bench reaching above my waistline. I was facing the street, and I felt fairly confident the judge would not waste his time with this nonsense.

However, I was aghast when the judge looked at the sheet of paper before him, and with a stone face said I was seen facing the schoolyard, masturbating. I bit my tongue. I almost told that judge, in a knee-jerk reaction, where he could stick that piece of paper. But, almost as quickly as that reaction came to me, I realized what was happening. The court had to drum it up; otherwise, it would be felt as such a waste of time, money, and effort of all the people concerned. In hindsight, I don't blame the court, jail, or cop that busted me.

Once I knew what I was being charged with, I felt I needed some people behind me. What follows are three letters from persons who know me and were willing to write these letters, which will hopefully keep me from anymore time behind bars.

The first of these letters was written by my landlords of the apartments where I have lived for the past eight plus years. They have only been managing the apartments for close to a year, but I have a good rapport with them, as I did my previous managers.

I asked my doctor if she would write the second letter, and she was nice enough to comply.

The third letter was written by a cop who I have known for all of his life. Dave happens to be my younger cousin, who has futilely tried to lead me away from this life of crime. However, I tried to explain to him, I had no control over this. It was, as appeared in a previous Superbowl, merely a costume malfunction.

Andrew and Genell Basurto:

Christine Weigen:

David Santiago:

I wanted to begin with this little event because it somewhat displays how I've handled other more consequential events in my life. Over the years, I've had to let a lot, simply roll off my chin.

November 23, 2003

To Whom It May Concern:
We are writing this letter on the behalf of Richard Fernandez.
We are Andrew and Genell Basurto, resident managers for Sara vale Apartments, 936 Azure St., Sunnyvale Calif.
We have known Richard Fernandez as a resident of Sara Vale apartment complex for one year.
In that time, Richard has never shown any inappropriate behavior, anger or disregard for others. He is always polite, considerate and well mannered. Richard gets along well with the other residents of this apartment complex.
Richard is also very responsible about paying his rent on time and has never been late. It is obviously to see he has a high regard for his well being since he is always groomed and dressed so well. Richard can often be seen walking around the neighborhood; he does this to keep himself fit.
We would do well to have more tenants like Richard Fernandez living at this complex.

Thank you for your time,
Andrew and Genell Basurto

Planned Parenthood
Mar Monte

604 East Evelyn
Sunnyvale, CA 94086
408.739.5151
408.992.0627 fax

Nov 18, 03

To whom It May Concern,

Re Richard Fernandez DOB 10-17-52

I have been Richard's physician since 8/27/98 and provided medical care for him on a regular basis.

Richard has requested that I write a letter in his behalf for the purpose of using it in his defense in a Court room setting.

During the numerous visits at our clinic, Richard has always been pleasant, cooperative and very conscientious with regard to his health care needs. He has never demonstrated any inappropriate behavior, or language. He has always gotten along well with our staff and it has been a pleasure to provide medical care for Richard.

I hope this is of help.

Sincerely

Christine Weigen M.D.

CHRISTINE WEIGEN, M.D.
6__ E. EVELYN AVE.
SUNNYVALE, CA. 94086
PH.#(408) 739-5151
FAX #(408) 992-0627

To whom this may concern :   12/15/03

Subject: Richard Fernandez   From: David Santiago, Jr.

                                              Occupation: Police Officer

I am aware of Ricks' recent arrest for Indecent Exposure and would like to comment on his character and behavior. Since his head injury as a teen, he has been constantly rehabilitating and attempting to help others with his several books on the subject. He contributes his recovery, in large part, to maintaining optimum health, mentally and physically. He drinks gallons of water every day and has tried to counsel me on the values of this routine. He also walks almost everywhere he goes, causing I'm sure, a need to relieve himself (bladder) often. I have no doubt that, although he was too embarrassed to admit it, he was just trying do this when he was accused of the crime.

The day he was released from county jail he called me and I went to his apartment. He said that the police searched his residence but found nothing that would lead one to believe he was connected in any way to pornography or anything involving children. In my business I am aware that most pedophiles will use the internet to enhance their efforts, so I asked Rick to help his cause by allowing me to access his computer files and e-mails. He agreed without hesitation and gave me his password. I can honestly say that I found not a shred of evidence that had anything to do with even the slightest of improprieties. Several months worth of e-mails were still listed, and I checked his old mail as well as computer trash bin.

The absence of any pornographic materials in his apartment, as well as my knowledge of his personal habits and character, lead me to say with confidence that Rick is merely a victim of his own handicap, and not a sexual predator as the witness, I'm sure, mistakenly believes.

I have been a police officer in Santa Clara County for 23 years and can be reached at (209) 404-8118 if needed.

Sincerely,

David Santiago, Jr.

Preface

I had finished writing this book. I wrote this explanation for a judge I will face, in short order. This has simply been one more experience that puts another feather in my cap.

Your Honor,

*   First of all, I'm very sorry for any inconvenience this may have caused anyone.

*   In 1971, at age eighteen, I was going nowhere fast.

*   I had my parents buy me a three wheel, former mail truck, so that I could attend a junior college in the area.

*   Having no direction at all, I ended up wrecking that small car, but putting my life in a direction for the better.

*   I remained in a coma for nine and a half weeks (sixty-seven days), following being hit by a drunk driver.

*   However tragic this may sound, it was one of the best things to have ever happened to me.

*   To rehabilitate most efficiently, I had to make sure my health was in top form. I use various methods to acquire this. And drinking at least eight glasses of water daily has

been a key ingredient to my very good health. I start each morning by drinking two medium-sized glasses of water, washing up, and then drinking two tall mugs of hot black coffee.

*

With my limited memory, it took me nine years to obtain my bachelor of arts degree and then my certificate in gerontology. After I graduated, as well as when I was a student, I had compiled hundreds of hours of volunteer work in my field. The number of days I missed, in that entire ten or so years, can be counted on one hand.

*

Over the years, the government has spent more than one and half million dollars, and that is *not* counting the numerous hours I spent in front of rehabilitation as well as academic counselors and job coaches, among others, on the road to my rehabilitation. I am currently looking for work, after I have compiled more than eleven years of paid work, since my graduation.

*

Over the last few years, I have written a very informative book on just how I managed to rehabilitate from such a striking disability.

*

I pay my bills promptly and completely from my unemployment/disability checks I receive each month.

*

In the book that I have written, which has yet to be published, I will have to stress this one drawback that drinking so much water can have.

*

Back in 1978, when I was in junior college, in one of my human behavior classes, the instructor had everyone in class perform a highly abnormal act. After this was done, we were supposed to write a two-page paper on how everyone around you reacted. I was very reluctant, but while shopping one day in the market, instead of pulling items off the shelf, I did my shopping from other people's carts. When I was reported to the management from an old lady, I stopped. I wrote a fairly good report after that. One of my fellow students strolled into class one day naked as a jaybird. He was wearing nothing but a paper bag over his head. There were holes in the paper bag for his eyes. When he reached the front of the class, he pulled the bag up so the teacher could see his face. This was the time when streaking was in vogue.

Acknowledgment

A special thank you goes out to Anne. Her friendship and tireless assistance were important factors in the production of this writing.

1

I started my rehabilitation on a positive note. I rarely, if ever, look at myself in negative terms. This is very strange, for I used to view, probably like many of you, the disabled as if they were creatures from another planet.

However, rehabilitation has been the only recreation that I have needed during this long trek. Everything that I do revolves around my disability. It has been this way since the start of my rehabilitation, and I no longer notice it. I have found it to be like hitting a home run, getting a hole in one, shooting and making a three-pointer, or any similar sports analogy. You don't stop after you make your first touchdown; you play until the time expires. The time hasn't run out yet, and I am still enjoying the game.

Rehabilitation, for me, has been a game that I never lose. There is very little risk involved, and I have numerous people on my side.

Disability is not something that I'm ashamed of or wish would go away. It's just there, the same as having five fingers on each hand. I'm not continuously pouting about not having six fingers on each hand. I merely work with what I have. I realize that that's easy to say, merely for the fact that most people do not have six fingers to begin with. It would be a waste of time brooding about not having six digits. Instead of wasting all that time, I have spent it learning all the other things that I can do with just five fingers.

I realize now how important it was for me to learn the difference between work and play. When I was first released from the hospital back in the spring of 1972, I couldn't keep my mind on anything for longer than a couple of minutes. My father purchased a number of board games for us to play. These were all right for a while, but I quickly learned how damaged my brain was.

To my benefit, I don't get too caught up in extraneous events. I give each outside activity the attention it deserves. At the beginning of my rehabilitation, I quickly became interested in table games because they were quick, and I could win at them. The first couple of years, I could not watch a baseball game because I would quickly lose interest. However, by the third year, the 1975 season, I could watch all nine innings and still ask for more.

Games, sports, and entertainment all have their place. In fact, baseball let me know that I could keep my interest on one thing for an extended period of time. I recall the good feeling it gave me after two plus hours of keeping my attention riveted on one thing. I realized that I could build from there.

The trick is to make it an enjoyable process. I didn't let things that didn't promote my rehabilitation get in the way. Even with all that I have accomplished, I am eager for the next challenge. It is enjoyable, but that is only because I remain in the game. I would have nothing without this head injury, much less the sense of self I now possess.

Presently, I have an A.A., B.A., a certificate in gerontology, am a certified nurse's assistant, have an activity director certificate, have several years of work experience, and a plethora of life experience. However, I am still on the treadmill, and I like it.

Over the years, I have had a few people who have known me for quite a while tell me that they didn't know that I was disabled until after I told them. At times, it felt like someone else was doing all these things that I have done. Nothing in my history would signify what I have produced.

What has allowed me to accomplish all that I have over the years is the tremendous feeling of self. This is not an outward façade (if it were, it would only be destructive), but, rather, there is a man inside who never stops cheering. Before the accident, I didn't have much pride. However, having survived something as traumatic as a head injury has given me much inner pride.

I had never had this feeling prior to the accident. I always felt as if I was lacking in some respect or another. It has been a complete turnaround, and I took very little risk in the process. There's no other way to go but up. What has provided this sense of self is the same drive that kept me alive while in the coma. From the day I began my rehabilitation, I felt as if this was something I could do. You could say that what this injury has done was to instill confidence in me.

While writing this book, I sat in northern California, and my parents lived in a very comfortable retirement home only a few blocks away. However, even though my folks were quite content with the old folk's home they had resided in for the past two years, my sister yanked their cords and had them move close to her. My father was eighty-seven years old, and my mother was close to eighty. Yes, even though I felt very comfortable with my aging parents nearby if they needed my emotional support in any way, I felt I could replace my continual visits by a couple of phone calls every week.

It was a very thin line. I could have gone either way. I can only speculate as to why things turned out so well. I would have to guess that this is why I'm writing this book. As I write, I peel off layer after layer of my disability. Don't get me wrong. I suffered a multitude of setbacks—any few of which would overwhelm most people. It could have done the same to me, but, with the assistance of my brain damage, I could not retain much in my head to worry about it.

Being disabled has not been disabling. To the contrary, it has opened many doors. It would have been to my detriment had I allowed it to consume me. Instead, I simply made use of what was at my disposal, which included a great many things. Luckily, I used these things judiciously, so as not to burn myself out.

I never had a cushion before, and this disability provided just that. The only way you can fall on your face with an injury such as this is to give up. Giving up was in my nature before I received this injury. I used to be an expert at throwing in the towel. I never found gratification in the process of climbing a steep hill or meeting a great challenge.

Giving up was never in the cards. I simply reached for the stars and pulled down whatever I could. Each success built on the next. There were not many failures, simply because when you begin from the ground up, everything is an accomplishment. So, if you fail at an attempt, you don't have very far to fall.

I don't know what I would have done without this head injury. It provided a necessary challenge in my life. It was a win–win situation for me. Even with a serious head injury, as long as I steered myself in the proper direction, I was a winner.

I was such a darn flake that I doubt very seriously that I would be alive if not for the accident. I, no doubt, would have fallen through the cracks of this society and would have never taken advantage of all the things that were at my disposal. If I had continued to live the way I had been living prior to this accident, I would be considerably less than I am now, having endured the endless challenges of my disability.

Just as there are two sides to a coin, there is a good side to disability. It has given me no setbacks that I couldn't overcome or simply avoid. Maybe we're going about this the wrong way. There was a time in this country that if you were born a certain ethnic race, your whole life was scripted beforehand. Now, on the other hand, there are all kinds of services and programs that can help you dig yourself out of the rut you are in. Disability is what got me moving in a positive direction. I have found it easier to accomplish things by realizing the hardships that I have already been through.

A person doesn't know how much he has until things start getting taken away. I realize that this might sound trite, but there's so much truth in this statement. Before the accident, I had a very poor self-image. If someone was to have told me back then that I would have survived an accident of the magnitude of the one that I have survived, I would not have believed him. I would probably have asked him if I could have a little of whatever it was that he was smoking. This is even without taking into account all the rehabilitation that I have plowed through.

What truly made it not difficult was that after my head injury, I could not remember how much I had before. I essentially began at square one. I have allowed my deficits to work in my best interest. All I had to do was accept what was and work from there. I started over. One could say that I was given a second chance. I didn't squander it. I turned my life around for the better.

In many ways, I turned my disability into an asset. Take, for instance, this book. Would anyone be reading this if I were just an ordinary writer, discussing a head injury from the point of view of a person who has never suffered one?

I believe the biggest asset to my condition was my refusal to look at the whole picture. I simply took one bite at a time. I realize this sounds as though it is very unbelievable, but disability is what you make it.

It is the attitude that one takes toward his condition that determines what he will or will not be able to accomplish. My acceptance of the nature of my condition, along with my continual work to minimize the effects of it, worked very well for me. It's like anything else—work, education, relationships, and essentially everything else in life. It's what is put into it that determines the outcome.

I accept my disability with open arms ... yet, I fought it tooth and nail from the beginning. I don't remember ever feeling sorry for myself. I did not do this consciously. I just never took the time to sit down and lament my circumstances. Disability is like a two-headed beast. To get anywhere, I had to turn a blind eye toward all my deficiencies and yet simultaneously fight diligently to overcome them.

My inabilities to do this, that, or the other never clouded my thinking. I worked with my shortcomings to lessen them. If others want to feel sorry for me, so be it. However, if I ever felt downtrodden, it would kill my spirit. With all the help I acquired from outside sources, the battle was considerably less of a strain. If I hadn't gotten all of the help that I received, I would have given up the struggle at the very beginning.

I simply had to sidestep a lot of the crap that tends to stifle all the normal folks out there. I work from where I am at. I don't worry as much about the outcome as I do about the process. It pumps me up to realize how many deficiencies I have and how, despite them, I have managed to keep myself in the game.

My brain has failed, and it has failed me in so many circumstances that it would have been easy to give up on myself. In fact, it would have been a hell of a lot easier to just throw my hands in the air.

I just let things happen as they would. I have failed in so many attempts that the failures don't even register with me anymore. I don't let it concern me. There is just so much I can't do, as opposed to someone playing with a full deck, that it just would have been one more added handicap to worry about it.

I couldn't have done it better if I had planned it. I am able to explore my achievements, and at the same time, I have a safety net underneath me at all times. It is unlike when I was fresh out of high school, when no slack was allowed me. As a result of my disabled condition I was, and am, given all the room I need. I put a total of nine hard years into higher education. If I had needed anymore time and money, then I am sure that it would have been granted to me.

With this assurance beneath me, I didn't have that stress that I am sure gnaws at other students. How would you like to be able to study whatever you want and have someone else pay for it? How would you like it if you didn't have to worry about your GPA and were saluted for the mere effort you put forth? All you have to do is acquire a severe head injury.

Sure, a severe head injury is one of the worst afflictions that can be laid on your doorstep. However, there are a multitude of good things that come your way because you are disabled. A lot of these things are tangible, and just as many more are intangible.

I don't ever recall singing the blues concerning my plight. That is, unless I had contrived this song and dance to reach my desired end. I never had so much attention and positive strokes delivered until I acquired this injury. I'm so glad that I used my disability and not vice versa. If one looks at disability in a positive format, then things turn out for the best. Concern and help are received from everyone. Money and services are provided and so forth.

I do things for my future, but I don't neglect to also work for today. It's easy to follow a procedure. However, it's a little more difficult to begin that procedure.

To start such a program as this, one first must be aware that one exists. Then, he must realize that he possesses all of the necessary amenities to make it work. Next, he has to have the drive to follow through and must surround himself with the right people. The fact that I had so many amenities at my disposal was the coup de grace. All these services, money, and people were essential.

To put that first foot forward, in relation to my rehabilitation, was the hardest part of this journey. However, it was much less difficult, I imagine, than doing nothing and living with the consequences. I chose to dive right into rehabilitation with both feet. I unconsciously realized that this way I wouldn't have to blame a half-assed effort if I landed on my face.

I am very grateful that I had a love life, although brief, before my head injury. I can speculate what it will be like when I throw my hat back in the ring again. After the first initial clumsiness, it will be a piece of cake. All of my past girlfriends, throughout high school and afterward, provided me with memories I can build on as well as cautions that I should take.

If I never had my past experiences with girls, I'd be in bad shape. No one can ever say to me, "You don't even know what it tastes like." Fortunately, I have literally vaulted this hurdle. All the present-day divorces—although caused by a variety of reasons, one of the biggest being our growing Senior populace—assures me that I didn't miss much.

The subject of women, if I let it, still tugs at my heart, but that's no big problem. In fact, it's gratifying reassurance. I'm every bit the man that the preinjury Rick was. In fact, I'm much more a man, for the mere fact that I'm much more knowledgeable. I'm a man, and still I rise to the occasion as any other man would under similar circumstances. However, I'm smart enough to realize that I'd only be assaulting myself if I let the horse get out of the barn, until I suck all the juice out of this disability.

I understand that I'm the same old guy I was before my injury, only a hell of a lot more knowledgeable. There is power in knowledge.

I'm not speaking primarily about the facts found in books. However, true life experience has much, if not greater, significance. I shudder at the thought of never having had the opportunity to acquire this injury when I did. If I were still alive, I'd be a shadow of what I am at this point. I would never trade places with the uninjured Rick. That guy didn't have anything in comparison to what this guy has.

I'm now the guy that I've always, in the back of my mind, dreamt that I could be. Everything has since fallen into place. Brain damage is a terrible thing to waste—you can quote me. The terms handicap, disability, and crippled have, in the past, always seemed so ominous. However, it was only after I had suffered these setbacks that I pushed forward.

I realize this sounds simplistic, but it's all in the way you look at it. I accept my head injury as a part of me. However, I never could have done more than I have done without this injury. I would never have known all that I have inside of me with this injury. Essentially, a little had to be taken away, so I was able to reap much more.

All clouds have a silver lining. If one needs proof of the validity of that statement, all he has to do is look in my direction. It was important for me never to waste too much time in sorrow. That would only bring me down lower, and grief doesn't produce anything positive.

My lack of effort before my head injury was, I can testify to that at this point, the main ingredient to my lackluster past. However, this injury has opened up a whole new part of me that I have henceforth explored for all that it is worth and with little fear of failure.

Embarrassment was a big part of my former lack of effort. I lacked drive because making a fool of oneself, I felt, went hand in hand with sticking your neck out. Disability was an easy way for me to try my hardest, with little concern about failure. With my condition, I only failed if I didn't make the attempt. Before my injury, I always feared getting a little egg on my face.

Before my accident, I was unsure of myself. Overcoming this monster put quite a feather in my cap. I took a head-on approach, subconsciously and consciously, toward my disability. Disability is a little wimp. It's only as large and obstructive as I make it. I learned how to turn deficiencies into advantages, mainly by a positive outlook.

Essentially, the same will to survive, while I was in a coma, redirected to rehabilitation. This shift was pretty easy. All I had to do was stay on course. It was a fight I could win, and it was a fight in which essentially everyone was on my side. I could only lose if I did not put forth the effort in a positive direction. I simply pushed forward and rarely looked back.

Everything has fallen into place, but this would not have been possible if not for my attitude. It was, of course, not only my positive attitude but the forward push I maintained. This positive attitude, which I maintained throughout my rehabilitation, is still a mystery even to me. I never had a positive attitude about anything throughout my preinjury days. This attitude built upon itself. The longer I remained positive, the more things benefited me. However, the most important part of this was that I had to put forth a genuine effort toward all I did.

I never thought I could be in control of myself. Health wise, socially, academically, and personally, I was a flake. Actually, nothing bothers me. Before my injury, the least little thing perturbed me. I had no control, or at least I felt that I had no control, over everyday occurrences.

I was afraid of my own shadow. This was not an outward projection of my feelings; in fact, I felt I covered my feelings very well. However, anything I did that involved the least amount of risk prompted deliberation. Before my accident, I was a perennial worrywart. Anything and everything had its chance to cloud my thinking. I felt I had no control over anything that occurred. However, I was a master of disguise. I could cover up most of my fear and trepidation around the majority of my peers.

Before my head injury, I was walking the proverbial tightrope. Apprehension about this or that kept me from going along the correct path. It was almost as if I was afraid of success. This head injury has given me tremendous emotional strength.

I'm not saying I was a basket case before this injury, but only I now feel as if I can handle most occurrences that might befall me:

death of a loved one, if I were to become destitute, or most anything else. Emotions are nonsense because they are not rational. They are things you do when you don't think. Things like love and marriage are big emotional situations— I rest my case.

Before my injury, I was never a person who would lose my cool, fly off the handle, or even make snap judgments. I would have to guess that this is what helped me through this long journey. It's good to be at ease with yourself.

My injury has brought forth a side of me that I only vaguely knew existed prior to my accident. I always wished someone would come along with a magic wand and magically transform me into the person I could be. Everything is nearly the direct opposite as to the way things were prior to my accident. However, on the other hand, I've always had the ability to do all the things I have done since the injury. However, I seriously doubt I would have called forth these abilities, if not for the cushion this injury provided.

Actually, this head injury saved my life. The inner strength it brought forth was always there; however, it would have remained dormant. Everything is nearly the direct opposite of what it was prior to my accident. At no time in my life have I been so sure of myself and all that I can do.

I cannot comprehend doing all that I have done without having the safety net of this disability underneath me. Never in my life have I ever pushed myself. I was always the type who took what came, and the majority of the time, I suffered the consequences. Before my accident, I never tried hard in school. I never went out for any sports at school or made efforts to be anything special in regards to much of anything academic. I merely tried my best to float by with little resistance, but I wouldn't say this was a bad thing. At this point, I can see the benefits of putting forth a little initiative.

Having this brain damage made me realize that I didn't want to set myself back with drugs, alcohol, and other needless things. If I count up all the things I've received since my head injury and contrast them with what I've lost, then the comparison wouldn't make me change my love of this injury. My brain damage has overwhelmingly been to my benefit. It has helped me more than it has hindered me.

With all the good things that have happened to me and how well I have handled the bad things, I still allow small occurrences to eat at me. There is just so much stuff to concern myself with through this rehabilitation process that it would have slowed me down significantly if I would have become bogged down with a poor self-image. With all I had to deal with, I didn't need my self-esteem to be one of the small things to bring me down.

Even though I allow little things to bother me, they are not all consuming. I have the ability to prioritize, and thus, I never lose clear perspective of what is truly important. I guess this is important because I try to resolve most everything. It is important for me to know which things to let go of.

I'm very grateful to have latched onto this positive mode of thought. Negativism would not have let me get out of the starting blocks. Feeling sorry for myself is worse, I feel, than others being concerned about my condition. You can use, in a constructive mode, all those you feel can help.

I've never complained about my condition. Eventually, I inertly realized that I would begin to feel sorry for myself if I did this. It would take the wind out of my sails. Grief does not inspire me to move. In fact, it just swallows up time.

No one wishes to board a sinking ship. With my constant reaching for higher plateaus, I have found many people willing to lend assistance. I don't know if it was instinctive, but I knew I would not get anywhere if I felt bad about my condition.

Many things were offered to me, and I used them properly; they made my disability seem all the more acceptable. Multitudes of freebies were and are thrown at me. Yet, if these things were not used properly, then they could do more harm than good. Everything provided to me—understanding or any shortcuts provided to me simply because of my condition—if used improperly, could have certainly set me back further.

I began to think that I was special. It was a good feeling to note people around me recognizing the effort that I was putting forth. I never had so much positive attention paid to me until I began to climb this high mountain of rehabilitation. When I first began to walk after my release from the hospital back in the spring of 1972, I would walk short distances around the neighborhood. People around town who, before the accident, would not give me the time of day would stop me to talk.

Some disabled persons allow all the benefits provided to inertly shame them. Everything was hard. I simply closed my eyes and plowed forward.

There is no losing, unless you simply give up. It's similar to horseshoes. You don't score any points until you throw the stupid horseshoe. There was and is no shame to being disabled. The majority of persons around me would marvel at my spunk. It's almost as if everyone around me became my surrogate parent. They wouldn't chastise me if they knew I was giving it my all.

Everything worked so well for me because I made a genuine effort. I eliminated halfhearted from my vocabulary. However, I must confess that it was easier for me because I didn't have far to go to reach my limit. All the stuff I had to give up—women, drugs, alcohol, friendships, leisure time, relaxation, money, and so forth—was no loss at all. All I had to do was make a wholehearted attempt.

I found that if I just accepted what was and worked from there, things just seemed to fall into place. Regrets and feeling sorry for myself take too much time, and they don't resolve a blessed thing. Efficient rehabilitation has no time for regrets or anything else that wastes valuable time. I threw everything unnecessary and unimportant, in respect to my rehabilitation, out the window.

It helps when you realize what you cannot do. I found that many things I could not do were not worth doing in the first place. There was never any self-pity in regards to my mental and physical state. I feel that I can attest to this because feeling sorry for yourself is just one more disability. No one likes to help a whiner. A sports team that does not believe in itself will not find very many fans who are willing to believe in them.

If being disabled were constantly on my mind, then it would leave very little energy to pursue much more productive avenues. In a strange kind of way, my brain damage helped me resolve much of it. I couldn't hold information long enough to fret about it. I'm always moving forward, even at this point. Many of the times I failed in one attempt at something, I simply tried another way. If that didn't work, I simply chalked it up as unimportant. I had to realize that not everything was going to go my way.

It's a never-ending process and a quite enjoyable one. In the beginning, I suffered a great many losses, but I couldn't hold that regrettable information long enough to stifle me. In this way, it was like a two-edged sword. Harboring regret would have been the largest obstacle. However, to hold onto bad feelings, you have to be able to remember much of the details.

It's hard to get people to jump aboard a sinking ship. So, when people noticed me putting forth a genuine effort, the majority were eager to lend a helping hand. I needed people and their help. I was amazed at how the people I knew before my injury, who I never gave a second thought to, became an essential part of my rehabilitation.

I never became angry about having brain damage. Brain damage is simply a part of me. It would be like a person being angry that they have a foot—it's just there. I simply use my brain damage and disabilities to lessen them.

I never wasted energy in anger. I needed all my energy to rehabilitate. I didn't consciously conduct myself in this manner. I suppose this was merely inbred. You learn how to walk, and you see the value in having a foot. I used my brain damage as I did my feet. I never fret because I have feet.

I only wonder how I will do. However, I gained security in the fact that I looked at disability and all the incongruities that go along with it and didn't blink. I spent nine years in higher learning establishments. I held on to the four full-time jobs, totaling seven years of work experience. At the present, I work two part-time jobs, and I find it very manageable.

Everything for the past number of years since my head injury has seemed to have gone swimmingly. However, just lately, I've begun serious contemplation over finding the woman or women of my dreams. It would put the brakes on my rehab, but what the heck!

Like a priest, it has been no big deal. I've had other more prominent things on my mind. At present, I work a little over forty-six hours a week. I feel okay, and I'm ready to jump into the relationship ring. This is not even mentioning the close scrape I had in my younger days. I only do productive things, no matter how insignificant I may feel them to be. I don't engage in destructive things, no matter how enjoyable they might seem to be. I don't overeat. I don't drink. I don't smoke or use drugs. I don't have any conflicts with anyone. I only owe my next month's rent. I take very good care of my health. I am not overly concerned about my son's plight. I will fix what I can, when I can, and I am either going to heaven, or I am going to hell. That's a sure thing.

I realize the reason for my good feeling has got a lot to do with the correct choices I have made. It was easy for me to do this, but I had to get rid of a lot of baggage first. It was easy to start at the bottom. It made every accomplishment a major one. Productive things were hard for me to accomplish at first, but nothing good comes easy. The trick was to never remain complacent. I don't know where I got this ability, but, for every hill that I scaled, I was ready for the next.

To continue to move forward, I had to have that initial drive that I summoned up at the beginning of my rehabilitation. At present, I am on cruise control. I simply maintain that push forward. I stay away from alcohol, drugs, self-pity, negative attitudes, laziness, and a wide spectrum of things that will bring me down.

This is not saying that I am not doing anything. On the contrary, I'm just not struggling as hard to pursue my goals. I put myself in that positive direction, and everything seems to work out fine. It's easier doing positive things than doing the least that I am capable of, as I did prior to my accident.

If I were not going in this direction, then I would in no way remain stationary. Being disabled, if you're not trying your best, you do not remain stagnant. You inevitably fall in that pit of self-destruction. One of the most significant things I discovered was how to use and not be used.

The positive feeling I have about my disability helps those around me as well. It's easier for people to communicate their feelings. It's not as if everyone around me is walking on egg shells.

I'm very glad that, at this point, I have all this behind me. I wouldn't change a thing. Everything I have in my past, whether good or bad, has enriched me. My goals at present are not predominant in my thinking. They will happen when they happen. At the time of this writing, it's now close to ten years after I completed my first book, and it has yet to be published, but even that is not so imperative. I have two part-time jobs that I enjoy. I am in good health. I have no conflicts with anyone. Even though I do not have any close friends (those whom I could confide in), the fact that I never made enemies helps me get along with everyone.

Having surmounted obstacle after obstacle gives me a sense of self. The trick for me was to not waste time resting on my laurels and contemplating past achievements, but to keep my sights set on the future and to keep going.

Before my injury, I had no direction. I also didn't have any cushion. The head injury provided both. There are many sides to disability. One of those sides is where one does as little as possible and tries to live off the sympathy of others. This, for me, did not work.

I'm happier at this point in my life than I have ever been. This is not a sudden or recent realization. This is exactly how I felt and still feel throughout my rehabilitation. I realize now that it was the direction that I needed. I found that direction through various means, but, largely, I found it through the proper use of my disability. Along with this direction, I was provided the funds to sustain this voyage. I was able to use people to their delight. In what other situation is this possible?

At one of the places I work (a Senior day care center in the community), I was guarding the door, and this very sweet old lady was sitting next to me and said, "You're very handsome." This short, extremely slender, as well as withered, lady, who always had a smile on her face and what seemed to be smoker's cough in her throat, took me aback. It was almost as if this ninetyish-looking chick was making a move on me. I merely chucked and coyly thanked her, all the while keeping an eye on her hands, fearing she might grab my behind.

I feel pretty good about the compliment she gave me. I realize she's more than forty years my Senior, but you've got to take it from where it comes. I get along very well with women, although I'd much rather bullshit with the guys.

15

I am very fortunate to have taken rehabilitation by the horns. I've noticed many other disabled persons with horns stuck in their asses. If you allow your disability to control you, then it will be very difficult to keep a job or to do much of anything else. I never thought of myself, even before my injury, as someone who could keep a job. I always thought that working for a salary was something unattainable. I guess I always had some grandiose opinion of work. However, work is vacation when compared to rehabilitation. I have been doing both for the past three years.

Work gives many tangible as well as intangible things. However, rehabilitation is virtually unnoticeable and quite slow in your own eyes. The trick for me was not to get caught up in counting my accomplishments. I just needed to keep pushing.

At one of my jobs, there was an elderly man suffering from some kind of brain disorder. He spoke very little and frequently displayed his angry side to me. One day, while outside in a fenced area, he bolted for the door and strode outside in what seemed to be a definite purpose.

This man, no taller or heavier than me, was as stubborn as they get. We walked off the grounds and onto the sidewalk. My bladder was bursting. We passed a few bus stop benches, which looked very inviting. I knew I'd lose him if I stopped. I was keeping up with him, so I coyly began to talk to him as if we were in conversation. He seemingly was following my talk, and as I inadvertently turned the corner, amazingly, he turned with me. After walking and talking a bit more, I once again turned the corner. Now, the Willow Glenn Villa, the place where I was working, was only a few blocks away. To make a long story short, I got him back, went to the head, and pissed a river—all in a day's work.

There was another incident that brought a smile to my face at the same Senior day care facility in northern California where I work. There's an elderly lady, in her mideighties, who is taken there from 9:00 a.m. to 3:30 p.m. each day. She is Cuban. I speak to her in English and in my broken Spanish tongue. She has a good sense of humor. She is only slightly mentally affected by a condition related to her age. Unlike Puerto Ricans, who have a reverence for the Spaniards, Cubans have a derogatory quip: "Viva Cuba. Viva

España. Los Españoles nunca se bañan, ni con Aqua Carabaña." The translation of this goes as follows: "Long live Cuba. Long live Spain. The Spanish never bathe themselves, not even with the Aqua Carabaña." Aqua Carabaña is a very strong laxative found in Cuba. You can derive from this quip that the Spanish are both thought of as filthy and full of shit. It seems as if the Cubans call it like it is. However, for some reason, the Puerto Ricans have a lot more respect for the Spanish.

My life with a head injury compared to that of one without a head injury can be viewed in a simple tortoise and the hare analogy. I will eventually get where I am going. However, for the person who is not as directed as me, he might take any number of paths. I thank my brain damage for allowing me the ability to appreciate this fine piece of machinery we all have above our shoulders.

The brain is such a reliable machine; however, it needs a lot of time to rebuild. However, this cannot be done if you thwart its rehabilitation with drugs, alcohol, and so forth. Brain damage taught me patience.

Patience as well as doing the right things to promote my rehabilitation are two of the many factors involved. Patience is the key word. It has been close to twenty-eight years since my injury, and I'm still noticing improvements; albeit, they are ever so slight.

Doing this, that, and the other with a head injury builds confidence. A lot of the stuff I have done would and could not have been done by others who have not sustained such an injury. My brain damage is a wonderful thing. It lets me know just how well the body repairs itself. However, lots of time, patience, fortitude, and giving up of simple pleasures are a large component in this process. A lot of other things I had to give up were not much to begin with.

My brain damage was a blessing in disguise. In the beginning, my lack of memory did not allow me the power to ruminate about my situation for long stretches. To suffer the consequences of anything, you must be able to remember what's bringing you down. I merely let bad thoughts slide off my back.

My brain damage also alienated me from all of the so-called normal people. Yes, all of those people who have abused alcohol and other substances are not working at their highest point as well as all of those people who got married and divorced in short order. Those who are workaholics are in the same boat as those who misuse their bodies in other ways, and the list goes on and on. If I had not been so busy trying to rectify my many disabilities, then I just might have become one of those persons.

I never felt bad about my condition. I realize that that only defeats you. Being able to recall just what it was I should have felt downhearted about would have placed my rehabilitation on a slower track.

I've worked continuously against my brain damage. It's always there, and it's a never-ending battle, but in no way do I regret having this head injury. I can never lose this battle unless I give up the fight and allow it to consume me. It's a win–win proposition. There's no loser. I'm competing against myself. I only lose if I quit.

If you look at all your achievements, and disregard the setbacks, then you'll be amazed at what you can do. At present, I don't desire much. Everything will come with time. I have surpassed everyone's expectations. Can you say that?

I have met more and different people as a result of this injury, and, of more importance, I have learned how to constructively use each. I can and I have had open communication with doctors, instructors, and other important people, as well as the alcoholics, drug users, pushers, and other extremes in our culture. All of this has taken place since my head injury, and I feel I derived from it the best that I could.

This is not to say that I have become an extrovert overnight. However, with the confidence gained from confronting this monster that is disability, I have little fear that anyone is better than me. Prior to my accident, I was never very sure of myself around others, but, with this head injury, I have virtually a carte blanche. Interaction with others has been widely broadened. Without this head injury, my extroversion would not have flourished.

I am alive, while the majority of persons would be dead. I was given that ball at the beginning of my rehabilitation, and I ran with it. At the start of my rehabilitation, I envisioned every one of my accomplishments as a big one, but I never rested. There was always one more hill to climb.

What made all this rehabilitation stuff work, I have to speculate, is the good feeling I always had for myself. I was able to maintain this feeling even at the lowest points during my rehabilitation. Before my accident, I was nothing, and I knew I was nothing. This injury opened my eyes.

I don't pat myself on the back every five minutes. I allow others to do that for me. In fact, that would only promote a lackadaisical disposition toward my shortcomings. Remorse is a waste of energy. I neither had nor do I have time for regrets. I simply turned negatives into positives.

I have never had as high of an opinion of myself as I do now. However, this is how I felt throughout my rehabilitation, and even at my lowest point, I never felt sorry for myself.

It didn't really matter how well or poorly I did. It was just the fact that I was still in the game that was important. I kept my eyes on that elusive goal. I didn't know what or where it was, but I remained focused upon discovering and reaching it.

It was as if I planned all this, and all I had to do was follow through with a sufficient amount of effort, and I'd be successful. In all honesty, it was not hard. It would have been much harder if I would have just let all of the benefits this disability provided slip through my fingers. It seems as if every plateau I reached was substituted by another seemingly reachable level. Never before in my life have I been goal oriented. This disability provided me with a goal and with a method for reaching that goal and with many perks along the way.

Working at a slower pace is quite comfortable for me. I don't feel I can handle stress. I have a Latin friend who works serving meals at one of my places of employment, and he will often hear me state, while he is within earshot of me, "Yo puedo hacer este trabajo dormido." This simply states, in Spanish, "I can do this job while in a coma."

It's weird. I like this head injury. It has given me much more than it has taken away. Yet, I'm kicking it in the ass every day. Every day is a challenge, though each day is much less of a struggle now than in the past. The remarkable part about this is that I don't shy away from them. This injury gives me something to do, and I never lose, as long as I'm in the fight.

This void in my life has been filled quite nicely by the struggles with my head injury. I have many things lacking in my life because of my head injury, but I don't waste time in senseless mourning. If that were the case, I would have a much harder time, simply because that wastes too much energy. I felt good when I discovered different ways to beat that hopeless syndrome.

I had too much empty time before my injury, and being the lazy type that I was, I chose the easiest diversions. I now substitute the fleeting enjoyments experienced by others for the lasting improvements that I have made.

I'm just your average all-American boy. If you were to see me on the street, you, no doubt, would like to take me home, and sometime in the future, you would like me to marry your daughter.

Everything seems to have just fallen into place. It seems as if I was just destined to do things in the way that I have. It is true that I did not plan the way that I was to rehabilitate; however, I was at the helm, and I steered clear of anything in the way.

My history is what keeps me going. The incidents that occurred in my past seem surreal. Even though I act similarly to those around me, as I have in the past, all that I have done and accomplished in the past seems as if it were fabricated.

What I have inside me must be inside the majority of men. It is only that circumstances vary so greatly that only a very small minority will have the necessity to use this power, and even fewer will choose to do so.

I didn't have time to concern myself with the feelings of others. I merely remained on that track forward and kept pushing. There is a trick to it. If done right, people almost thank you for letting them help. I use others in a manner that's beneficial to both the giver and the beneficiary. To the countless instructors, health care workers, fellow employees and others that have helped me, my hat goes off to you, regardless of the fact that you reaped as much or more than I did. Let's not forget the tax payers who financed much of my rehabilitation and the endeavors I have pursued as a result.

I don't know if it was intentional on my part, but it seemed like every time I made improvements, it was as good for the person helping me, as it was for me. No one loses in rehabilitation.

There is too much to do when you are trying to repair the brain. You don't need to add one more disability, such as regret, to the list of hardships. I had to work along with my brain damage to minimize the effects of it. If I did not accept it as part of me, then it would have only been a greater hardship to endure.

Several years back, arguably the greatest and most famous boxer of all time, Mohammed Ali, employed a tactic that I also have used. He called it rope-a-dope. In doing this, he would rest against the ropes, while his opponent would exhaust all of his energy throwing a multitude of punches to Ali's midsection. Similarly, I never burned up too much energy in grief. I merely did what I could.

I am a new person. I build from here. I have all kinds of assistance, understanding, and so forth. I'm grateful that this injury essentially cleansed my soul. I don't have any unsupported or unsubstantiated fears. I remember, before the accident, I had so many fears. It hampered my thinking.

In fact, as I look back on it, this head injury had been somewhat of a vacation. At present, I'm concerned about few things, and I merely fix those things that I can. I do not ruminate senselessly, as I did in the past.

I like where I am right now. There is nothing in my past that I would change if I had the ability to do so. Can you say the same? Not to denounce you, but, what the heck have you done in your life that is remotely comparable?

Perspective, my brain damage has given me time and facilities to gain a heck of a lot of perspective. It has allowed me to judge what truly is important. This feeling grows on you. However, during the process, there were numerous things I wished were different, but, I realized, if everything goes your way, then it does not build strength. Everyone goes the extra mile for you when they realize the genuine effort you're putting forth.

Divorce, bankruptcy, alcoholism, drug use, and so forth are all self-inflicted. Are you a better person for having been through it? However, this head injury was, in many ways, self-inflicted, and everyone around me, including me, can state I'm much better for it.

It's not over until the fat lady sings, as they say. At present, she's merely clearing her throat. This injury, I probably stated this before, has made me a stronger individual, and I continually get stronger. This is opposed to the period before my head injury. I seemed to be sinking deeper and deeper into oblivion. I realize that's a bit overdramatic, but it certainly fits the way that I felt.

I still have a long way to go. This will never end until the nails are pounded into my box. I take that back because I prefer to be cremated. I feel confident that I can grapple with any incongruities that come my way. I realize all that I have done could not have been done without the help of others. I thank my lucky stars that I was wise enough to use all the help that was offered. This is the only thing that I deserve credit for.

I've received a lot of help throughout the years, and I feel I must say something that is being overlooked by the majority. I owe a great deal to all of you in this country. And because of the course of study I engaged in at school, I feel I have a bit of knowledge in this area. Something radical must be done to save our country's youth. At present, it seems as if we're wearing blinders. It seems as if we're too stupid to look down the road. The expense that Seniors incur on this society is inevitably the cause of many of our problems. Our future generations are the ones who will feel the brunt of this. The idea of throwaway kids and keepsake Seniors is entirely ridiculous.

The AARP should open its cataract eyes. With all the money and power they have, they should do things for the up and coming generations. However, like spoiled children, they're just out for theirs. The Senior population could make a truly significant difference if they truly cared. I hope history paints a clearer picture of what Seniors have done for this nation. I realize that I'm biting the hands that feed me, but this same hand is slapping our nation's youth in the face.

I'm sure all of us remember President Clinton. In my eyes, his presidency was a time when this country was elevated to new heights. From time to time, some of his body parts also shot for the stars, but, unfortunately for him, this will not sit well for his legacy.

However, for others it just might. Monica Lewinsky, not surprisingly, wrote a book. *My Million Dollar Lips*, I believe that's the title of it. I'm uncertain of the value of a book like hers. I'm doubtful that she wrote much of it. However, there are always persons out there who can turn much of anything into cash. I guess I'm no different. However, I feel I can give a little hope in an otherwise hopeless scenario.

I don't feel as though there will be many people who will pick up this book for curiosity's sake. I feel and hope that people will pick up this book, and all of my former writings, for inspiration. Can you imagine the time and effort it took for Monica Lewinsky to write her book? It took me close to five years to write my first four books. Monica barely took her lips off of Bill Clinton's body parts, and the next day, the book was in the stores.

This is disgusting. The information this book provides matters very little to anyone, that is, unless you plan to give the president a good time. Such a book like that is merely entertainment. However, books like mine might simply go unnoticed. Even though millions in this country have a greater need for the information that is delivered in my writing, it might go unnoticed, because mine might not be flashy enough.

However, I provide valuable information in stimulating format. I am shooting straight from the hip. Things that have happened to me very well could or might have happened to you or someone close to you. America, if it wants to continue prospering, must get its priorities straight.

My rehabilitation has been a most enjoyable experience. Though the president's little romp must have provided him with much pleasure, it hasn't provided anything positive. It's ironic. The president is currently suffering the consequences of his erections, and the guy he beat in the last election, Bob Dole, is advertising medication for erectile dysfunction. Is this country consumed by sex?

It is humorous because Dole got screwed in his bid for the White House, and now he's advertising a product that will help you screw a bit longer. Look at all I have done without the benefit of a warm body close to mine. Could that be the reason that the country is not aspiring as well as it should, considering all it has at its disposal?

This is bullshit. In other countries, men have women on the side, and no one thinks anything of it. When I went to Puerto Rico in 1976, my cousin, about twenty years older than me, had an extra woman, and no one, not even his wife, thought much of it. Yet, you and I are spending millions of dollars on something that is none of our business.

My entire life has been made better through the luxury of a head injury. What I actually did was point myself in the right direction. Like that proverbial snowball rolling down the hill, I merely picked up steam as I went along.

It was, the way things have fallen into place, as if I had a guiding light that I've been following all these years of my life. It is a comfort to me to realize that things couldn't be in any way better for me. As I write this, I'm now forty-six years old, and I expect my heart to keep pumping for a bit longer. However, I don't know how I could have made it successfully, as I have, without this head injury. As I look back on it, I couldn't have scripted it any better.

Surviving this head injury has given me the distinct impression that I have done what I was put on this earth to accomplish. Can you say the same?

It was almost as if my life were scripted beforehand. Everything just seems to have fallen into place. I was born to be head injured.

All the while, during this rehabilitation, I've been hard at work. However, this is not the kind of hard work that exhausts you. On the other hand, it has propelled me. I've never been so completely exhausted that I wanted to throw in the towel. I might have stated this before, but this needs repeating. This head injury has given me far more than it has taken away.

In the short amount of time I've been on this planet, I've done everything I could ever have wanted to accomplish. I have yet to have my first book published; however, I'm sure it will get out there.

This injury has given me time to explore my inner capabilities. If not for all this injury has given me, there would be a void in my life. I seriously believe that without my head injury and subsequent rehabilitation, I would be missing a great deal in my life.

It's almost like doing something that you're proud of—like, for instance, graduating from college, being happily married, raising a family, or any number of things that can give you the sense of justified pride.

If I didn't have the accident in 1971, if I were not dead, in jail or in an otherwise unspectacular living condition, then I surely would be an empty person.

I might have said this before (I know I have, but bear with me) this injury was sent from above. This is not saying that I believe there's anything besides atmosphere up there. My head injury has rounded me out. Don't get me wrong. I'm not saying that I've been blessed with this head injury. Head injuries, for the majority of persons, can be a pain in the ass. However, if you remain vigilant and unwavering in your approach to thwarting the many incidents that tend to hold you back, as I did, then things just turn out better.

The advances in my life that have resulted from my injury are incalculable. If you knew me before the accident, then you could argue the point that I could have descended a bit further—but not much.

Change, in my situation, was a beneficial thing. The changes this head injury provided were wonderful. I believe this was because I worked with it and didn't allow it to consume me. I venture a guess that if you'd ask any person who knew me before my head injury, they'd unequivocally implore that I'm a much better person now because of it.

My parents, no doubt, would be the first to acknowledge my remarkable recovery. However, they would wrongly not take credit for a large part of it. More mistakenly yet, they would take credit away from me and give the glory to some outsider in the sky.

This injury allowed me the advantage of many things. All I had to do was not become overwhelmed by it. Only the strong survive. This is not 100 percent correct in relation to the battle I had to wage. It was a combination of a lot of things. I never knew I had the ability to sidestep the many pitfalls one encounters while rehabilitating. I never knew I could dance. However, with this disability, I glided across the dance floor like Fred Astaire.

Before my accident, I was like a rosebud waiting to blossom. With all the services, money, professionals and so forth at my disposal, I definitely bloomed. How many of you reading this know what you are made of? Prior to my accident, I was like you. Oh sure, you can make all kinds of assumptions, but you truly are in the dark until something like this comes along.

All I needed to do was continue trying. I gave an honest effort and never bit the hand that fed me. Of course, I did things my way, and I sometimes concealed what I was doing from people who were helping me. Yet, the end result is what counts.

The several counselors I went through during this voyage were all quite important. Be they rehabilitation, academic or just persons on the sidelines wishing to help, I used them to my best advantage. I used the majority of my counselors in a most proficient manner, and that was essential. The reason counselors are there is to help you deal with your disability. That's what they were there for. You have to use the people and the things that are available to you. They're using you. Without you, they'd need to find a different line of work. Even though I became very good friends with my counselors and others who were lending their assistance, I was most concerned with myself.

This head injury has been my pot of gold in many more ways than one. My head injury gave me confidence I never had before the accident. I found inner strength. As I've stated before, I learned how to use people constructively. I concentrated on building myself up physically and mentally. My injury pulled me away from bad influences. I currently make sound decisions about my future, and I no longer allow my emotions to steer my thinking. Plowing through this head injury has been like a game for me; as long as I remain in a positive direction, I cannot lose.

Since my head injury, most everyone around me is very willing to help me along in that positive direction. These are the same people, I'm sure, who would not give me the time of day prior to my injury. My head injury has also given me great self-confidence.

Before my injury, I was like a leaf blowing in the wing. After my injury, I took a much more directive approach to my life.

I am neither proud nor ashamed of my condition. However, I'm very proud of the way that I have handled it. I am quite obviously disabled. There are numerous things that I cannot do as well as the next guy, but I don't think about it. I can't sing, dance, or play the violin, but I don't lose any sleep over it.

My feelings, I would have to guess, are similar to those that you have. There's no way in the world I'd accept a disability with open arms. However, I have made it one of the best things that has happened in my life. I would have to guess the feeling of disability is to the majority of persons out there something short of horrendous, but, for me, it was all in how I used it. I never let it pull me down for any extended period.

The disabled feeling, thinking that everyone around me is in some way better than me, never pervaded my thinking. I'm not saying it was never there. I just never gave it fertile ground to germinate. I didn't view my brain damage as a deficit. That was the other guy. I merely sucked it dry.

I used my disability like having a rich, childless uncle who always tended to favor me, and in the majority of the cases, his name was Uncle Sam. Disability begged me to use it. It was like a prostitute that would never tire and would quite regularly pay me.

I would have to guess that it was a good thing the majority of other disabled persons were not using their disability as well as I have. There is only so much pie to go around. I am very glad to have gotten my slice when I did. Let others feel sorry for my condition. Just don't call me late for dinner. My disability is the hungry infant. The government is the swollen breast.

Disability could have easily had its way with me, but, through much good fortune, I grabbed it by its tail and made it dance to my tune. With all my deficits, it is amazing that I never felt bad. I looked for ways to use them.

Before my injury, I had a take what comes attitude about almost everything. I did not like this one bit. However, it's too hard to change course midstream. I never liked to work for anything. I never had endurance. I don't even remember working for anything. The word effort was not in my vocabulary.

I never went out on a limb. I took what came with the girls that I knew. All my friends were merely tagalongs, like me. I did not like work, or even play, if it involved effort. If you accept things as they happen, then it means you do not have to plan anything, and you do not have to take the blame if you fail. That was one of the biggest handicaps I dealt with prior to my injury. I am totally different now. I look before I leap.

If I had never acquired this injury, even though I was always a tad more cautious than my peers, then I no doubt would have jumped off the deep end a few times, and eventually, I would have drowned.

2

I was fortunate to be able to instinctively realize what would have the possibility of working and what would require too much work with not enough benefits in return. Sometimes, the person trying to assist me didn't know exactly what would fit. I know I had to honestly open up and work cooperatively with whoever was trying to help me. For the majority of the time, this worked. For the few times that the helper and I didn't click, the other person and I simply went our separate ways.

People and organizations who try to assist the disabled, particularly the head injured, must realize that one size does not fit all. I realize that that sounds simple, but I have had to reiterate that more than once to many of the people who were trying to help me.

One of my academic counselors, who had known me for a while, had seen me on campus one day. I was sitting alone and having a cup of coffee when she passed. I greeted her, and she greeted me. We exchanged a few words, and then she went on her way. I thought little of this, until I saw her a few days later for a scheduled appointment. I came in to thank her for all she had done for me while I was a student there. I was about to graduate, and she was one of the key reasons for this.

We had talked for a while, and then, right out of the blue, she inquired about my romantic needs. This is something I will elaborate on in greater detail in a future book, but I felt this is where I could make a better point of it. If I were to have encumbered myself with *any* nonessential activity, then I would never have made it this far. You have to pay the piper to get this far after losing as much mental, physical, and social abilities. I feel I have made the correct decision in that respect. In reference to the success/failure rate among couples today, I feel I haven't lost much.

This seems as if it is an overly simplistic reason I have for the large amount of success I've experienced over the years, but I have to thank my parents for the bulk of my accomplishments. However, it was not so much for what they did, as for what they did not do.

I owe everything I possess to the manner in which I confronted this head injury. Also, much of the credit has to be given to the people who surrounded me, once again, starting with my folks. There is no way I could have done what I have done without my parents. It was not that my folks had any expertise in rehabilitation advice, but they provided the atmosphere and support for my rehabilitation to germinate. In the back of my mind, I realized how much I had put them through with the car accident and subsequent disability, and I needed to keep that push alive.

I'm still the same guy that I was before the injury. All the things I do still have to pass through that same sieve they would have had to pass through before this injury. However, at this point, I control the size of the mesh in that utensil, and I can determine, with fairly good accuracy, which elements I should allow through that strainer.

After all these years, everything that confronts me is met head on. I no longer try to skirt things or hide them under a rug. I sublimely realize that, in the long run, everything catches up with you.

All things work out better this way. If I fall on my face, as I've done from time to time, I only pick myself up, learn from my mistakes, and continue. In fact, when something pulls me down, lifting myself up only makes me stronger. If you think about it, rehabilitation is a process where it's hard to lose. Even slight effort is better than none at all.

As long as I stay on my feet and continue throwing punches, I'm a winner. Writing this book is merely a continuance of my overall positive outlook. Who knows, maybe later in the fight I'll throw this disability a sucker punch and land it flat on its back.

My rehabilitation, where I have been the key participant, is a win–win situation. There are no losers. However, to be a winner, I've found that you have to be the person in the ring throwing the punches. Although the persons in your corner can help you, you must use their support to strengthen your own punches.

My rehabilitation counselors provided the money to pay for school, buy the books, and pay for transportation. My academic counselors advised me of which classes to take, what programs on campus would assist me, and where I could obtain even more financial aid, if need be. On not-so-rare occasions, if I would need a tutor, I was led to one who might best help me.

However, once again, I had to be the one with the fire in my belly. I don't know what I ever would have done if I did not have this drive. I can only guess where this drive came from. I would have to say that this drive was placed there by the fact that I realized how much I put my parents through, as well as how good it made me feel at how much I could do after having sustained an injury such as this.

I'm presently enjoying all the aspects of my disability. The most important aspect, among many others, is the way I have viewed my disability. My personal outlook on being disabled had to be a positive one. Before I became disabled, I viewed disabled persons as freaks in a sideshow. However, unlike at the sideshow, I was careful not to look in their direction. This was done partially out of respect for them, but largely because I was afraid I'd catch it.

I believe that if I had not stepped out on the dance floor, disregarding what might be said about my feeble attempts to dance, I might as well have chopped my legs off. Being begrudged about being disabled would've been a large impediment. I didn't need any more things standing in my way.

I simply didn't concern myself with what I had lost. It would've exhausted the majority of my time and energy. I needed an abundance of both. Instead, I gave more attention to what I could achieve. I never felt depressed. There was always something I had to do. The majority of the time I could do it.

I couldn't afford to waste time. I can't pinpoint what it was that gave me the power and the stamina it took to wrestle with this disability. However, maintaining this drive was one of the easiest things I did.

I can't explain how I did it, but I never let my disability swallow me. I rejected pity from others, and I certainly wasted no time on self-pity.

All throughout my rehabilitation, I maintained this positive outlook. I've realized now, this is the only way that I could have sustained this long, drawn-out course. The only people who will hop aboard a sinking ship are others who themselves are failing to bail out water aboard their own vessels.

At this point in my life, everything seems to be going my way. The reason for this, in my eyes, is that I've maintained a positive direction and seldom wavered. What I feel was most important was that I never felt sorry for myself. There were times I fell on my face, but, with the help of others, I picked myself up.

There was a teacher's assistant, among many other assistants throughout school, named Mary, who helped me tremendously. We maintained this friendship for many years, and it has provided me with much inner pride.

To bring myself this far, I had to have a love of self. This isn't bad. If you don't love yourself, you're no good to anyone else. If I didn't love myself, then I would never have come this far or even lived through the period when I laid in a coma.

This love of self, something that was very dormant before my head injury, was what kept me distant from a lot of things that could have destroyed me while traversing through this maze of disability. I'm not an outwardly egotistical kind of guy. However, it is the pride I have in myself that keeps the coals burning. That is the driving force. Without love of self, you're nothing.

I have to confess, it was not so much the love of self that promoted my comeback, but the fear of where I'd be if not for the effort I put forth. However, that fear, in and of itself, can be construed as self-love.

This is the first time in my life that I have felt so directed. I'm going to ride the crest of that wave for as long as I can. I shudder at the thought of having to go through life without this cushion of disability. This head injury has been what I needed in my life. Without it, I would've been consumed, like so many others, by the simply inconsequentialities of life.

At present, I'm not overanxious for anything. At this moment, my first four books haven't been published, I haven't yet thrown my hat into the ring concerning my love life, and I work two jobs but only make enough money to survive. However, the drive I've gained throughout this struggle will remain my entire life. Through patience, I have gained so much over the years during my rehabilitation. I don't worry about a thing.

Before the accident, I had no self-confidence. I felt as if I had not done a thing for myself. The only thing I could take credit for was screwing up. The admiration of self pushed everything forward.

Realization, although very sublime, that I have done things most have not encouraged that feeling. The concept of self was an illusion before my accident. Although I was always looking out for my behind, I didn't put forth the energy to do a good job of it.

First off, to get anywhere, I had to like myself. I had to recognize that all I had been through has only made me a stronger person. It didn't detract anything from me. I didn't need anyone to sound my horn—that was a given. However, the only one who could hear that horn was me.

I never let the little setbacks resulting from my injury get in my way or slow me down. I let all little setbacks go by the wayside. If I would have allowed myself to be encumbered by all the trivialities, then it would only have been a larger disability than I already had.

I didn't let any thoughts enter my head that would fester and eventually pull me down further. I did this consciously, but, as time went on, I did this on a subconscious level. In fact, I built on these incongruities. It made me feel more competent to be able to proceed even after such setbacks. I patted myself on the back a number of times, but I was always careful not to wallow in that stuff.

33

Actually, little setbacks would turn into major accomplishments when I managed to surmount each obstacle that presented itself or simply sidestep those I could not.

When I first began to walk after my exit from the hospital, back in 1972, I had a horrendous limp. This was caused by my right leg having to be connected by a couple of metal pins on the femur bone. My femur bone was protruding outside my skin, for a good amount of the time, while I was in a coma. Doctors could not operate on it till my fever went down. When they thought it was safe enough to operate, they did, with much success. However, might right leg is about a one fourth of an inch shorter than my left. Regardless of that, my continual walking over the years has made the limp undetectable.

Everything just keeps on flowing as long I don't stop to ponder. Over the years, with this head injury, I have done more positive things than I could have done without this disability. The motivation that grew, simply because I was fighting and conquering this beast, was seemingly endless.

I was given this disability, and I had to run with it. If I would have remained still, then the opposition would have piled up on me. I took advantage of my offensive line and am still running toward the goal post. The trick was to not look back and regret the losses. In my case, there was not much good to be lost.

I shudder at the thought of sitting on my hands throughout this disability. I can only imagine how tough it would have been for me to live with the fact that I had so much at my disposal and let it slip through my fingers.

Getting an education, which was a tad more difficult than for the average student, was time well spent. If I hadn't gone to school, then it would have been considerably more taxing. If I had done nothing, or even less than I have done, it certainly would have been the reason for my downfall. Simply realizing what I let slip away, it is my guess, would haunt me the rest of my days.

My head injury has been my savior. My disability led me through a tough part in my life. I needed a major setback such as this, but, moreover, I needed all the help that flowed my way. Christians have their Christ, Buddhists have their Buddha, Jews have their

Judaism, and I my disability. I have received much more from my disability than has been taken away.

I was in a deep hole before my accident. There was no way out. All I had was a shovel that begged me to dig deeper and deeper. However, this disability was a rope hanging down from the top, with numerous cheerleaders at the top encouraging me to pull my way up. All kinds of assistance was rendered to me, as well as numerous pats on the back as each new level was reached.

There were teachers, rehabilitation counselors, librarians, student assistants, and bus drivers, and the list goes on and on. Everyone is willing to lend a hand, as long as they know you are putting forth an honest effort. The trick is to take as much as you can use, and make sure you let them know of your gratitude. This does not mean I had to be thanking people left and right. I thanked them simply by the progress I was making.

A good number of people will bend over backwards for you. The trick is not to let anyone break their back. There will be, more than likely, a time when they will be needed again in the future.

I found myself laughing at others around me more than at myself. It's humorous how the majority of you nondisabled people will tend to self-destruct. There are numerous methods you employ to do this: overeating, alcohol consumption, marriage followed quickly by divorce, cigarette smoking, drug misuse, lack of exercise, and so forth. Although, I must admit that laughing at others was merely done to preempt laughing at myself, which would only slow me down, and I didn't need any more impediments.

Laughing at others was a way of protecting myself from bad feelings that might have developed about my condition. I merely pointed myself in the opposite direction of everybody else. Not much more thinking was necessary. That was good, because thinking was a limited commodity for me at that point.

With all the difficulties involved with living with a disability, I discovered that being an unmotivated jerk with all your faculties was much worse. Essentially, I had all my faculties stripped from me. I learned what real struggles were. However, I was never distraught because there was always a way that was presented in which I would come out the winner.

I was more disabled before my accident. I didn't have the knowledge or motivation to do what I needed to do, and I did not have the energy. You have to consider that there was a time I could do very little physically and even less mentally.

I had to rely on the good persons around me to point the way. However, I had to have the will and the blind faith to pursue this course. I would have to say that it was what I had inside me and the manner in which I was raised that deserve the majority of the credit.

As I look back, from time to time, I realize how easy it would have been not to have put forth the effort. At the beginning of my rehabilitation, I blindly reached for all I could have attained, and blind faith motivated me. The snowball rolling down the hill analogy applies here. However, since there are so many plateaus while rehabilitating, you must be prepared to occasionally self-propel that snowball.

As I traveled along this road of recovery, it became easier and easier as I picked up steam. At this point in my recovery, I don't feel any less motivated to push forward than at any other time. However, at this point, I have a lot more tools at my disposal.

For close to fifteen years after my release from the hospital, I chose not to drive. It was one of the better choices that I made. Before my accident, I don't remember walking any further than my high school, which was about a half mile away from my house. However, after my accident, walking from place to place liberated me. It became an essential part of my health plan.

At present, even though I drive to a majority of the places that I go, I still walk whenever I can. I also take the bus whenever it's convenient. Exercise is very much a part of my rehabilitation. Before my accident, I don't know that I would have been able to even so much as spell the word.

You have to understand, with all of my inabilities, especially at the start of my rehabilitation, I had to view things lightheartedly in order to deal with the majority of them. This is not saying that I thought my head injury was a joke, but, every time I fell on my face, I had to pick myself up and continue.

With this head injury, I was given a plethora of shortcomings. Every aspect of my being has been affected. I can see why a large number of head injured people get involved in illegal drug use. It's a method of escape. Fortunately, I found other ways to deal with this large stone that is now tied to my leg.

I can't think of one thing concerning my disability that I didn't meet head on. This is not saying I defeated every difficulty that presented itself. I just didn't back down. If I would have been encumbered by the mere fact that I possessed this disability, then it would have exhausted much of my energy.

I had to take most things with a grain of salt. However, at the same time, I had to work diligently. The way I did this was to merely plow full steam ahead. If it didn't come out right, then I couldn't blame anyone, not even myself. Over the years, I have found myself laughing at some of my own antics. Nothing was ever taken—or had to be taken—with a do-or-die attitude. I simply did my best, and I let the chips fall where they landed. I survived nicely with this cushion of disability.

All throughout this disabled venture, I've had to balance my concerns. I've had to choose which thing to take seriously and which thing to "ponle pitchon y dejalo volar." That last statement was a courtesy of my mom's vast archive of Puerto Rican quips. It simply means to "throw a rock at a bird, and let it fly away."

I was told once that I had a dry sense of humor. I never really understood what that meant. However, I have a distinct impression that it is what brought me this far. Actually, I'm further than I ever thought I could have gotten. This was even before I acquired this head injury. The few thoughts that would run through my mind before my head injury about my future were very brief and somewhat frightening. My future always looked less than bright. I just tried to stick my head in the sand and let tomorrow bring what it might.

My sense of humor and my ability to laugh at my situation, not necessarily at myself, have helped me enormously. It's not an outward laugh, but merely a sense that I should not take things too seriously. I fully understand that that would only have destroyed me. It smoothed over a lot of rough edges to confront a disability of this magnitude, whenever I used laughter as a protective device.

Even at the rare moments I laugh at myself, I instantly realize it's not a terminal condition. I spin anything in a manner so that it is beneficial to me.

My health maintenance over the years kept the rehabilitation engine running. I exercise regularly. I eat the correct foods at the correct times and in the correct proportion. I take vitamins and other beneficial supplements to keep myself strong and healthy.

My inconsistent health, although I was never seriously ill before my accident, was the source of my lackluster approach to most everything. When I toppled each little health concern, each victory made me stronger and more prepared to face the next. My good health allowed me to confront this disability head on.

My health practices, not in order of their importance, are water intake, proper foods in the proper quantity, daily exercise, good dosages of fresh air and sunshine, never letting things stress me out, maintaining good relations with all, never letting the lack of money slow me down, and never involving myself in family problems ... the list goes on and on.

Good health built upon itself. Good health promotes good health. It provided me with the spark I needed to keep this rehabilitation engine running. My continual good fortune provides fuel for this engine.

At the present time, I don't have any destructive vices. I don't overeat; I eat the right things; I don't drink or smoke; I exercise regularly; I have no enemies (perhaps because I don't make close friends); I don't have any family problems; my monetary stature at present is lacking, but it is of no great concern to me; and I have no love interests at present, but I am sure that will develop. I am not in debt. I now have a different sense of self. I eventually will complete my life by falling in love, getting married, and so forth.

As far as how I will conduct myself after I get off this rehabilitation treadmill, your guess is as good as mine. However, I am surprised at the stamina I have. Nothing I ever did before this head injury would give anyone even the slightest notion that a person like me could accomplish as much as I have. It's a good feeling to have done so.

I found there were many things I could do to effect a change for the better if I only remained diligent. With this head injury, I went into most things blindfolded. However, with my tenacity and the direction from others much higher on the ladder than me, I fortunately went in the right direction.

I was fortunate enough to realize the proper direction to take. I don't take too seriously the things that I cannot change. However, it's the constant work I put into my rehabilitation that makes it seem effortless. For me, I would have to guess, it was the lack of pressure that was placed upon me.

This enjoyable task will never end. I'm very satisfied with the way things have turned out. After all I have been through and overcome, I realize I should be overjoyed. However, that is not the case. There's always one more hill to climb ... and that's the way that I like it to be.

Before this head injury, I never took pride in myself or what I was doing. I have made a dramatic 180-degree turn. Likewise, I'd be somewhat disappointed if my rehabilitation stopped here. All that I have done since the acquisition of this injury should have left me satisfied. However, I don't think I will be until the undertaker secures the last nails in my coffin. Even at that point, I don't think I'd be able to refrain from telling him that he had a dead-end job.

It's a slow process, but, on the other hand, it's just my speed. I have learned to enjoy this ride. Even the many frustrations are a kick when you realize they are no match against your determination. It's something I never lose at. All I have to do is simply put forth effort.

Getting used to the slowness of rehabilitation was easy. Instead of regretting my deficits, I found enjoyment in realizing how many I could conquer. I find enjoyment in flowing successfully through this molasses of rehabilitation.

It puffs up my chest to realize, from time to time, I was fortunate enough to use my disability as constructively as I did. If this would have been a rapid process, then I would not have enjoyed the ride as much. I would have to guess that the reason behind why I find rehabilitation so enjoyable is because it gave me time to enjoy the process.

There was a lot of guidance within me. I simply needed to flourish. I also needed boundaries. Rehabilitation provided these elements in spades. Along with this inner guidance, I also needed guidance from the outside. This head injury provided all the assistance I needed and then some.

I wasn't exactly like a leaf in the wind. I was a leaf. However, I floated on the currents that I assumed would cause me the least amount of resistance. No direction with all your faculties is considerably worse than a clear path ahead of you, even with a lot less to work with.

I was a lost bullet, and that bullet was directed straight at my behind. Life before my head injury was considerably worse than life with it. I had no direction and no willingness to search for guidance.

My disability escorted me through all the rough parts of my life. While my main concern was putting myself together, others around me were busy tearing their lives apart. Many a friend and relative have had their lives rearranged by way of marriage and subsequent divorce. A few of my former associates were locked up for a while, and those of my friends whose lives were not taken by the abuse of drugs are presently suffering the after effects of their indulgences. Even my friend who became a cop in northern California realized that he could have done better than he has. However, it is me, a person with a serious disability, who feels the most fortunate in my circumstances.

Ironically, and thankfully, this head injury saved my life. What it did, essentially, was put me in gear. My disability has taught me so much. I would never have learned the many things about myself that I have without this injury.

No books, movies, instructions, or anything else could have taught me what this head injury has taught me. This was similar to the credit-or-no credit, pass-or-fail system offered in some classes given at school. Fortunately, I passed. In fact, I think I made it on the Dean's List.

I have received so many pats on the back on an ongoing basis. This helps provide me with the fuel that I need. A good number of these pats are issued by yours truly.

Without this injury, I am certain I would be a perennial clock watcher. I would be continually thinking there'd be something better that I could be doing. However, to be realistic, there isn't very much to be done than that which I have already done. In part, the reason I find joy in my work is that I can finally do something for someone else.

It's like constantly winning. However, this is no fluke. It's not like winning the lottery. I make efforts to continually rehabilitate. It's a constant struggle, but it doesn't bother me in an exhausting manner. I feed off all my accomplishments.

I enjoy the process of rehabilitation. I guess I will enjoy it the rest of my life. This is something I can never lose at, unless I simply lose the desire to get better. I continually improve my condition, so it makes little sense to quit moving.

Rehabilitation has become part of me. I continually work with it. Just like I'm always health conscious, I dress appropriately and do a plethora of other things to compensate for my disability. It's not a chore. Again, I enjoy it. Each day goes by with little concern for the small stuff. My reduced abilities don't play on my mind. I feel I have good control over my disability. It's a wonderful feeling.

3

I worked with my head injury. I didn't fight it. In all the time that I've been disabled, I've never regretted it. By regretting this disability, you essentially let it win. I worked with my disability and let it work for me.

My disability was like a member of my professional sports team. This member would continually be a large draw at the box office. Even though this guy would make continuous errors, step out of bounds and make flagrant mistakes, the crowd loved him and would continuously fill the stadium. This person would play in every game—the end result is what mattered.

It wasn't that all things dealing with this disability fit me like a glove. However, I was able to withstand the many ups and downs provided by my disability. Nothing I did or said would be held against me as long as they were done and said while I was pushing forward.

It seemed like I had always been searching for something to back me up all the years before this head injury. With this injury, it seems as if I have found the perfect entity to show me the correct path to follow, as well as the financial capabilities to follow it.

Having this disability has provided a cushion that I have always been looking for. It seems, throughout my youth, this head injury was always looking for me. However, at that point, I wasn't ready to let it find me.

There are many things you can learn through the process of rehabilitation, such as patience, understanding, personal strength, the correct use of others, and using your own faculties to their maximum potential. The list goes on and on. The entire rehabilitation process has given me a valuable education in life.

If head injuries weren't so costly—my tab is getting close to the one million dollar mark for all the services—then I would recommend head injury to the bulk of youth who are misguided. However, there is no guarantee that anyone can use their disability as efficiently as I did mine.

My rehabilitation taught me patience. The good part about my disability was that I always had a cushion I could fall back on if I failed. If I ever fell, I knew there were people around me who were willing to help; this was the key element.

As long as I was pushing forward, the right people would get in my corner. Disability became my friend that I could use. This friend had sympathy, compassion, and empathy, and along with other things, this friend had loads of money. I rarely dwelled in my predicament. I merely shuffled my feet and kept moving.

The loss of many of my faculties, the majority of them being mental, was a blessing in disguise. I can only imagine how it would have been if I would have allowed my situation to consume me. The way I avoided the depression derived from disability was to be consistently working toward that elusive goal of complete rehabilitation. I'll never attain it, so I will on this track as long as I live—why not enjoy it? Brain damage wasn't so hard to live with … I just never let it swallow me.

Good attitude was and is still important. Disability is a funny thing. I found myself numerous times laughing at my disability and almost never at myself. I used humor along the long, winding road of disability to inspire myself.

I haven't laughed at myself yet. I found many things concerning my head injury humorous. I laughed at my injury not at myself. There is a very fine line when you try to separate the disability from yourself. Even though I've always accepted the fact that I have a disability, the disability isn't me. It's like having a bad haircut. Even though that hair cut will be with you for a while, it's not necessarily a part of you.

Disability is something that set me apart from the rest. In a way, I was liberated from all the shackles of being normal. I don't have to compete against anyone else. As long as I put forth effort, I'm a winner. Disability has a bad rap. There is good in everything; you simply have to look for it and remain patient.

My disabilities have given me a greater sense of self. I was nobody until I acquired this injury. It gave me a purpose in this life. Before the accident, the only purpose I had was to see how well I could shuck responsibility. What a stroke of good luck! If not for this head injury, what the majority of you might see as a misfortune, then I would be in dire straits. Good things come in strange packages. If not for the life-threatening, horrific car accident, my life could have been in a serious dilemma.

In contrast to the way things occurred in my life before my head injury, where I felt I had very little control over what happened to me, I'm currently in the driver's seat. Control of things seems to be at my finger tips. My preinjury self was in control of squat. It is the best feeling I have ever encountered.

I rarely, if ever, let my disability have the upper hand. My disability built me up. I was able to rise above it. What worked for me was to just keep going. I worked at diminishing my disability little pieces at a time. I rarely was overwhelmed. This way, I was never tempted to quit. Disability is a little punk. The trick is not to let it transform you into an even smaller punk.

I am proud. Even in those beginning years of my injury, I never let it overcome me. I believe it was because I never let my spirits bring me down. I never felt sorry for myself. That would merely compound my disability. I've always felt that if I lived through what I lived through, then the sky was the limit.

My rehabilitation could have very well been put on hold at the start of my comeback through various miniscule happenstances. However, because of the use of various commodities that were placed in front of me, I was a kid let loose in a candy store. However, just as easily, I could have been a bull let loose in a china shop. I could have let all the extra benefits slip through my fingers. I could have refused to enter higher education when it was right there at my finger tips. I could have thrown away the money that was given to me on drugs, fast women, and other nonessentials. I could have milked everyone's compassion and thus do as little as possible to rehabilitate. I could have neglected my health, and the list goes on. However, all these things that could have set me back were just as easy to stay clear of.

It could have very easily swallowed me numerous times. However, it was just as easy to remain in the fight, since there weren't any rewards for giving up on myself.

The energy, fortitude, and courage needed in overcoming large obstacles were always there. Only, in my case, this entity was consistently dormant. A belief in myself, which was something that was absent from my being, was suddenly generated with the onset of this disability. The belief in my inner workings increased as I undertook that slow uphill climb. Rehabilitation, in my case, was a great confidence builder. As I kept improving, at a slower and slower pace, I climbed the next hill with that much more vigor and stamina.

I had no memory of ever defeating anything, least of all something as grand as the many deficits I have encountered. And, seemingly, all I had to do was put up the fight. Encouragement from others pushed me forward. However, it was always there. That's because I always surrounded myself with others who were right there when I needed them.

This disability is me. It isn't like an extra arm or leg that's just in the way. I work on it to diminish its hold upon me. It was never something I wished I didn't have. I use it like I use most anything I can find to help me through the muck.

I didn't see myself and my disability as two separate things. As time went on, I accepted it. I realized that fighting against oneself is a waste of energy. I didn't need one more thing to fight against. I simply accepted what I couldn't change and put a good portion of my energy on the things that I could.

My disability is the part I'm continually trying to improve. It's like steadily lifting weights. There's little urge to quit when I steadily get bigger and stronger. Even at this point, I continue to strive. It's remarkable because I never thought I could juggle—least of all the number of bowling pins I have in the air at this point. There is a valid reason or excuse for my actions and every outlandish thing I say or do. It was my understanding and acceptance of the situation that allowed me to push forward. I never laughed at myself for doing foolish things. I understood and went on.

I never looked at my disability as a joke. In no sense was I laughing at myself. Laughing at myself would make me feel like a fool. This would have stopped me dead in my tracks. I merely bit the bullet and proceeded forward.

Before my accident, I was selective in my association with others, and I stayed away from those who enjoyed working for what they had. Since I didn't like work, I chose others who held the same values. None of my former close friends were ever aspiring to do much of anything. However, through trepidation, I was careful not to associate with those who were likely to choose the deep end as their final destination. I always, with my low self-esteem, chose the bottom of the barrel types. Leaf-in-the-wind personalities were what suited me. I guess you can say that I was the same type of individual.

However, at this point in my life, I don't seem to need people like I did before my injury. It seems as if I needed people around me at that time to reassure me that I was all right. At this point, I realize that I don't need that reassurance, considering what I've been through and how far I've come. Considering what my friends of the past provided me with, I feel I can do much better without them. In essence, I have come to like this guy, who is me. I never before had this feeling. I always thought I was lesser than most, and I can now say retrospectively that none of my pals were any more than me.

Even at times when I can't overcome obstacles, I'm still a winner. This is simply because I stay in the fight. This is in direct contrast to the way things were handled before my accident. A leaf blowing in the wind would knock me over.

The reason this disability hasn't swallowed me is because it's a fight I can never lose. It's like lifting weights. The more conditioned I get, I'll be able to lift heavier weights. I don't get immediately discouraged because I can't press two hundred pounds. I work on what I can. My good health and, moreover, my regimen of practicing health policies are what keeps this engine purring.

Ironically, it's a fairly comfortable place to be. Virtually everyone is cheering for me and, at the same time, willing to assist me as long as I keep trying. Self-pity would've slowed me down, and unavoidably, I would have begun to believe myself. Because of my disability, I consider myself somewhat less than everyone else and, at the same time, on a higher perch, considering my comeback.

This is a good feeling. I receive money, services, and help when I need them, and at the same time, I have a good feeling about who I am and how far I've traveled. With my disability, I have been awarded a self-confident feeling I never knew. It's strange, for I had to be brought down to the lowest level I've ever experienced.

I found more good in my disability than bad, but this was only because I was in search of it. I looked for all the good, and amazingly enough, there was a lot of good that was buried beneath my disability.

I had to be able to overlook my disabled condition in order to master it. Let me rephrase that. It wasn't that I overlooked my disability; it was only that it didn't matter all that much to me. It is the same as the fact that I can't dunk a basketball at my height, five feet nine inches. I simply don't dwell on the fact that I have all these deficits. I would be a miserable character if I were to have exhausted my time fruitlessly in the arena of self-pity.

I realize it's all in how you look at it. For as many deficits I found with my disability, I found just as many, I can say considerably more, benefits just by the use of this disabled condition. Complaining about this or that would have been the easiest thing to do. However, that only keeps you in the spotlight for a short while. I found that by continually doing productive things, that spotlight never dimmed. I found that I never lose when I don't give up. Feeling sad about my condition, or feeling worthless, would have been like putting on the brakes before I even started.

There is humor in most any situation. Those events where I could find none, I simply looked the other way. That is, I didn't dwell on things that brought me down and the things that I couldn't change. I had to use humor so often during the rehabilitation venture that I forgot that I was using it. I never was the joke. Of course, I did laugh at myself from time to time, but I wasn't the joke; merely, it was the situation that I found myself in.

I looked the other way, concerning all my deficits. I stayed on my feet. I rolled with the punches and even sustained a few that hit below the belt. I had so many things wrong with me following this head injury that no one, aside from myself, would have faulted me if I didn't come back as far as I have.

If I were to have enumerated all the setbacks and all the difficulties I was having, then this would have consumed all of my time. I found that not being so conscious of my rehabilitation and refusing to get discouraged about my condition were key aspects. Fighting with my disability gave me something very constructive to do.

I can't remember ever being disheartened over the fact that I was disabled. Of course, there were instances when I'd feel overwhelmed. However, there always seemed to be more than one way to skin a cat. Feeling sorry for myself was something that, remarkably, I never mired in. It would have been easy, and justifiable, to fall into this pit. I can only attribute my success to my background and the elements I had inside me from birth to be the things that kept my head above water.

When I awoke from the nine-and-a-half-week coma, I couldn't remember what happened to me, who I was, or who anyone aside from my family was. I couldn't walk, use the toilet, feed myself, or hold any information in my head. I lacked emotional control, and you could infer anything else and not be far off the mark.

You don't know what you have until you have some of it taken away. I now, unlike before my accident, fully understand what I have. I am more satisfied with my rehabilitation. It's like losing everything you ever had without suffering the anguish of that loss and then finding all those things and then some. My life has been refurbished.

The majority of other disabled persons I have met over the years aren't looking down the road. I found the majority are focusing on the here and now, which is all well and good, but my focus is the light at the end of this disabled cavern. My close contact with, although no personal involvement with, other disabled persons throughout the years has kept me on track along this process. It's like being a former drunk. To keep on the straight and narrow, you refrain from keeping company with the former crowd. One of the biggest reasons I didn't like to associate with other disabled people is I didn't like to think I was disabled. This, I believe, kept me pushing forward.

Before my accident, disabled persons always made me feel very uncomfortable. Now that I understand what disability is, I tolerate other disabled people, but I don't make a habit of associating with them. I don't like to own up to my disability unless it provides windfalls. My disability has blown many my way over the years.

Challenges were never my forte. I would have to say skirting was my stronger point. Disability is a challenge. It's very continual. Overcoming the many setbacks is also a challenge, but this is something that is very rewarding to accomplish and, thus, not such a tiring aspect.

I overcame the largest challenge there was, and this was the temptation to quit. It was always there, but I have always maintained the drive. It was same drive that sustained me during the sixty-seven days I laid in a coma. It is that same engine that has me writing this book while simultaneously working two jobs at forty-eight hours a week.

It's amazing. Throughout my life, I've always been a devote quitter. However, through the use of this disability, there has been no justified reason I should quit. Things are just so easy when you remain dedicated.

It was as if every negative was turned into a positive, simply by the effort I maintained. This was the best situation I ever found myself in. By continually trying, this is a game in which I have never lost. I didn't deliberate about all I lost previously. I merely tried to gain back as much as I could.

Before the accident, I was a lackluster individual. However, my head injury changed all that. There's no failing when you are rehabilitating. You only fail if you fail to attempt. Before my accident, I feared failure, so I never tried.

I never became tired of all my accomplishments. I was on a treadmill, and I never became exhausted. I would have to assume the reason why me and my disability and rehabilitation clicked was because of my fear of failure.

There are plenty of bad things that went along with being disabled. I luckily never dwelled in the negatives. I don't recall ever sitting on my disability. I found many more opportunities for the simple fact that I was disabled. I exploited my situation. It was a friend I could use, and it never complained or took things from me. The only way my disability took from me was if I dwelled on my shortcomings for too long. The process of rehabilitation was my friend. I embraced it.

I was on a road. I had much assistance as well as understanding people around me, money given to me, no time restrictions, and a plethora of other commodities at my command. I was that proverbial kid in the candy store. If I were to have felt bad about my situation or hated the process of rehabilitation, then I would have gotten nowhere.

I was living within myself. Of course, there was a world going on outside of me. However, I merely stayed the course and took what came. I found rehabilitation to be as difficult as I made it.

Rehabilitation is an arduous journey. At the same time, it's been a piece of cake. Even though there was only a very dim light at the end of the tunnel, I didn't let that dense fog that surrounded me deter me from my course.

I simply turned a blind eye to all the difficulties I confronted and went forward. It's easy to sidestep a lot of minutiae that can trip you up. All I had to do was keep stepping forward. One important thing I had to do in this road to rehabilitation was to never think of myself as lower than anyone else, simply because of my condition.

It was to my benefit that I found the whole process of rehabilitation an interesting as well as challenging voyage. Never before in my life had I taken on a challenge so readily. Now I realize it was because I had a cushion to fall back on.

In the fall of 1971, I won the lotto. Disability was the horn of plenty. There was just so much available so long as I gave it my best. There's no other way I could've gotten all of this.

With this head injury, it's almost as if I have found a treasure chest. So many things are simply awarded to you. The list of things goes on and on and is too lengthy to enumerate. So, you will just have to take my word for it. Pennies from heaven, but not only that, I spent these coins in a very judicious fashion.

Important people, such as doctors, nurses, rehabilitation counselors, instructors, academic counselors, social workers, and the list goes on, are at your finger tips. These people wouldn't have given the old Rick the time of day.

God helps those who help themselves. In reality, it's other people who help those who help themselves. I had and have a multitude of difficulties with my disability, but no one wants to hear me whining, least of all myself. I didn't do this consciously, but this is what kept my rehabilitation motor running. I simply wore blinders throughout this whole rehabilitation process. Conscious and subconscious efforts draw people around you wishing to help. The opposite is also true.

Rehabilitation grew on me. I simply put one positive foot in front of the other. I didn't allow the struggles to overcome me. The majority of people, after noting the effort that I put in, would bend over backwards to help me. This effort wasn't an essential part of my makeup. At the beginning, I had to make a conscious effort, but, as time went on, I found myself putting in all my effort with little forethought.

From only remotely having confidence in myself to knowing it was I who pulled the strings was a refreshing change. Ironically, with this head injury, I feel that I'm more in control of things than ever before in my life. I never had this feeling prior to my injury.

It seems, and has seemed throughout this rehabilitation, I've been the one calling the shots. I realize this isn't one hundred percent true. However, I have been the motivational force behind the whole voyage. I don't brandish, at least consciously, all of my accomplishments in front of anyone's nose. In fact, this book is the first time, I believe, I've ever tooted my own horn.

I was consumed by poor health or should I say I was not one hundred percent health directed the majority of years before my injury. Having control over most aspects concerning my health leaves me with much free time to pursue other aspects that deal more directly with my rehabilitation. Good health is the foundation for successful rehabilitation. People, in my eyes, must find their own optimal health.

Over the years, I have learned much about the way to correctly tackle this giant. Disability is a monster, but, through the proper procedure, it can be tamed like a puppy. I fortunately fell into disability at the correct time with the proper frame of mind so as to squeeze the most juice from this lemon. And with that juice, I'm adding the proper amount of sweetness and making a refreshing lemonade.

Head injuries are so commonplace in this era. People should be aware that there are many ways to skin this cat, and who better to tell them than someone who has also sustained one? I wouldn't doubt if you personally know or are related to a head injured person. It was important for me to receive this blessing when the head injured population began to explode. I was on the cutting edge.

In my parent's tongue, there is a quip that is normally used in reference to Puerto Ricans, but it also can be used to describe the head injured. "Head injured persons son como aros blanco, son donde queran." Translation: "The head injured are like white rice; they are everywhere."

I never looked at my disability as my enemy. It merely provided me with obstacles to overcome. I overcame the majority. I went around the rest of the obstacles. Disability is tough. It's a lot tougher than me. I innately knew this from the start. So, rather than hit my head against the wall, I used that wall in various ways to promote my comeback.

My many disabilities have been my friend. Becoming angry at my situation was no good. It seemed as if people were willing to help me in any way possible. Putting a bad face on disability would be like biting the hand that feeds me. My mental attitude about my condition was one of the prominent factors. I never kicked myself or blamed another for my condition. It was mentally exhilarating for me to conquer or simply push aside each little obstacle.

I never thought of myself as something to laugh at, but some of the things I did were quite humorous. Inherently, I didn't laugh at my plight as much as I overlooked it. The way that I've avoided constant deliberation about my poor set of circumstances was my equally constant fight against this foe. It's an open field. Rehabilitation can be accomplished in many ways. The trick was to never give up on myself. In and of itself, rehabilitation has provided me with constructive rehabilitation. It's difficult to explain, but it was the process of rehabilitation that spurred more rehabilitation.

Even though I should be satisfied with where I am at this point, my eyes are still fixed on the future. I can't pinpoint how this is done, but, in certain respects, I made the process of rehabilitation work for me. Rehabilitation gave me a lot to do, while a good number of my peers were destroying themselves.

I was never (post head injury) satisfied with my accomplishments. That's what kept me moving. I know that I've said this before, but it bears repeating. I only wish that I can maintain that movement once I have done all the things I want to, but, then again, the thrill is in the hunt. Nothing has ever satisfied me as much as this drive I've maintained over the years. It more than makes up for my lackluster past.

Ironically, before my head injury, the objective was how far I could push myself back. It would be better said, "I'm okay; you're okay. Let's stick our fingers where the sun don't shine." The "I'm okay; you're okay" nonsense didn't hold water because I was sliding into an abyss.

If you're disabled and you feel this way and fail to strive for all you can achieve, then you'll certainly need a bit of luck if you hope to make anything of yourself. Let's be realistic because if a person would simply accept who they are and not try to better themselves, then not many, if any, advances would be made.

Everyone is my friend. I make no enemies. I don't place anyone below me. However, I don't let anyone beyond this shield I brandish. I don't give a hoot what people think or have thought about my introverted nature. I made it work for me, and that's what matters.

I don't have to be a certain way, and I do not need to do certain things to please others. I realize this sounds self-centered, and you're right if you think it does. To lessen the poor effects that certain groups around you can have on your rehabilitation, you have to be selective in the group you associate with. I excluded everyone from my circle of close friends. I never had to do anything the others did. I was genuinely my own man. Lack of close friends was pivotal in the success of my rehabilitation. Definitely, close friends would've slowed me down.

What I find to be important in life, particularly while rehabilitating, is to keep on friendly terms with everyone. I played no favorites; that is, I tried to be on friendly terms with everyone. Making enemies spoils the whole rehabilitation process. This doesn't mean I embrace everyone. I just don't alienate anyone.

This is only partially untrue. When I was attending school, all nine years of it, I distanced myself from other classmates. I had better friendships with instructors than with my fellow classmates. I felt below other students in the fact that they were not dealing with a serious brain injury. And yet, I felt above them because I could use my disability to gain the instructor's understanding. By not being the typical student, I didn't have to worry about who was my friend or how many friends I had, and by not being a close friend to anyone, I did not have to worry about who was or wasn't my friend.

I didn't need any bumps in the road. Disability is bumpy enough. This way, I didn't have to be continually thinking about how I should act toward this person or that. It was easier this way. I was always on the constant. This brought a better outlook for my goals. It takes energy to be continually looking over your shoulder.

You can acquire more rehabilitation with honey than with vinegar. You can quote me. It's human nature. People want to help a person who takes responsibility for their shortcomings more than those who try to displace their responsibility.

I never made enemies. I realize now that that was one of the smartest things I did. Everyone was vital to my rehabilitation. Relationships I maintained with people were essential. I had to be able to judge which people would help or hinder me throughout my rehabilitation and divide my time accordingly. I managed to keep my relations with most people on a positive note. Even those who were supposedly there to help me at times held me back. Luckily, I was able to distinguish one from the other. It seemed as if as long as I maintained a positive push, there were people and financial assistance to help me along.

All the right people root for you when you are actively rehabilitating, and wrong ones fall by the wayside. I had no longing to be with my friends of the past, and because of my disability, they also tended to shun me.

I was like fly paper. As long as I maintained a positive glow, the right people were attracted to me. It's human nature. Few people willingly hop aboard a sinking ship when they notice passengers merely lying on the deck sunbathing. However, if they notice you fervently bailing out water, then you stand a better chance of getting help. People want to be on the winning side. It's human nature. You probably have your share of close friends and just as many reasons for needing them as I have for not needing them, and I'll raise you five.

I did much better without close friends. In this way, you don't exclude anyone. There are no demands or expectations placed on you. Close friend are needed when you have free time to spend. This free time is generally expended fruitlessly. I can see where a lot of people would disagree with me. However, probably the same number would disagree with me if I met them at the altar and told them that this union just might not work.

Don't get me wrong. I relied on many people, only I did so on my terms. In the past, close friends were my downfall. You can throw lovers into that soup also.

Before the accident, I had no direction whatsoever. This injury helped me find myself, as well as gave me goals to achieve. I wasn't happy with myself before the accident. I didn't know where I was going, and I didn't know how I was going to get there. I have gained a much greater sense of self than I ever had before.

A few weeks before the accident, I remember telling my mother, when she asked me what courses I was going to take in school the next semester, a phrase that was a worn-out cliché at the time: "I need to kick back a while and find where my head's at." My mother quickly returned with a Puerto Rican phrase that slapped me right in the face. She told me, "Vete la mierda." This has the English equivalent of "eat shit!"

At this point in my life, I tend to push myself. This isn't hard at all. In fact, I find joy in pushing myself. It's something I can do and reap many rewards. Before my accident, I tended to allow myself to be pushed. Life, at this point, shows me no great challenges that I fear to meet head on.

Using the correct people was essential. Essentially everyone I came in contact with was used. I don't use people to their detriment. It merely worked toward my advancement. Virtually everyone I came in contact with posthead injury was important. Essentially, it was how they were used that made them important.

If you use people in the correct fashion, then the majority of them enjoy being used. However, you must go one step up the ladder in relation to the people around you. My former friends, before my accident, were used also. All along the way, as they were sinking lower and lower, through my usage of my disability, I was creeping higher and higher.

A big plus in my comeback has got to be the way that I feel about my circumstances. I accepted my disability, and I didn't need friends or lovers to rub salve over my wounds. There isn't any need for friends. You make everyone a friend. I make no one my enemy.

I have no enemies. Even my disability, something that others might think I deplore, has been a useful tool over the years. I could've easily made people dislike me by flaunting or rubbing their noses in my disability. I only used these stances when I was certain, to some degree, they wouldn't work against me. When you make close friends with one group, you tend to polarize yourself in relation to others.

In days of old, running away from reality was about the only exercise pursued by me and my cohorts. While we're on the subject of friends, something that happened the other day took me back to the days of old. The other day, I went to a department store to buy white spray paint for a chair that I have. I didn't look too carefully at the can, and when I got back to the apartment, I found it was clear lacquer. When I was buying it, the cashier made me show some ID. I guess some people still sniff that. Back in the old days, that was a cheap high. That's how Rueben "The Crow," my late buddy from the old neighborhood, destroyed a multitude of brain cells in his head.

It's easy to do that stuff along with other things that distort your thinking. This is especially true when you have no goals and plenty of time to pursue them. Later on in life, when he was not in jail or prison, he graduated to selling heroin and eventually to using this drug. Even while in his youth, The Crow never seemed to aspire to do much of anything.

Rueben's mind was continually off in the ozone. Clear lacquer became one of the Rueben's best friends, aside from anyone who had a little loose change. Rueben is currently sniffing spray in oblivion. I wonder if they allow that stuff down there; after all, it is highly flammable. He died a few years ago on an overdose of heroin.

It is wrong for me to make snap judgments about anyone, except maybe myself. However, I can't with any sincerity say that anything good happened to the lot of them. The list of my former friends sounds like a role call at the morgue. In reality, I have not heard a thing from any of those few who survived. For all I know, the majority of them could be decent, respectful taxpaying citizens. Yes, who knows? The ones who are still among us are doctors, lawyers, or candlestick makers. Jack just happened to be one of my associates who passed away. Then, Bear, Conejo, Paul "Cherry Pie", Weasel, and a few more also have taken their last breath. I haven't been back to the neighborhood in a few years, and I'm sure there are a few more on the respirator.

Rehabilitation is a task that incorporates all of your waking hours. Even as I'm writing these words, I'm busy rehabilitating. I'm a very healthy person at this point. Ironically, I can attribute this to my disability. All my health practices, and even some more that fail to register in my consciousness, have added lubrication to the machinery of my rehabilitation.

I had to maintain a good feeling about virtually anything. Without my health, I'd be up a creek with no paddle. Poor health would've been one more obstacle. My generous water intake, enough sunshine every day, proper food intake, chewing my food adequately, time of day food is eaten, exercise, and emotional balance are beneficial to me.

Maintaining good health was an overall key to the rehabilitation lock. I've learned over the years that, without my health, I could have done nothing. The poor health I endured throughout my youth helped sponsor my lackluster achievement of my younger days. Each health procedure I used built upon the next.

Before my accident, I had a piece missing. It was as if I was trying to roll my vehicle with three wheels when it needed four for optimum efficiency. Poor health is like a rock tied to your leg. You can still move; however, it is done less efficiently. In contrast, good health builds upon itself. It's like a snowball rushing down a hill.

Optimum health brings forth optimism. It is one less obstacle in front of you. Just realizing I was able to conquer this foe put another feather in my cap. I had to remove as many obstacles as I could when it concerned my rehabilitation. My health, or lack of, played a prominent role.

Good health works hand in hand with improving mental functioning. One hand washes the other. This certainly rings true when it concerns health and rehabilitation. It would be like trying to wash your car without soap, rags, and so forth. It could still be done, but it would be much harder and done less efficiently. Everything works together. If you have a severe pain in your toe, it'll color everything else you do. My good health, combined with my positive attitude, was the key.

My health maintenance is a relatively easy process to follow. It gives me much more than it takes away. I had nothing but time. By maintaining my health, I could use this time productively.

Everything I've attained since my injury can be traced back to my good health. In the years of my lackluster performance prior to my injury, I didn't know I was in the driver's seat. Even if good health were to have been harder or more time consuming, it would be worth it. Poor health would've been another disability I would have had to contend with.

The trouble with me is I didn't prioritize my actions before my head injury. I took the easiest things to come along. There was not a tangible reason to keep up good health. I, like you perhaps, couldn't sustain this health regimen without tangible payback. The only payback I would have received at that time would have been very intangible.

Keeping a strict health regiment meant I had to use my brain to keep everything in proper order. This mental exertion, being only remedial, was quite gratifying. As each ritual was added, I'd mentally kick myself after seeing how easy it was and how beneficial it would have been if I only had practiced these before my head injury.

Health maintenance is so easy, but I can see how easily it could take a backseat if you let your mind drift. It was easy for me to put health number one on my agenda because there was a tremendous payback.

Maintaining good health feeds on itself. Good health was so easy to maintain, it's a shame I didn't know this beforehand. Simple practices have to be maintained for the whole process to work. As I incorporated one good set of practices, another set, as it seemed, was waiting in the wings.

The healthier I became, the greater the pursuit for healthful practices became. The better I felt, the greater the will to maintain that feeling became. I could almost say that once I began these health practices, they fed on each other. Feeling good helped encourage that drive forward. Alternately, poor health would just be one more obstruction in the process of rehabilitation.

Not knowing how to maintain my health before the accident, and hence suffering the consequences, I didn't want to travel that route again. It's similar to conquering this disability. I have to remain ardent in my struggle.

This head injury put me on the right track. Yes, my head injury was a savior. It not only physically set me straight, but it also emotionally and socially set me straight. I still exercise regularly. I no longer go the gym down the street at my cousin's apartment complex, but I do simple calisthenics to keep in shape. I'm five feet nine inches, have a medium frame, and I'm 160 to 165 pounds. I've been this way for a few decades.

I do a few set of exercises each night before I shower. It takes but a half hour, and I feel in very good shape. My overall health consciousness over the years has brought me this far. So I won't abandon it midstream. My last physical exam was a couple of years ago, and I truly surprised my doctor. With the look of astonishment on his face, coming back with the lab results, he told me that I had the insides of someone twenty years my junior.

It's so easy to care for your health. However, one must be motivated and committed. There must be a reason, I believe, deep down inside to motivate you to carry out this procedure. Motivation—that is, you have to have a reason for doing this or that to continue the upkeep of these practices—has to be present.

Ability to remain stringent to these practices wasn't hard. It presented a challenge. In the back of my mind, I had an objective, even though this goal was quite foggy at that time. Good health gives continual rewards. It allows you to do your best, whatever that might be. Even though I'm not as successful in my attempts as I'd like to be, this force behind me is what keeps me striving. After a while, it's very easy. It's like tying your shoes. Once you know how, it's quite simple.

I was born with a good set of genes from my parents. There was nothing else outstanding about their health, but it gave me a good foundation to build upon. My father was the last of ten kids. His father died before he was born. His mother had to be quite strong. My mother's mother died when my mother was in her teens. The stamina my mother had to posses must have been enormous. Even though her father had a thriving bakery, my mother had to deal with my grandfather's lust-filled behavior with different women. He carried on like this before, while my poor grandmother was on her deathbed. My mom and dad had to show some strong qualities to survive their youths, which were somewhat unique for the era that we're talking about.

I am in no way special. What I have done, is merely take advantage of my situation. I was fortunate enough not to be consumed by it. I give a good amount of credit to the way I was raised. There are others who have survived essentially the same thing I have, but they will go unnoticed.

With all that I've done throughout my rehabilitation, as well as a lot of the destructive stuff I did prior, I feel as though I have done a lot. However, I realize this could be done by virtually anyone. I am nothing special. I'm no different than the majority of you reading this. However, I'm such a poor reader I would've lost interest and set this book down a long time ago. I simply used all or most of the elements I was provided and maximized their use.

However, if I were merely reading this book, and had a person close to me who had suffered similar injuries, then I would be extremely skeptical that he could use his plight as effectively as I have.

Without my disability, I wouldn't know up from down. My disability has given me much more than it has taken away. In fact, can't think of one deficit that has not turned into a positive. Yes, I can't think of one negative that hasn't been flipped into a positive. The key word here is "think." You can think anyway you want. Of course, there are several things I suffer because of my disability, but they amount to nothing as long as I don't allow them to bother me. I was too busy doing positive things to allow the negatives to consume me.

Being able to turn such a dire set of circumstances into a positive outcome is one gigantic feather in my cap. Learning how to change bad into good was a process that was totally foreign to me in the preinjury days. However, with all the compassion and understanding I received, I'd be a fool if I didn't remain on a strict course.

By overcoming, or simply sidestepping, the ravages that this injury has left me with is an enormous ego booster. Thinking I was on top of the world, it was amazingly easy to look on the bright side of my disability. I simply had to take my disability as given and go from there.

As long as I didn't stand downwind from the pungent odor of my disability, I continued my rehabilitation. I didn't let my situation consume me. There was just too much room for improvement. Most things I did were for the betterment of my condition. If I weren't advancing in one way or another, I'd be stepping back. It was fairly easy for me to distinguish between the two.

I, fortunately, didn't waste time. With a disability, you slowly move forward, remain idle, or slide rapidly back. When I first awoke from a coma in 1971, I jumped on the treadmill of rehabilitation. I found it easier than feeling sorry for myself.

I don't recall any time during my rehabilitation, including now, where I didn't have an objective. With disabilities, there's no time to dillydally around. It seemed as if the more positive things I did, the more positive things I could do.

Up until this point, I haven't overtly tooted my horn. However, at this point in my rehabilitation, I can share some of my knowledge and experience in a form that would be helpful to others. Parents, doctors, teachers, and essentially everyone will gain useful knowledge from my books.

I didn't realize how valuable firsthand knowledge can be, but as things began to collect in my storehouse of information, the outline for this book and the ones that will follow began to surface. I speak with candid knowledge that only a person who's lived through it can. It's like reading a book about the Holocaust written by a statistician as opposed to a book written by a Jew who survived a Nazi death camp.

With all I've experienced throughout my rehabilitation, not very much at this point can stump me. I can't remember the last time I was ill and remained in bed for any length of time. I have no unwarranted fear of sickness or disease or any other variety of intangibles.

Having to confront this head injury using my own strength has built character. This was something that was seriously lacking before my injury. I would have to assume this would have to do a lot with the maturity I now posses, as opposed to anything else.

At this point, I have hopes for my future. Before my accident, I never had any plans for tomorrow. My head injury was a blessing in disguise. Very little scares me at this point. This is unlike before my head injury, where I was taken aback by my own shadow.

In my opinion, which is the only opinion that truly matters to me, I have done the best I could with this disabling experience. Disability didn't work me over. I wrestled it to the ground through various means. I worked it and took the best I could from it. There is much good that can be derived from a situation like mine. It merely has to be searched for.

I can think of no other way I could have handled this disability in a better fashion. I don't believe I ever let it have the upper hand. I always felt in control; even at the very beginning of my rehabilitation, it was I who made the decision to open my eyes after lying in that comfortable hospital bed for several weeks.

Before my injury, I was a lost bullet, and I didn't like the feeling. I feel better about myself and my situation at this point, decades after my head made contact with the asphalt, than any time in my history. At present, most things are going my way. I can attribute this to the luxury of time that was given to me and time that I took in regards to my rehabilitation. Actually, I learned the ins and outs of the process.

4

My sense of self is innocuous. That is, it doesn't tread on anyone else's territory. I don't profess to be better than anyone else. I realize this is self-destructive. However, I do realize that I have strengths, and I try to build on these and laugh at my inabilities.

I have many physical and psychological disabilities as a result of the brain damage I suffered in my accident. My outlook helps me to deal with these things effectively. I realize that there are many things that I cannot do, but these things don't bother me as much because I don't dwell on them. I feel I'm better off than you, but I think that's the way everyone should feel about themselves.

I've rarely, if ever, lamented about my condition. In the rare instances I have, I did so strategically. This disability is just another part of me. I don't see it as a third foot or an extra eye in the middle of my forehead. It's just there.

I've used my disability, as I am using it now; otherwise, it would have used me. I've always used it as if it were another part of me. I could almost classify it as a talent. It's as if I could sing or dance very well. I'd certainly utilize that talent. The same is true if I could dig a ditch well—you'd always find dirt under my fingernails. I have accepted the bulk of my limitations and simultaneously fight continuously against them so as to not give them the upper hand.

It's been a wonderful voyage. Before my injury, everything I did was done with a bit of trepidation. I was afraid of falling on my face. However, postinjury, there was no fear of failure because I didn't fall very far, since I was already on the ground.

I thought very little about head injuries before my car accident. The little thought of them was quite dismal. However, in actuality, my head injury saved my life. I don't specifically remember ever giving brain injury laborious thought. From a distance, those shoes appeared very large, but, when I approached closer, I realized they fit me like a glove. Before my injury, disability was scary to me. It was the other guy's problem, and I wished it to stay right there.

I always pictured disabled persons as being from another planet. I never differentiated the head inured from all the other disabled. They were all in the same boat, and that boat had many holes in it and was sinking fast. I, in no way, wanted to hop aboard.

Gradually, from the time of my injury to this point, the pendulum began to swing in my favor. Even at my lowest point, back in 1972 at the beginning of my rehabilitation, I felt in control. Though that control was felt only on the remotest level, it was control I managed. Yes, disability was better than I ever thought that it might be. Even though my thoughts about others who had disabilities hasn't changed that much—for me, disability has been my horn of plenty.

At this point, I feel in control. People around me don't, I believe, feel comfortable telling me what to do concerning my major life decisions. I erroneously thought disability was the same in regards to everyone. Others with disabilities tended to turn me off. However, I now realize that is because I wrongly assumed that this was something I could not handle, but the opposite is true now.

Before my accident, the term disability was so foreign to me that it was frightening. It was them, not me, and I wanted to keep it that way. Disability, to me was like having an extra foot growing out of your forehead. How things change.

In my preinjury days, disabled persons were like creatures from Mars. If I were to pass one on the street, I couldn't make eye contact with them. They essentially gave me the creeps. However, at the start of my rehabilitation, I began to see all the advantages there were to being disabled. More importantly, I began to use these benefits constructively.

Disability, to me, is like having blue hair. Of course, it was somewhat difficult at first getting used to these blue locks. With time, though, I realized all I could receive merely because these strands held a different tint. If I wouldn't have accepted it from the start, I couldn't work against it.

The road toward improvement was a difficult one for me to follow. However, if I would have merely thrown my arms into the air and given up, then this would have been harder. I found rehabilitation to be an easy road to follow. All you have to do is use the correct path. By the correct path, I mean a positive mental attitude. With all the negatives you are given with disability, you don't need another one. People came out of the woodwork to help me with my rehabilitation. I feel this was simply because I accepted my disabilities and didn't place blame on anyone, not even myself for my shortcomings. I merely went forward from where I was at.

It's almost as difficult as falling off a tree. All you have to do is make the effort to let go of the branches. In essence, you must take a venture into the unknown. You must be willing to continuously work for something you're not sure will ever pan out.

It would have definitely been to my detriment if I were to have ever looked back and realized all that I let slip through my fingers if I had not used my situation to its fullest potential. Sure, it was hard, but trying to live with the fact that I had missed so much if I had just fallen through the cracks of this disability would have been many times worse. I don't know if its age, maturity, knowledge, the sense of self, or what it is, but I feel much better than any time in my life.

Sure, there were rough times throughout this disability, but this was for the better. I had to see what I was made of. The trick was I would always wear blinders. These blinders were placed in such a position so that I couldn't see the towel and, thus, never throw it in.

Let's face it. I have a serious disability, but I have never felt better in my life. This is definitely because of the way I handled the incongruities that this disability has presented. I am speaking now of the part of my life that has had to suffer the complications of this head injury. It's not so much that I had a terrible upbringing; on the contrary, I had many possibilities. If I would have been the academic type, then I'm sure my father would have put me through school for as long as I thought I needed. If I had a special talent, or whatever, then I'm sure my folks would have stood behind me. I had many possibilities—not too much unlike the majority of persons. So, after throwing away all those other possibilities of my past, I wasn't going to shy away from taking all that I could from this situation.

Disability is a weak little punk. There are so many ways to overcome it. It's fruitless to despair. It's almost as if you're afraid of something that's not there. The good feeling I had toward my disability was, for the most part, internal. If I would have been outwardly overjoyed, then it would have worked against me.

When you're kicking disability in the ass, you have no time to feel sorry for yourself. Even when I wasn't successful in one venture, the mere fact that I was in the fight made me a winner. Feeling sorry for oneself, takes a bit if not more energy. It wasn't as if I was always blatantly defeating this monster. However, when you're continuously battling this foe, it makes you successful in a lot of other ventures.

To me, my disability has been no big deal. Disability was similar to a cushion. I simply look at it as I do my inability to sing or dance, and life goes on. I've always accepted my inabilities to do this or that. At the start of rehabilitation, there were many things I found to be a challenge to work through. The inner gratification this provides lends the fuel to keep the motor humming.

I genuinely feel my disability will be a benefit to all those around me and to those who read my writings. At the start of my recovery back in 1972, there was nothing, to my knowledge, out there like the book you're reading at present.

If I would have died as a result of the car accident, then I would have missed out on so much. Moreover, if I would've allowed my disability to swallow me, and not vice versa, it would've been to everyone's detriment.

We are all connected to one another, no matter how independent you might think you are. This book is simply repayment for the portion of good I received from so many generous people throughout my rehabilitation. Everybody wins when a disabled, especially head injured person, can triumph over his shortcomings. Moreover, it's such a waste if a person allows their disability to consume them.

There are so many good people in this world. My disability tended to bring them out, and my continual reaching for higher levels brought these people out in spades. I and everyone else were like a team. I could not have made it this far without everyone around me. However, it's like everything else; everyone must be approached in the appropriate manner … It's remarkable. I feel so good with all the deficiencies I sustained. This is because I realize how good I had it in the past but failed to utilize the majority of the things I had at my disposal. Even with all my disabilities and things others might view as impediments to a happy life, I feel much better, at this point, in comparison to how I ever felt.

Before my injury, I had a set up. I threw it all away. If this weren't true, then I don't believe I would have pushed myself so hard. This isn't because I had such a hard life. It's conversely because I had everything and just didn't use it to my advantage. Even if I never had the accident, I don't believe I would have ever excelled as much as I have. I had to have this little shaking up to stir the pot and start me in the right direction.

There are just so many things I have reaped with this disability that I can't fathom ever accomplishing what I have without it. I couldn't have made it this far without the constructive use of my disability.

I guess you can differentiate me from other disabled persons who try to ignore their disabilities and go from there. I've tended to milk my disability and then go from there.

Unlike if this were another human, or something tangible, I was in debt to no one or to any one thing. I just finished watching a snippet on the *60 Minutes* news program. There was a one-armed man who had made his disability, along with his acting troop, work for him. In certain ways, he is like me. I use my disability, and I don't overlook it.

I thank my lucky stars for the severity and the ability to bounce back from an injury of this magnitude. All the parts just seemed to fit perfectly for me. However, I realize at this point that this in only because I rolled with the punches.

If I had to do it over again or if I had scripted all of this beforehand, then I couldn't have done a better job. I truly can't think of anything better to have happened to me. As long as I kept active and traveled in a positive direction, things just went my way.

If I ever would've stopped to smell the roses, or more relevant to my condition, paused to pull the thorns out of my ass stuck there as a result of falling on that rose bush many more times than I would like to remember, then I wouldn't have gotten a thing done. I didn't realize this at the time, but I was climbing a steep rock. If I stopped my climbing, I wouldn't remain in the same place. However, gravity would pull me further down.

Sitting around doing nothing, I fortunately had the notion would be worse for me than trying and failing. I never let grass grow under my feet. "An idle mind …" certainly rings true for this head injured person. Remorse takes time and energy. It thwarts the process.

This disability has been one of the most important things in my life. I'm speaking now in positive terms. I can't fathom, considering my lackluster youth, doing anything positive with my life if not for this injury. This rehabilitation stint was much easier for me than the previous years before my accident. During all the years of my youth, I had little direction. However, with this massive head injury, I had direction as well as a multitude of people and services thrown into my lap.

As I look back on all the years of my rehabilitation, I realize that it hasn't been hard at all. However, it would've been significantly harder if I wouldn't have tried. I would have second guessed myself to death. I would've, more than likely, compared my situation to my lackluster youth and justified the whole thing by accepting the fact that I'm a born loser.

It was very important I never felt downtrodden because of my disability. I was always at work to thwart whatever it produced. I never felt less than anyone else. Let me clarify that. I knew I was substantially less in the mental and physical realm, but I never let it eat me up.

Always, in the back of my mind, there has been a crowd cheering me on. Equally, as motivation was building, it never booed when I dropped the ball, as I do from time to time. In fact, in a different kind of way, I have always felt as if I had a bit more going for myself than the average Joe. If I would've continually felt less of an individual because of my mental, physical and social condition, then it would have taken some of the steam from my engine. I needed all the force I could muster. There was always something productive to do.

Patience had to be learned. It was not inherent in my makeup, but learning this was easy, for I had no other distractions. Do you, I'm sure you do, remember the tortoise and the hare? I have to satisfy myself with much smaller gains at a very slow pace.

I feel one of the keys to my ongoing rehabilitation is my patience. It has already been almost twenty-eight years since my injury, and I'm still rehabilitating, but at a much slower pace.

Patience is and was the key. When I was laid off my position in 1993 in southern California, I fruitlessly looked for work for the next two years. However, when I came up to the northern portion of the state, I found two positions that I currently hold in less than a month. Even though it was only about four hundred miles from my place in southern California, northern California opened up a few doors for me. There is an exit for everyone.

I have been on a perpetual treadmill for all these years. It has made me stronger both mentally and physically. I never consciously or subconsciously bragged about myself. That serves no purpose. In fact, that just exhausts time. My time can be used more productively. If I were continuously tooting my horn about this or that, then it would definitely draw wind from my sails.

The unegotistical belief in self is more productive. I just let everything go in one ear and out the other. This goes for bad as well as good. Thinking and worrying about my condition would've only slowed me down. The fewer things you have to concern yourself about, the easier it is to make it. Actually, that is the only way to make it.

Having come from where I did, understanding others, especially disabled persons, isn't such a difficult task. I no longer have to worry about myself, as I did before my head injury, as well as my rehabilitation up to this point. I can now concern myself with more extraneous things, as opposed to the me-first method of rehabilitation. Now, I find understanding others and their concerns an easier task.

Now that I have a bit more time and know who I am, I can concern myself with other things. In my field, gerontology, it's easier for me to relate one-on-one with these Seniors. They're going through something that I've been through. However, they're on a downward trajectory. This book is a form of help for others. It's possibly the greatest help I can deliver. Although this book doesn't render a step-by-step account about how I rehabilitated, it does give hope to the millions who surround the head injured.

I didn't need one more deficit in my makeup, as a lack of money would've been, if I had let it. It was all relative. I made do with what I had. This frugality must have been built-in. I never suffered because I had less than others. I merely rolled with the punches. I kept my expenses down. I'm very good with money. I realized debts can stifle you. I only live off the essentials. I realize this will change in the future, but I have no regrets for the way I've handled my money throughout my rehabilitation.

If lack of money would've been a problem, then everything else would have followed suit. Living on such a low an income was a challenge that I undertook with little remorse. I didn't know what it was like to have lots of money in my pockets, so it was no loss. I found that an outside push, as well as financial assistance, is great. However, if you combine it with a push of your own, then you will reap the maximum rewards. I feel that not putting forth much effort and allowing things to be done for you are like paying for sex and not having the gratification of working for it.

Places and organizations that try to help are a good source, but you must initiate that inner drive. Organizations and such prime the engine, but what I needed was the internal engine to burn that fuel. I, luckily, found that motor deep down inside. In fact, I don't see how rehabilitation can be accomplished without the two entities working hand in hand. It would be like trying to build the tower of Babel. Even though all the workers were speaking in the same tongue, they could not agree on what type of health coverage they wanted and the size of the deductible … not a brick would be laid.

I never had people skills before the accident. I had a good deal of apprehension when it came to conveying my ideas to another person. I chose the easiest way. My friends tended to be those who wavered on the lower end of the social spectrum. I've found that one doesn't need to have a cluster of close friends to be complete.

I needed time to find out who I was before I could ever attempt to discover who you are. I wouldn't say, at present, that I'm a people person. However, I've lost a lot of the trepidation that would impede upon any relations before.

I was shy around the opposite sex and didn't make friends of the same sex very easily. I was in sad shape back then. I didn't know how I could fix that. I would mutter to myself. "Maybe a time out?"

My thought pattern, at this point, is very clear. I realize it can get fogged up in the future, but just realizing how much I've accomplished by refraining from simple pleasures for this interim will easily make up for it. I gave up a little and gained a hell of a lot more. It's a cheap high. I could've used substances that others were engaged in, including sex. However, I subconsciously realized this wouldn't be life enhancing. It would be similar to when the well was dry, and the guy down the street and I would saturate a rag with clear lacquer spray paint and sniff our way into a different reality, not necessarily a better one.

Presently, I feel very comfortable with my ability to judge up from down. This would have been impossible for me if I would have involved myself with drugs, alcohol, the opposite sex, or a myriad of other things.

Thank heaven for small favors. I credit having a former love life for the endurance I presently possess. It's like not smoking. I don't crave smoking, because that's not an animal need. Over these many years, I have simply prioritized these needs. It's like a person falling off a cliff. If given a choice, any thinking man would choose a sturdy rope tied to a large rock than the arms of a scantily clothed beautiful woman, no matter the shape of her biceps.

Sex has been around a long time. In fact, that's the reason you and I are here at this moment. Sex will not take a hiatus when

I decide to throw my hat back in the ring. I still have the animal desire that I've always had, but I have the intelligence to know I'm not ready for that now.

There's still a bit of my life yet to complete. If I were to jump into the fire at this point, essentially without an asbestos suit, I would undoubtedly get burned. There are a few things I still have to do before I throw in the towel on this rehabilitation stuff and throw my hat into the ring concerning love. I can do no worse than the bulk of other Americans who have an equal success/failure rate.

Over the years, that animal hasn't died. Conversely, he's a lot more fit and a hell of a lot more intelligent. With the mental and physical difficulties I have at this point, I'd be much better than I ever was in my past, as ironic as that might sound.

I often have thoughts about throwing my hat back into the ring and having a love life. Even though I feel like that would be a piece of cake after all that I've been through, there's still some trepidation. I might gag on that bit of pastry if I indulge before I do everything I want done. I still have to get my first book published.

It's difficult to explain. I guess it would be like an ex-smoker for the past ten years after being a moderate smoker for the previous twenty. Then, through the miracle of science, they develop a pill you take every day to offset the harmful effects of nicotine. All the rest of the negatives would still exist, such as the stench, discoloration of teeth, stains on your fingers, smoker's breath, and so forth. The question is … will you pick up the habit again? Thank heaven I've never picked up that addictive trait. However, when I'm ready, I will jump into that love game with both feet and similar cravings.

The key to my rehabilitation has been patience as well as determination. It will happen when it happens. Presently, although very content, I'm not exactly where I'd like to be. I have no doubt I will get there, whenever I am meant to.

I think I'm very mature at this point. However, I want a few more things before I turn on that switch in my heart. If I were to jump into a relationship at this point, when I'm essentially half-baked in reference to where I'd like to be, I'd end up regretting it.

There was a time when that was predominant in my thinking. However, now that I've had the luxury of this extended time out, I feel a bit more certain than the average Joe on the street. I don't know if it's because I'm older and wiser. There's not much proof that age makes any person wiser when it comes to relationships, but I feel I won't make a mistake and haphazardly fall in love.

There's time enough to fall in love and have three or four relationships with educated women. When I throw my hat into the ring, I want to be able to walk back in that same ring, and if it begins to close in on me, dance and pick it up again.

Even like ten or so years ago, I was very willing to throw my hat back into the ring, but it always seemed as if I had other priorities. I have the same longings for the opposite sex as I always have. I'm ever so grateful to have had the smarts to put all that stuff on the back shelf for all these years of my rehabilitation. All the time, energy, and legal fees wasted by all these people who have gone through that marriage or serious relationship quandary have merely been a waste of time and energy.

I saved myself a lot of trouble, headaches, suicidal thoughts, and so forth by cleaning up my act since that brisk night in 1971. It will be the same as if I have been in a time capsule for all those years. However, the big difference is that I grew intellectually and currently have a lot more sense. And while in that time capsule, I have witnessed others through the window that surrounds the capsule do senseless things.

Love can bring you down just as easily as drugs or alcohol. If I had been using drugs throughout this excursion of rehabilitation, then I wouldn't have had the stamina that was required. Love is a cheap and expensive habit. Like drugs and alcohol, it can be used effectively, but this is difficult, and very few accomplish it.

While we're on the topic of drugs and alcohol, I have to get this tidbit off my chest. Oprah and all the rest of the talk show hosts and hostesses are merely masturbating you. All the time you've wasted in front of the TV, what has it brought you? Are you smarter or able to handle your problems better? An even better question would be can you remember any of the topics discussed last week on any of her programs? I rest my case.

Wake up America. It's show time. If you genuinely believe you can gain knowledge by listening to a person who might have loads of charisma and not all the factual data you need, then you're merely satiating your mind with palatable tidbits of information. I'm not putting blame on talk show hosts because they are in a business. They make money showing you things you want to see and telling you stuff you want to hear—even things you might not want to hear or see. They might give you correct information, but there's hardly enough time or depth in their coverage to scrape the surface of most any topic covered by the majority of these people.

When I think of the vast sums of money these people rake in, it causes me to wonder if we would rather see an end to the problems displayed on these shows or simply remain as voyeurs. Now that I've got that off of my chest …

I realize that little snippet was off the topic a bit, but I felt it had to be said. Look at all I've gotten done, just by remaining in one direction. All these talk show hosts and the rest are doing very little, but making their pockets full at your expense. With all the time and attention you've paid these people, are you any better than before?

It would've been an outright shame if I had never had the opportunity to search myself and pull out the side of me that always lingered there until the apropos moment. I needed, throughout my youth, a safety net underneath me. This injury has provided just that.

I had no fear or embarrassment. When you begin from the bottom, it's an accomplishment just to be putting forth effort. All these abilities regarding what I have done after my head injury have always been there. However, I feel it was a cushion provided by my disability, which was the missing piece in the puzzle.

I wouldn't recommend it to any of you out there to go out and suffer a head injury. However, to those of you who've already experienced one, I'd like you to know there's another side to the coin. The brain is such a complex mechanism. It immediately begins to repair itself once it's been damaged. We have millions of cells up in our head that wait for the right time to awaken and take the place of the cells that were killed. However, they take their sweet time to do this.

I feel good about myself. This is nothing I could've said prior to my head injury. Before my accident, I never felt good about myself. What I displayed to others was a mere masquerade. And if, say, I were to survive to this day without having suffered this severe head injury, then I seriously doubt I could enjoy this self-satisfaction that I currently do. It has already been such a long time since my head made contact, in a forceful manner, with the pavement, but I'm just beginning to smell the roses on the other side of the curb.

My injury released the fight I had within me. It's not so much the fight I have inside, but, for lack of a better word, the cunning I posses. Ask yourself, "Have I done everything I could have to become what I'd like to be at this point?" Maybe I could've said this if I had not had the accident and the following rehabilitation, but it would've been an empty statement.

I looked instinctively for all the benefits that could be derived from being in this condition. I never whimpered. That music didn't sway me. The words "poor me" were not in my vocabulary. However, during the few times, very few times, when I sensed it could help me over a little bump in the road, I put on my dancing shoes. Living off the pity of others dilutes a person's will to do for him or herself.

The well runs dry quickly. There's only so much concern others can show you before the moisture evaporates. Too much pity from others simply promotes self-pity. That's a waste of time. Time is of the essence. Rehabilitation takes time. It was fortunate for me that I didn't need or want pity. That would've only held me back. I steered clear of those who merely wanted to show their concern for my situation and provided little in terms of help.

It seems as if I'm prepared to meet every challenge that presents itself head on. This differs greatly because, before my head injury, I would tend to skirt anything that presented a little work. However, since my injury, I know there will be people and things beside me to lend a helping hand. This is contrary to before my disability, where I believed no one would assist me. It's hard to fail with my head injury. The only way I can fail is by not trying. Even the few failures I've had, none of which I can remember, are overshadowed by all the successes I've had.

It's easier to perform when you have a cheering crowd (friends, relatives, and associates), cheerleaders (teachers, counselors, and so forth), and coaches as well as management (uniforms, stadium, concession stand, and the like) all at your disposal.

When I had a valid reason to fail, ironically, it became much easier to succeed. I milked the reality of having less for all it was worth. I have become rich in the process. I had less responsibilities and commitments, and no one but yours truly to answer to. I began with nothing after my injury, and the gradual build up of my mental abilities was very encouraging.

Having limited resources, as it pertained to knowledge, made every inch forward a giant leap. Educating myself, going to school, and so forth were easier with this head injury. The only way I can describe it is it's easier to keep track of your finances when you are poor, in contrast to if you had all the money in the world.

Disability gave me a constructive deviation. I was no longer doing things my peers were. At this point, a good number of my friends are either busy pushing up roses or else they have found steady employment making license plates.

I feel as though I've just completed a critically important part of my life. Without this disability, I'd be nothing. I merely flowed with the tide of this circumstance. Disability begs to be used. I can't think of where I'd be at this moment without having this life-altering event take place in my life.

I could've never done as much as I did without the luxury of this handicap. As it turned out, this was one of, if not the best, things to ever happen to me. I have never had any reservations or regrets, and this remains true.

A variety of things also happened to me, some bad and others good, but I wouldn't change a thing. As I look back on my years of rehabilitation, there is very little I wish I would have done differently. I haven't in the past, or even at present, given it more than a cursory review. It seems as if everything has worked out very well for me. I'm sure there are some things that could be changed that would make things better, but I worked with what I had, and that made it even more self-gratifying.

I'm satisfied. If I were able to look through a crystal ball before that eventful night in 1971 and foresee all the benefits this injury would provide, then I wouldn't have avoided anything that might have prevented it from happening. Rehabilitation is totally individual. What I might see as a grand accomplishment, you, even as another disabled person, might see it as trivial.

I realize, as I write these words, much time has passed since my head made contact with the asphalt. The time has passed in the blink of an eye. What made everything go so well was that I was always in a positive direction.

Luckily, I've never been consumed by time. Things will happen when they do. I continue with this positive direction, and even though it was at times very hard, I notice it less by keeping my eye on the end of that tunnel. With my head injury, things have happened at a significantly slower pace. Even though everyone and everything have continued to surpass me, I don't let it sway my direction. As the clock ticks, it ticks in my favor. This is simply because I've maintained this positive direction.

Things are harder for me, of course, but I just accept everything as a given and don't let it swallow me. I'm swimming upstream. However, I don't get caught up in the endless struggles so much that it makes me want to quit. Lamenting about this or that, and there were so many, is merely a waste of time. It will bring your emotions to a lower point.

Remember President Reagan? He was called the Teflon President. Not much stuck to this guy. I am the Teflon handicapped. I have let all the discouragement, feelings of inferiority, and lack of social contacts fly out the window. We were all born without the ability to fly. Imagine all the time you'd waste and things you'd fail to do simply because you were too busy lamenting the inability to fly. I accepted what I was left with and never stopped working on what I could improve.

I keep my eyes on the goal post. I will reach them when I do. I'm enjoying the process of running downfield. I have the suspicion that when I finally reach the end zone, it will be anticlimactic.

I have no dire need for anything. Love, sex, money, and fame will come when it does. I could cross the street tomorrow and get killed by an angry old lady who hits me with her cane as she speeds by. Fate is a tricky thing. However, I found that fate can be manipulated. I have been in the process of altering fate's wishes, even before I realized what I was doing.

This head injury has taught me a great deal of patience. It has also given me a great deal of foresight. With the great amount of patience that I have acquired through this head injury, this patience will breathe life into forever. I'm afraid at the end of the trek that there will not be no more hills to conquer. Hopefully, I'm wrong, and something else needing my dire attention will present itself.

I found that by taking an active part in dismantling my brain damage, it tended to strengthen me more and more. My brain damage was a little wimp. There was relatively little that resulted from it that I couldn't topple or otherwise find a way around. It was war from the start. No matter how many times I tried and failed, there were always those around me who put me back on my feet again. This was true when I was attending school and trying to rebuild myself physically, as well as mentally, because I'd always find enough money to do the things that pushed me forward. This was something I never lost at. Not only that, I had people all around me at my finger tips who would help me along the way.

I instinctively found ways to render it useless. I had and I have a disability. Disability isn't me. That, I found, was the best way to confront this monster. It's hard to judge how I did this, but I never let it have the upper hand. I believe that this is particularly because I kept moving. With all that was at my disposal, I did all I could. The only thing I had to pay back was not with success, but with my continual push forward. I had no other concerns. All I had to do was plow ahead. I had a hard time getting to where I am at this point. I would not have made it if not for this cushion of disability.

For me, this head injury has been a great learning device. It has helped me with education, social status, knowledge of self, and other's perception of me, and it has given me a cushion to explore with little fear of failure. I never make a fool of myself, others give me credit for my courage, and my health has definitely benefited from the need to start from square one.

It's not that I needed a rough road to struggle through. In reality, what I needed were others around me to perceive me as having a rough time. That automatically developed a cheering section around me. It was better than making a fresh start. I had a lot of things already done for me.

I found ways to use others, though not destructively, to benefit my comeback. However, this is definitely not a comeback because in no way do I want to be back where I was prior to my injury. At this point, everything is manageable. Before my injury, I was not in control of anything. Being somewhat in control of my situation wasn't something that just fell out of the sky. I had to work at it. However, unlike the past, I found enjoyment in the process of the struggle.

I now have structure in my life. I take care of myself physically, try my best to get along with everyone, I work at two places (and do a good job at each), and take care of most problems as they come up. This is a surprising change. I was once a person who did the least I possibly could, and I merely scraped by. However, at this point, I enjoy challenges. That is, I enjoy challenges that I am sure will end in a positive result.

If I didn't have the need to improve, provided by this injury, I know I would've self-destructed. Actually, none of the time posthead injury was spent twiddling my thumbs. At the time immediately following my injury, I didn't have the coordination to twiddle my thumbs, so I had to exhaust my time doing things that provided results. I'm making up for all the leisure time I had while in a coma.

I'm a thinking animal first. I'm working in excess, I exercise regularly, I'm writing this book, and doing other things that take up much of my time. This is something I never thought I could do in the preinjury days. I'm very satisfied with the way things turned out after my head injury. This head injury has provided me with challenges that were surmountable, if I only tried. Before my injury, I was lost. At age eighteen, I was too tired to do anything positive. Not doing anything positive led me in the direction of doing negative things. Drugs, alcohol, and doing other illegal deeds were rampant in the area where I grew up. After a mere taste of the negatives, I was saved by this injury.

What I found after the injury was myself. There's no other way, I have to assume, that I ever could've done what I have. I would've been too caught up in doing whatever those around me wished. It's so easy to go either way. It's a little scary when I think of it. Of course, if I would've just sat on my hands, the opposite would've been true.

The struggle has made me a better person. The drive I used to stay afloat while in a coma is the same push that I'm using now. This was just what the doctor ordered. I needed the struggle this injury provided in order to see just what I had. Also, the financial assistance, as well as all the key people who would help me along the way, was also a great help in bringing out this side of me that was previously dormant.

There are many things I did before the accident that contrast what I do today. It's almost incredible. What is more noteworthy, however, is that underneath everything, I'm still the same character.

All in all, it was me who had to move, and I also had to have people around me assisting me in that movement. I, for whatever reason, never shifted the blame for my condition onto anyone else. I never even blamed myself. I have to guess, I realized that that would only stifle me. Of course, I don't wish to slight my parents. However, without this disability, I, more than likely, would have unjustly shifted the blame for my lackluster life onto them.

My parent's lack of push worked for me. However, if I didn't have this inner drive, then their lack of direction would've placed me in the lion's mouth. I don't wish to minimize other pertinent things that dealt so largely throughout my rehabilitation, but, my mom and dad were very significant. Even their belief in God played a constructive part in my rehabilitation.

The church is not a solid foundation. If all the leaders and parishioners suddenly bent to the right, then so would the church and all of its followers. It's a disgrace. The church has to go with the times. The church has to bend with the demands of the followers. A few priests and pastors have been caught with their hands in the cookie jar. Other clergymen have been caught with their hands in other lurid places. However, their congregations merely turned the other cheek.

Divorce used to be a big no-no. Now, as divorce numbers rise, the church dances to whatever is being played. The church is no different from this capitalist society. It seems as if people who have little hope for their futures, such as divorcees, parents of divorcees, drug addicts, ex-cons, and so forth fall into the belief system.

However, even my nonbelief, which I will expand upon in later writings, played a significant role in my rehabilitation. I needed things that I could push against, that were not necessarily going to push back, to give me strength during my rehabilitation. I needed to find power, and just the fact that I was pushing against something my whole family and close friends were relying on for emotional support built a good amount of power for this guy.

If I didn't have the strength that was elicited by this injury, then I would have found little direction at all. This is not saying my parents would not have liked me to follow the direction I eventually did, only they did not have the expertise needed to guide me down that road—very few people do.

Many of the problems nondisabled persons suffer through are self-perpetuated. The help and concern you can derive from others are limited. However, when I discovered the gold mine of this disability, I received much more than I ever expected. The resolution to this disability also had to be self-perpetuated.

People who need external gods fail to recognize the god they have in themselves and, thus, allow a whole multitude of things to destroy them. If you believe in yourself, then you don't need any external force. That notion didn't just present itself to me the other day, it built up over the many years I've struggled with this head injury.

Beyond a shadow of a doubt, this head injury saved my life. I can't see how I could've lived my life any happier than it has turned out. There were times before my accident when I was with all my senses, and I'd ask myself, "What's my purpose?" Now I know. I shudder to think how my life would've turned out without the interruption of this head injury. There'd be so much good stuff left uncovered underneath the refuse that engulfed me.

Before the accident, I didn't know who I was and what I was capable of doing. I was headed down the dark path of self-destruction without a flashlight. I was an airplane without a pilot. I did not have anyone or anything to guide me. I was left with only my basic instincts. I couldn't find a soul. Then, the enormity of this disability came, and it steered me in the most correct direction I've ever been on in my entire life.

I not only understand my condition, I accept it, which is very important for me. Otherwise, I would have wasted too much time brooding about my situation. I feel, when I finally open my heart, I will do much better than I ever did in my past. However, first of all, I'm human ... make your own assumptions.

Like the majority of you who don't play professional football, I stay on the sidelines and watch. It's safer that way. I don't have any safety pads, and I can't run worth a darn.

I still listen to classic rock. The Beatles, The Rolling Stones, Black Sabbath, Pink Floyd, and other rock bands of the late '1960s and early 1970s bring back good memories. If you were a youth at the time, then you just might understand what I'm talking about. I feel I can enjoy the feeling of being a footloose youth. However, I was less concerned about tomorrow at that point than I am at this time. The music of those bygone days brings back good memories. Even though at that time, I was both mentally and physically at my lowest point. You can say that was the classic Rick.

The music doesn't bring me back to a happier time. This is the happiest time of my life. At the point prior to my accident, I had no goals, and I didn't feel the need to find any. I would get lost in the music and let tomorrow take care of itself. This is the only time in my life that I have been able to achieve so much. I guess part of the reason I like the music of that past era is because I can realize how much I've gained by simply steering clear. Now, however, I'm able to enjoy the music without me, or it, having hidden agendas.

I've done more in my life than I ever could have expected while growing up as a lackluster youth. My head injury has turned me around for the better. Before the accident, I accomplished nothing or should I say nothing that I could be proud of. However, with the blessing of this injury, I have done much more than I could've ever hoped for. If I were to die tomorrow, then I feel I have accomplished more than my fair share.

Even if I weren't able to get this book published and no one was to know how I did what I did, just the fact that I did it would be of some comfort. Disability is of great importance in my life.

A thought just crossed my mind. Hell, I couldn't have chosen a better thing to have happen to me! I don't smoke cigarettes, use drugs, I rarely drink alcohol, my monetary situation is comfortable, I don't have any ex's, I have no enemies, I'm in very good health, I like and am liked at both of my jobs, I am an excellent driver, I don't reach for unattainable goals, I've given my parents more than they've ever expected, I feel extremely comfortable with my situation, I haven't stepped on any toes in getting to where I'm at, and I'm a very unique individual (something I have always internally been in search of). Even though at this point I've had more than anyone, including myself, could've ever expected, I'm not satisfied. This isn't egotistical or braggadocio. It just is.

If I were a blind person, then I would like to be similar to Dr. Stan Greenberg. I worked with Stan as his driver back in 1991–1993. Stan didn't let his limitations stand in his way. Stan and his sidekick, Slate, were a good pair. Slate is Stan's guide dog. I only wonder if I could handle such a disability as his with such ease. Stan is a very intelligent man. His mind is like a storage box of information. All essential, as well as nonessential, facts about everything are at his fingertips.

His blindness made my disability seem trivial. However, this man took the whole reality in stride. He seemingly knew everything about most things and never flaunted it in front of anyone's face. He could stand toe to toe with you as if he was speaking to you on the level of a college professor or as one of the lowlives in the old neighborhood.

One of these days, I'll go back east to visit my old chum, Stan Greenberg. I wonder if Slate will remember me. I certainly will remember him. He put his teeth into me every time I made a wrong turn.

Even though it's been a tough road, this is a road that has taught me much more than any other I could fathom. What it taught me was all the power I had within, that was remaining dormant, as I "struggled" through life without a head injury. Just like attending and finishing school was a laborious task, I'm more than happy I stuck it out. As I look at it at this point, I wouldn't trade this rehabilitation struggle for any other option presented to me before my injury. I'm glad I had this experience with my head injury. I also doubt I would've regretted it at any time during my rehabilitation.Even though it was tough going all the way through, I fed off my small accomplishments along the way. There was always a silent applause from the crowd. Also, I would assume, there were those out there who might have wondered if they could have done as well if they had to plow through a similar disability.

Having taken this trip through this disabled experience over the years, I don't need any drugs to give me a new sense of being. The process of rehabilitation is similar to coming down from a night of experimenting with all kinds of psychedelic drugs. The only difference is that I have lingered in this process for over thirty years. There's no need to escape reality when you are brain damaged. I was consistently knocking and continually knocking at the door trying to get back in. It was a long, slow process, but I began to appreciate the journey and let the disappointments roll off my back. This disability was quite a rewarding trip.

5

Good health played one of the biggest, if not the biggest, roles in my rehabilitation. My ability to adapt to most any situation at work has a lot to do with my health. If I'm not healthy, then I'm shortchanging my fellow employees.

Being able to rehabilitate would have been futile without being able to control my health. The same holds true in the work arena. Being able to show up for work each day is important, and I haven't missed a day of work in over three years. I've only taken one vacation in that time period. That was when I took seven days in November to go down to southern California to celebrate both my mother and father's birthdays.

At work, I'm ready to do anything at anytime. I'm not pulled down by any sickness I might have. Everything I do hinges on my health. Probably, the same holds for true for the rest of you out there. With poor health, the average person can't hope to perform up to his abilities.

In the first fifteen or so years after my injury, I had quite an array of disabilities. All these disabilities were self-perpetuated. There was this mountain placed before me. I could have turned around and refused to climb it. However, even though there were many obstacles placed before me, there were just as many, if not more, remedies to assist me.

I suppose that it would have been just as easy and understandable if I had become overwhelmed by all the shortcomings presented by my disability. However, I confronted them one at a time. That, luckily, was all my mind could handle at a time. My lack of memory assisted me in the beginning. The mere fact that I would forget things minute by minute didn't allow me the luxury of ruminating on my situation. I simply took one step at a time.

Mental fitness goes hand in hand with physical fitness. To rehabilitate well, a person, I particularly, has to keep both mental and physical capacities in tune. Physical fitness is like breathing. It's habit forming. The opposite is true also.

It's like everything else. If you don't make a habit out of it, then you will tend to do less and less of it. Since my rehabilitation began, it has put me on this physical fitness treadmill. Maybe I should more correctly state that I put myself on this treadmill. It would have been just as easy to sidestep this exercise machine, but it was just as rewarding, in fact more so, to just keep moving my feet.

It could more correctly be analogized to smoking. There's really no dire need to exercise, but, once you begin in earnest, it's hard to stop. It seems as though ever since I began on this road to complete rehabilitation, I've incorporated a wide array of good habits that were formally left by the wayside.

Good health is instrumental. It's hard to prioritize which tactic is more important. Overall good health, which meant doing all things I could do to control my health, was one of the best tactics I've employed during my rehabilitation. Good health left me with time and energy that would have been wasted if I had been continually struggling with health concerns.

I used many methods while on this long journey of rehabilitation, but sticking to them was very easy once I learned the benefits. Rehabilitation without optimal health (the best health an individual can achieve) is like putting a broken-down cart before a disoriented horse. I placed my good health on the top of the list in regards to my successful rehabilitation.

This head injury has washed away many of the insecurities I've had festering within. A lot of these unsubstantiated fears were the ones that were holding me back all throughout my budding youth.

Hospitals, doctors, and antiseptic smells used to make me weak in the knees. Lots of old-time apprehensions have died. However, at this point, the thought of overcoming these self-inflicted maladies is an accomplishment in itself.

It's amazing. After awakening from a coma in late 1971 at Rancho Los Amigos Hospital in Downey, California, I didn't smell any alcohol whatsoever. Before my accident, my own shadow used to send chills down my spine. However, now, I tend to analyze things more. In fact, visiting the doctor, as I do from time to time, merely reinforces my self-confidence.

I'm currently in perfect health. I feel better than at any other time in my life before my accident, when I was a lightweight hypochondriac. I rarely see a doctor because I'm in such good health. However, I contracted the runs a couple of years ago (I picked up a bug that was circulating Willow Glen Villa, my place of employment, and my body was weakened because I was lifting heavy weights in my exercise program), and I was given a complete checkup. I'm very healthy, except for Hepatitis C, which I must have contracted way back in 1971 from a blood transfusion.

It seems as if all things work out for the good. This Hepatitis C would have remained hidden till a future checkup, and since I was always in such good health, I might have waited till it was too late to do anything about it. What I understand is that Hepatitis C can eventually eat up my liver. I currently see the doctor about every six months to check my blood. I had a liver biopsy six months ago and will have another next month, but, so far, my liver is in great shape.

It's been much healthier to go with the flow than to paddle upstream while tending to the disabilities that befell me. In an odd sort of way, my disability has become my friend. This, I feel, is the healthiest way to feel about my situation. I received all the benefits with open arms, while sidestepping the majority of potholes I've encountered along the way.

Before the injury, I never considered myself a fighter. With this disability, I don't necessarily have to fight against it. I merely have to absorb the benefits it renders. In my preinjury days, just looking at disabled persons would send shivers down my spine and would turn my stomach. However, with my acceptance of my situation (I don't recall ever rejecting it), it's been the most comfortable pair of slippers I've ever owned.

Positive things continued to happen to me. I don't put anything stronger than a hot cup of black coffee into my system each morning. With my maintenance of a clean lifestyle (no drugs, alcohol, close friends, or lovers), my successes build on themselves. Relationships can be synonymous with substance abuse.

It's similar to a snowball rushing downhill. I have no yearnings to fall back into my old ways. Of course, refraining from these particular activities, especially close relations with the opposite sex, can be trying. However, I balance that against all I've achieved because of this conscious restraint, and I applaud myself. Besides, in no time, I will have achieved all that I desire and will jump back into that tangled web of love.

The health practices I've adhered to throughout my rehabilitation were essential. I don't have to be concerned about this or that at this point, regarding my health. That takes time. I didn't, and I do not have, any time to waste.

Continual exercise played an important part throughout the rehabilitation process. Even at this time, every night before I shower, I'll do a few sets of calisthenics. My weight never fluctuates more than five pounds from 160 pounds. My good health was essential to my rehabilitation.

As I'm writing this, a feeling of guilt comes over me. Last night, my cousin came in from the Midwest with her husband to visit our aunt. I went over to her house, which is a few blocks away from mine, to visit for a few hours. I returned at an hour when I had no time to do my daily ritual of exercise. However, I realize that feeling will quickly diminish tonight when I begin my routine once again.

I walk to where I'm going whenever I have the chance. This can only be attributed to the long period of time before I had a driver's license and had no choice about the matter. Living the clean and healthy lifestyle that I have for many years now has not been difficult at all. In fact, it would have been much harder if I would have done it any other way.

I don't abuse any substances. I choose carefully what I now put in my mouth. Escape mechanisms are just that, escape mechanisms. I don't need, or wish, to run away from anything. I'm almost the exact opposite of my preinjury self.

More importantly than that, I no longer abuse relationships, as I did prior to my accident. That is a drug that can destroy me equally as much as any other—even more so because I still have the mental capacity to realize how stupid I was.

Up to this date, I have maintained the health kick that I've been on for years since returning from the hospital in 1972. I placed myself on this course toward optimum health almost at the beginning of my rehabilitation. With a heavy dose of determination, nothing has swayed me from it. Good health is what has brought me this far.

Keeping my mind and body fit is a very easy chore. In reality, it's not a chore, but a lifestyle. I am currently maintaining my hard, flat stomach; strong biceps; and even stronger legs. This is something I never attempted before my accident.

I haven't used a drug since the last time I smoked a little grass and drank a lot of beer with my cousin. That was back in 1974, I believe. I've seen the error of my ways and haven't distorted reality since that time. My cousin has also seen the error of his ways. He's now a cop in northern California, putting kids behind bars for similar deeds.

I feel that the reason there's such an abuse of legal and illegal drugs in this country is that people aren't maximizing their own potential. Improving things at home will make it less profitable for illegal drug cartels in other countries.

The need to escape, which drugs falsely satiate, should be made less a priority. Somewhere else down the line, the illegal drugs entering this country need to be stopped. If we simply eliminate the need to get away from reality, then the need for drugs will soon deteriorate.

We could work more effectively on ways to curtail illegal drug use. Perhaps, legalize them. It would be like food—many people overeat and become dangerously overweight. Legalizing drug use, supervised by medical professionals, just might be the route to take. What we have now is not working at all. We currently have a pill for erectile dysfunction being advertised by a former presidential candidate. President Clinton, after he left office, could come on television ads puffing on a marijuana cigarette, and when exhaling could say, "Now I can inhale!"

Prostitution can then be legalized, the government can tax it, and we can keep a lot of other illegal acts and diseases that illegal prostitution promotes in check.

If I keep things going the way they have, in twenty more years, they'll have to put me in a playpen. In fact, at no time prior to my injury do I remember feeling any better physically, socially, economically, or spiritually than I do now.

6

I employed a multitude of different things to bring me to where I am today. Living with a disability, I had to hone my attitude to be able to extricate the most I could from my disabled condition. I was lucky that I went into this disability with this kind of mindset. There were many avenues to embark upon that would produce positive results. My different living situations proved to have as many avenues. It only mattered which ones I took.

In 1977, five years after my release from Rancho Los Amigos Hospital, I moved back. Rancho had a halfway house located on the grounds, which provided free room and board for disabled persons trying to make it back from their disabled condition. This house was called Casa Consuelo.

Casa, in and of itself, was an educational process. Learning how to use people in a way that's complimentary to both parties was a skill I polished while living at Casa. My formal education is on par with my true life experiences; one complimented the other and vice versa. If I had only the education that I gained while at school, then I would have considerably less knowledge than I possess at this point. I feel very enriched from having lived at this locale. The realization that I could make it on my own, provided by three short years I spent at Casa, was an important element in this journey through disability.

Life at Casa was very similar to the way I approached any other aspect of my rehabilitation. I used Casa like I have and am using my disability. It was merely one of the tools I employed to get me this far. In and of itself, Casa was a learning tool that I used until I could squeeze no more use out of it.

I found the quiet and virtual solitude provided at this halfway house to be instrumental. I was able to see just how far I could extend myself mentally, and at the same time, I could learn how to regulate my relations with others. I quickly found that association with anyone, which included my fellow residents at Casa, would merely be a distraction. I honed my aloofness while at Casa. While attending school and living at Casa, I had to discover what educational process worked best for me.

It seems as if everything I did, including all the dancing I had to do, while living at Casa had only one objective. However, that objective encompassed many others. It's very difficult to distinguish what had been recreational and what had been specifically for my mental and physical rehabilitation. I feel that this is what has made it such an easy process. I'm able to determine if a recreation I'm pursuing is complimentary to any aspect of my rehabilitation.

They blend in with each other. There's no distinction between what is for fun and what is done to avert the conditions of my disability. As I continue to rehabilitate, which I will do for the rest of my life, I sense I will enjoy the ride more and more.

At this point, it seems as if the track that I set myself on, since the outset of my rehabilitation, has been a most enjoyable one. I doubt if I would have made it any other way.

I didn't realize it at the time, or perhaps I did, but I made disability a useful tool in the process of trying to minimize it. Skills that I learned in relation to dealing with people that I used so well while living at Casa also have worked very well with you so-called normal people.

Disabled persons, I don't wish to categorize them as all being the same, are as difficult to get along with as any other segment of this population. In fact, I found disabled persons less caught up in other trivialities of life that many of the "normal" people are drowning in.

It was much easier to get along with other disabled people than to try and associate with the nondisabled, so-called whole persons.

It's not only the factual data I picked up while attending school, but the real life issues I dealt with while living at Casa. I cannot dictate, verbatim, everything I've learned over the years. Still, true life experiences, like the ones I've had at Casa, remain embedded.

Living at Casa was very eye opening. The residents (about twenty) were chosen by their rehabilitation counselors as persons who could benefit from it. Essentially, we were the cream of the crop. It was there that I learned how well my positive attitude worked.

Life at Casa, all three years of it, was an important portion of my rehabilitation. This is where I first began to dance with my disability. At Casa, you were provided everything to help you make the transition from wherever you might have come from, such as your parent's home (as in my case), the street (as a few who lived there), other institutions, other hospitals, and the like. This was the first time I was able to truly witness how other people dealt with their disabilities.

Life at Casa didn't teach me the skills I needed to get along with people; it honed them. I feed off the fact that disability, which seems to swallow most, gave me such inspiration. It seemed as if I had these skills ingrained in me. With a wide array of personalities and having to confront an even wider array of disabilities, it taught me much about myself.

At Casa, I could witness first hand things that I could merely speculate upon before. The majority of what I had previously believed proved to be right on target. Casa provided a cushion. If ever I fell, something I can't remember doing, I'd bounce back up. I was able to get along with everyone. I found that was the key to my success there and elsewhere throughout this process of rehabilitation. Learning I was just one more cog in the wheel assisted me greatly.

At Casa, I simply maintained the positive direction I had been on throughout this rehabilitation process. There was no ranking in accordance to where you were at in your rehabilitation. Nevertheless, I still felt that I was at the top of the heap. Even though this was the cream of the crop in regards to disabled persons, I never met anyone there with optimism about their individual situation.

I was friendly with all, but I disassociated with the majority. As a matter of fact, this is the way I've been with everyone else throughout my rehabilitation period. In those three years, I made myself aware of just how much I was able to do with the proper use of people. The positive outlook was maintained and strengthened while living at Casa.

I derived many things from life at Casa. These things are just too numerous to list. However, these many things that I picked up at Casa are used throughout my day-to-day living, even at this point. One of the most important things that Casa helped me do was to cut the apron strings that I felt tied me to my parents.

Yes, I cut those apron strings before they strangled me to death. It was not that my parents were overly smothering. I felt the need to spread my wings. I used productively all the good psychological vibes I had received from my parents in those first few years after my release from the hospital.

Separation from my parents wasn't that dramatic. Living with twenty or so other disabled people didn't bring me down. In fact, I learned many ways to use the government services. I learned how much rehabilitation counselors could be of service as well as how much they can hinder progress. The maintenance skills that I have learned have come in quite handy. I sensed myself better than others did at Casa, in terms of managing my money and realizing that the government was there to be used. I maintained relations with all. It was a splendid place to study. It was also a variety of other good things.

I felt independent. At the same time, I was using the government, something that I still effectively do.

7

Counselors can open many doors for you. I made friends with the majority of my counselors. They tend to understand and lend a sympathetic ear. It was my rehabilitation counselor who opened the doors for me at Casa. We remained on good terms all throughout my three-year stay at this facility. That's where a good number of my fellow residents shot themselves in the foot. Counselors can offer a panacea of things that can help your voyage through disability. It makes sense to keep them on your side.

Just as with most things throughout my rehabilitation, I used my counselors. This was especially true when I lived at Casa.

Living at Casa from 1977–1980 was a very enlightening portion of my rehabilitation. There are just so many things I picked up that were of grand assistance to me. I will not risk listing them for fear that I might forget something. I was unable to imagine all the benefits that would come my way by simply moving from my parent's home, but Casa opened my eyes. This was something I needed.

Casa fit like a glove. There were rules I had to follow, but that's nothing. Living and associating with other disabled persons was, I feel, the easiest part of Casa. Frankly, I can't remember any bad points that I could list against Casa. It made me realize that I could make it on my own. I associated well with other disabled as well as the staff. I learned how to dance effectively. This was very important because simply by living there, it reassured me that I could dance with my disability.

The staff tried to remain rigid for the flakes, but I went by the program, and all was well. I would fix my own food, even though three square meals were provided every day. I kept my own schedules and regulated what little money I had. This was very important.

Casa was a perfect transition for me. I could go at whatever speed was comfortable for me and still be accepted. This was, of course, as long as I was proceeding in a positive direction. I remarkably built up and, to a certain extent, honed my abilities to grapple with disability.

It was almost as if it were a game. The only difference was that there were true life consequences involved in this match. Casa energized my rehabilitation. It was only five years since my injury, but I felt I had received all I could from life at home. I needed that transition.

Casa was merely an extension, a major one, of all the services I've effectively utilized. I found I could get along with people, run my game, use the services and so forth just as I did, if not more, when I moved in to Casa.

Life at Casa presented no problems. It merely honed the abilities that would assist me through the rest or should I say my continuing rehabilitation. Amazingly, everything seemed to click. My rehabilitation was right on track. The majority of my improvements just seemed to stagnate while I lived with my folks.

I had, and have, a frame of mind that is conducive to the rehabilitation process. What was very important for me at Casa was that I've always had that drive, but there it was allowed to flourish.

It was fortunate for me that others at Casa, for the most part, didn't have the same drive. It would be hard for me to try and keep up with others. I had to set my own pace. It wasn't that I was inherently better than anyone else at Casa, but I had this motivating force constantly pushing me. I used my disability to all ends.

I've never kicked back and relaxed when it came to this disability. Even though I've conquered the majority of my setbacks, I keep on pushing. Writing this book is something that is definitely over the pail, but this is also part of my rehabilitation.

It was a fine line I walked, but I mastered it to a T. I was on good terms with the people who worked there as well as my fellow residents. This was very simple. I merely remained superficial to all. This is true even today.

It was important that I remain close to everyone at Casa and, at the same time, distance myself. If I would've had conflicts with anyone, then it would have burned too much energy. I needed all the energy I could muster against this disability.

Being friendly with everyone is less mental work than keeping constant track of who to be friendly with and who to turn a cold shoulder to. This was the best thing I could've done. It paid me back in spades.

I kept to myself, not in an isolationist fashion, but I kept everything superficial. I simply tackled the task at hand. My first apartment was merely an extension of life at Casa. I didn't waiver much in my approach to anything. I believe the largest factor in my rehabilitation was that I was not led by anyone. I was self-motivated. I followed people's advice, but it all went through a filter, and in the end, I decided things for myself.

Living on my own was a breeze. It was much less a struggle than I had anticipated, but this was because I didn't waiver in the approach I took toward my disability. I approached, and still do, living on my own as another part of my rehabilitation. I have gone about it so didactically for so long that it has become a part of me. Every bit about living alone enriched my sense of rehabilitation.

Separation anxiety was not present. I did the most I could to make it a very successful part of my rehabilitation. It had only been five years since my accident, but I took it on. Encouragement from Pam, my rehabilitation counselor, as well as my father's ambivalent sentiment toward the whole idea, remarkably solidified my resolve.

Positive aspects of my rehabilitation were my education, work experience, ability to get along with others, money management, ability to use others, and counselors (I had about four during that time). I even used other disabled persons. Just by noting my ability to use this circumstance, I strengthened myself physically and mentally.

Confidence that I could make it without my parents was built at this locale, and this was one of the prime ingredients of life at Casa.

I'm very glad to have used this service while the time was right. Rancho provided me with so much. Beginning with my initial visit in 1971, while I was still comatose, the many follow-up visits I made after my release, the many times I did volunteer work there, and the many counselors that helped me were of the essence.

I believe that Casa is now in mothballs. I also understand that Rancho Los Amigos Hospital is now shut down. I'm very thankful to have gotten what I got when I got it. I went there several years ago, but it now looks like a ghost town. We are talking about a former army base that had a few acres of land on both sides of Imperial Highway in the city of Downey, California. The few times that I've been back since I stopped doing volunteer work there have brought back fond memories.

My first apartment in Carson gave me the notion that I could make it on my own. I was in a different world, and I liked it. I made no close friendships, and I was superficially friendly to all. I remained friendly to all and, yet, aloof to all at the same time. This is how it had to be done. No one was on the same level with me. That's the way that I liked it.

I couldn't drive. However, I was only a couple of miles from school and about a mile from the nearest grocery store.

There are a lot of intricacies you must wrestle with when you live alone. I felt I handled them quite well. In fact, living alone is a lot easier for me than living with others. When you live with others, you have to concern yourself with the wishes, priorities, and so forth of people you don't wish to offend.

My first apartment, as well as the one that came afterward, merely assured me I could function as well, if not better, than the next guy. There are certain things that have to be done, and I can do them. That gives me satisfaction. I liked the structure that maintaining a place gave me.

I am a tidy person. That is, I don't make messes. That way, I don't have to be continually picking up after myself. I would, and still do, pay my rent religiously on the twenty-fifth of each month. I never leave dirty dishes in the sink. I vacuum, mop, scrub the tub, and all the rest of the basins every week. I consider myself tidy. However, I don't do windows.

I found that if I was aware of what had to be done, and then, of course, did it, that it made living on my own a breeze.

Living on my own enhanced the rehabilitation process. I have no restraints. There is nothing that I avoid doing. I just have to watch my p's and q's and keep on truckin'. My immediate family lives a few hundred miles away, and I feel more than satisfied.

For the most part, I count on myself. I still need others around me, but I feel as if it's the way I use my disability that gives me the sense of self. All those years of having to rely on others, even though I realized I was using everyone I made contact with, was morale building. And now, more than ever, I feel as if I call the shots.

I find that it gives me a good feeling just knowing what I've been through. However, I don't allow myself to be drunk by that feeling. It's challenging. Every time I've lived in an apartment, three separate times over a six-year period, I've managed to make it, despite being on a limited income.

That's one more struggle I've overcome. All the different things you must overcome while battling a head injury simply adds more and more feathers to your cap. Even living on just enough to pay my rent and having enough money for only a few outside luxuries are a much better feeling just knowing what I've lived through. It's like a medallion I can hang over my fireplace. However, I've always been careful never to toot my own horn. Remarkably enough, with this head injury, I've always felt that there was a safety net beneath me.

If I would have never been able to drive again, then I would've adjusted. I remember when my rehab counselor suggested I learn to drive again. It was when I was just about to graduate from the first university I ever attended. That was the first time that it ever crossed my mind.

I don't use public transportation as I once did. However, if I had never used it, then it would have subtracted a lot from my experience. I gained much from almost ten years of daily bus use. Ironically, it gives one a greater sense of freedom. Riding the buses allowed me to feel that I was more in control of my destiny.

The use of bus routes and schedules, connections with different people, the exercise that is gained through walking, and the good feeling that is derived from not being harnessed to a vehicle are definite benefits. However, after seven years or so, I have tied myself to that umbilical cord once again. By getting my driver's license and then a car, after that ten-year hiatus since my accident, I'm once again being strangled as well as nurtured by that cord.

At the time of this writing, I'm no longer receiving state or federal funds. My living expenses (i.e., my room and board and other living expenses) were stopped after I began working full time. However, I still get free medical services. I believe Uncle Sam does this, so persons who are on disability payments will not fear going back to work and, thus, losing their medical coverage. I feel that this is a wise way to go about it.

I'm a fairly health guy, but who knows? I could be walking across the street tomorrow and sprain my ankle or something even less traumatic. This medical coverage is a very good thing. Even though I'm a fairly healthy guy, the secure feeling of always having medical coverage is one less thing I have to concern myself with.

I realize how much we all need the government. What I'm actually saying is I realize how much we need each other. The government is us. In fact, the less you think of the government, the less you think of yourself. The government, which means all of you, has been a great help. Very little of what I've done, and continue to do, could have been done without your help.

One year, at tax time, I owed Uncle Sam a little more than four hundred dollars. I just barely scraped up the money to pay this. The next year, I had them withhold a small amount from each paycheck. The following year, Uncle Sam owed me close to five hundred dollars. However, since the government had made a few errors over the years and had overpaid me, something that I promptly reported, they decided to keep that refund. In fact, that overpayment they made to me, over a three-year period, amounted to a little more than a few thousand dollars. In fact, I should be happy that they didn't throw my behind in jail.

One of the big problems in this country is that we haven't got our priorities straight. Almost everyone is trying to screw the next guy. It seems as if everyone is trying to swindle the person next to them. Several people in this country have their hands in everyone else's pockets—from your religious minister all the way to the cop walking the beat. Several people are trying to get away with as much as they can. It's the American way.

Several years ago, there was a heavyweight championship boxing match. I believe it was between Lennox and Holyfield. I didn't see the fight, which ended in a draw, but I'm sure it will be settled down the road at the cost of millions of dollars more from fight enthusiasts. Once again, it's the American way.

I'm only speculating, but I feel there will be a rematch. This match will obviously draw a bigger crowd than the previous one. The fight promoters will walk away like bandits. Do we enjoy being taken to the cleaners? I'm no different, and perhaps you're no different either. I now remember when I was in the market to buy a car a German American couple were selling their 1987 Golf Volkswagen for nineteen hundred dollars. I told Dave, my cousin, who's a police officer in San Jose, to play the handicapped card (draw sympathy by telling them I'm handicapped), and he got the lady to come down to sixteen hundred dollars. I guess I'm no different than the rest of America.

What the hell, they tried to rope-a-dope me. This German-speaking man was obviously in cahoots with this young lady. He just so happened to be a perspective buyer of this car during the same time that I was there. She made it seem as if I didn't buy the car, then this guy was going to buy it before me. What really confirmed my suspicions about this guy being a plant was that when I took the car out for a test drive, he was the only one that went along with me and my cousin. She stayed back home. Thus, all is well in love, war, and car purchases.

For being such an old car, it runs amazingly well. The same is true with the tactics I've used to pull me down this road of disability. I've certainly placed this disability through the ringer. This late in the game, I felt that using my disability, as I've done in the past, wouldn't work. However, I never lost hope. The use of this disability has served me well. Even if this is merely a false perception, the mere fact that I feel that I'm using my disability, and that it is not using me, adds fuel to the engine.

8

Everything postinjury was an uphill climb. This is similar to the way things were prior to the injury. However, all the barriers before the injury were self-imposed. I never suspected I had anything like what I found in myself after this life-threatening injury occurred. I always believed myself lower on the scale than most everyone. Though I never let it show on the outside, I always had an issue with a lack of self-confidence brewing on the inside.

The process of rehabilitation has been the best thing for me. It has shown me what I'm made of. I couldn't have chosen a better set of disabilities than if I had deliberated on it extensively beforehand. I would most likely state the same thing, if I had been given any other wide range of disabilities. It's all in how one perceives his condition.

I'm the same individual. However, with the assistance of my condition, I blossomed. I learned how to use people and things in a way that was good for all concerned.

I have not been doing all this rehabilitation stuff for anyone but me. There has been nothing altruistic about it. My ego is very deep down inside, for I don't feel as though I've done much more than anyone else could have. However, I realize I must have that strong will that helped me emerge from the coma.

Sense of self was nonexistent before my injury. In fact, that is what I feel I was searching for all those years beforehand. To me, everything is relative. If one thing doesn't happen, then another does or doesn't because of it. However, as far as my ego, that is what pushed me the extra mile.

It's strange because I never felt proud of myself before the accident. I wouldn't, in my wildest dreams, have believed I could do all that I have done since my head injury. I have always wanted something I could shine about, and this rehabilitation provided the perfect vehicle.

I lived through something that the majority couldn't have. This was actually the first thing I liked about myself. Being able to rehabilitate gave me an inner pride. Before the accident, I thought little of myself. After my injury, I utilized the same drive that kept me alive throughout the coma to pull me down an even rougher course.

My sense of self was a priority throughout my rehabilitations. I had to feel good about myself and my prospects for the future to keep this engine purring. For everything to work out right, I had to have an internal pride. For the majority of the time, I never knew this stuff existed. However, without this, I wouldn't have come this far.

I had to like myself and what I was all about in order to make all this rehabilitation stuff work. Actually, there's never been an outward display of pride. I believe that would have only slowed me down. Every little achievement built on the next. I had to take the success in small increments. I built on these small advances.

Take, for instance, when I had just come out of the coma. I asked my father to test my memory. I told him to tell me something and then ask me about five minutes later what it was that he had said. My father then told me the day of the week. I then tried to remember what he had said by repeating it internally over and over. By the second or third repetition, I had forgotten what he had said or that we were even conducting this small task.

He'd then tell me something like, "Your mom will be here in the morning." Then, he'd wait a few minutes, and I'd be repeating it to myself, but to no avail. I'd forget what it was he had told me or even that we were playing this little game.

This is ideal. How would you like to play a game and simply because you put forth the effort, you win? This is the way it was and is with this head injury. I never lost, as long as I was proceeding in a positive direction. Everyone, as it seemed, was on my side; I didn't waste my time with those who weren't on my side.

I was never very good at any athletic endeavor or much of anything before or after my head injury. However, if rehabilitation were a sport, then I would hit a home run, hit a hole in one, hit a tree pointer, score a touchdown, or any other such analogy.

I never thought it to be as if I were climbing a high mountain or, even less, as if this rehabilitation process were as if I were on a treadmill. Rehabilitation has been a form of recreation for me. It's enjoyable for me because I never lose. The least little accomplishments are inflated merely from the fact of where I came from.

I realize that the majority of persons wouldn't like to be in my shoes. That merely puts one more feather in my cap. I've done something in this life that few others have been able to do. If boxing is your sport of choice, then I have this disability against the ropes, and I'm issuing it multiple low blows with the referee looking conveniently in the other direction.

To look at all the ups and downs involved in rehabilitation, you must believe it takes a strong individual to weather the storm. However, I feel it merely takes a combination of a lot of things. I never knew I had anything inside me that could confront something of this magnitude.

Before my accident, I was the kind of guy who would look at others who seemingly had it all together and wonder why that couldn't be me. I never had much of an ego. However, after my injury, that's what kept me going. Sense of self powers this machine. I never thought much of myself prior to my head injury, but it is now the driving force behind my life.

That's the big reason why I had such a lackluster youth. Surviving this gigantic slap on the head pushed me to gain whatever I could. Everything I did posthead injury seemed as if it always went in the direction of bettering my condition. Everyone needs a little pride in themselves to go in a positive direction and then to maintain it.

Of course, by allowing people around me to assist me took some of the spotlight off of me, but, to the contrary, the light that went in their direction inevitably reflected back on me. If you don't give anything, then you're not likely to receive much. I put the majority of the load on everyone's back, and then I assisted them in moving forward with it.

It's best to let your counselor know most things about you, so they can do their best work. They don't shine unless you shine. You can analogize it to a football game. Your counselor is like all the players on your team. You are like the quarterback, and they will block, and such, but you have to be the one that runs though the openings they create for you. If you let them do all the work and don't do a little running through the openings that they have created, then there's little self-gratification.

In most cases, counselors will bend over backwards for you, if they see that you are giving a genuine effort. Counselors, either rehabilitation or academic, were used for all they were worth. I used them for my benefit, whichever way that I could.

I was very open with my counselors. I found that they could help in situations I had never expected. I liked to shine. Counselors, rehabilitation especially, have a small percentage of brain-injured clients who are giving it their all to rehabilitate. I took advantage of this.

About my third year after my release as a patient at Rancho Los Amigos Hospital, I decided to attend classes given there for the disabled. I was a student on the grounds (the junior college at Cerritos had some of their off-campus classes given there), where I met Pam, my third or fourth rehabilitation counselor, in about as many weeks. I was really perplexed. I asked her, "How many days are you going to be my counselor?" She told me that I had nothing to worry about. She was very correct. She remained my counselor for about four years. She provided the right push, as well as encouragement, when I left to attend the main campus, only a few months after I had been a student on the grounds at Rancho.

Pam was a very important factor at the start of my rehabilitation. The off-campus school that they had at Rancho was very lacking. Since Rancho was a former army base, the room that they used as the class looked like it was a barracks for the military, with desks put in for the students. The whole area seemed as if it were a remnant from something out of the 1950s. However, I paid regular attendance for the few months I was there.

At the time, I was interested in speed reading and had spent the previous year attending the public library daily for the mile-long walk it provided, as well as the time I spent reading. In the year I went to the library, I longed to read at a faster pace, as well as remember anything that I had read. I could do neither of these tasks with any proficiency. Since the school at Rancho was a satellite campus of Cerritos, I went to the main campus (about ten miles from Rancho) one day to see what I was missing. Pam eventually hooked me up with everything I needed to become a student at the main campus, and the rest is history.

There are just so many things a counselor, especially a rehab counselor, can do for you. It's senseless to make them your enemy. In my rehabilitation, my only foes were those things that got in the way. I did my best, and my counselors knew I was genuinely trying, so they in turn did whatever they could.

Counselors will bend over backwards for you when they know you are genuinely putting forth effort. I worked with my counselors, and we were a team. That didn't mean I wouldn't take advantage of them when it was in my best interest to do so. I treated my counselors as an extension of myself. I realized that this was a good part of me because it could do so much for me.

Counselors, whether rehabilitation or academic, have various tools at their disposal—use them. If you succeed, then they succeed. It's their job to help you. I noticed a lot of my disabled brothers and sisters were angry at their counselor. I realize, at this point, it's merely a form of projection. It's natural to try to place blame on someone else for your disability. Counselors are the safest target because they're not going to retaliate against you. At times, I treated my counselors as my audience. They will applaud you while you're performing.

When you come from a place such as the one I was in—I had a very large void between my ears and not much hope before the accident—you feel as if you have genuinely done something. Yes, the only reason I feel so self-assured is because of where I came from.

Work is fulfilling, because it lets me know all the time and effort I put in school wasn't wasted. Work isn't taxing or strenuous for me; it's an accomplishment. There's an internal joy in knowing I can work. It's just one more hurdle I have managed to surmount. There will be others, but this has been a large one.

My choice in careers fits me like a glove. Back in school, after my third year at Cerritos Junior College, with a choice of career paths, I went into Pat Cook's office, my academic counselor; rummaged through a few books strewn around her office; and decided to become a gerontologist. This was mainly because Pat was a gerontologist and prompted the idea, and what a wise choice it was. Essentially, I'm exhausting time with my clients until the grim reaper comes knockin'. I'm no longer on stage. I do what I feel is right. I don't make assumptions. I keep an impeccable work attendance record. I get along well with all my co-workers and participants in the program. Someone will actually pay me for what I do. This is amazing considering where I come from.

I don't look at it, as trite as this might sound, as me working for someone else. Somewhere down in my subconscious, I realize that I am doing it for me. Don't get me wrong, because work is work. However, I view it in a whole different light than the average schmuck.

As I see it, work provides me with a twofold benefit. I'm earning money, and I'm doing something I previously only remotely believed I'd be able to do. I don't earn all that much, just enough to keep my head above water. I enjoy both jobs. They are easy for me, and they create no stress. And, on top of all that, from time to time, I reflect back to where I've been.

At these two jobs, I'm just myself. I no longer try to be "super handicapped," as I did in my previous positions. I no longer try to be something I'm not. I work at my own pace, and everything is fine. Work is like the finish line of my rehabilitation. However, I know this isn't true. I will always be rehabilitating. The trick is to enjoy it.

The cards were initially stacked against me. So, occasionally, I had to play an ace in the hole. Very few people will kick a man when he's down. You could say that I work my disability. Disability can reap many things—services, monies, help, compassion, and so forth. I took only a fraction of what was available to me.

I could sing and dance with the best of them. I would, with a straight face, let them know my deficiencies and assure them it'd be beneficial. Especially in the line of work that I have chosen, my deficiencies are not seen as such an impediment, but, on the contrary, my disability gives me more insight. By allowing my employer to know my situation, it automatically puts him/her on my side. It was the same approach (some would say scam) I pulled on the majority of my instructors at school. I would let them be at ease with it, similar to the way that I've been handling it.

I must confess, however, it was the way in which I'd let people know about my disability that would win the majority over to my side. No one likes a whiner. Just the same, no one likes a braggart. Throughout my rehabilitation, I have been neither. With the exception of this book, and the ones that will follow, I have never tooted my own horn. I let others do it for me.

Being head injured has been the most dramatic thing that's ever happened to me. I accepted it, and I worked against it all the way. I never let it have the upper hand. Even at the start of my rehabilitation, when my head was full of nothing but air, I built on each little improvement. Every minute accomplishment was applauded by others, specifically my folks.

Before becoming disabled, I thought it to be one of the worst things that could happen to a person. When I saw a disabled person, maybe a lot like you, I'd look the other way. Deep, maybe not so deep down, I'd be thinking, *Why him and not me?* However, when I received this gift, I used it for all it was worth.

With this new identity, I found I didn't need people as I did before. However, in the same breath, I now needed a different set of people and to a larger degree. I utilize this power. I believe on the street, it's called shuck and jibe, bullshit in some cultures, and in another era, song and dance. This is what I needed to do.

It's strange; before my accident when I had all my faculties, it seemed I did nothing without friends. However, with this disability, I'm doing remarkably well without them. I built a tremendous sense of self with this injury, something that was missing beforehand.

Fortunately for myself, none of my friends of the past stood by me during my rehabilitation. If they would have, then that would have just meant one more cog in the wheel. I needed all the free space I could find away from influences of the past. Friends, for me, would tend to alter my thinking. With disability, I needed to think for myself.

9

This disability certainly has changed my life for the better. Having a severe disability doesn't have to be the end of the world. My disabilities created a whole new world for me. This knock on the head is what I needed to shake the cobwebs loose. I don't want to sound quaint, but, just as a frown is a smile turned upside down, disability is ability with its nose amputated.

In fact, I believe, no matter how bad off I was after my head injury with the way my mind was geared, I would've still made the best of it. Ironically, I believe, that if my disability hadn't been as severe, then I wouldn't have dug down deep enough for the resources I needed.

If I had never had been through this rehabilitation experience, then I'm certain that I would be a shell of what I am today. I needed this struggle to shake me up. It was almost as if I was born lacking this something that this disability provided so lavishly. My formal education and my true life education fed off one another. It seemed as if one complimented the other. The course of study I undertook, human services and then gerontology, were made easier because of my true life experiences. It wasn't as if the two experiences fit like a glove; however, through give and take, they eventually complimented each other very well. I can't say which one was more important. I don't believe I could've done one without the other.

Counselors are a tool, but, unlike a hammer or saw, these tools must be given strokes as well. I guess you could say that these strokes given are equivalent to cleaning and storing your tools in a cool, dry place after use. I use counselors for the exact reason they're put there. Counselors have so many tools at their disposal. It makes little sense to treat them unkindly. I've seen other disabled persons merely project their bad feelings that they had about their own condition onto the shoulders of their counselors. The counselor has enough on their plate without having to mend broken fences in their relationships with their clients. I followed their plans, spiced with my input, to make it more palatable. I never felt as if they were running the entire show.

It's wise to use counselors, teachers, and everyone and everything at your disposal. The key for me was to play the sly. I would use everyone, and they didn't even suspect, so I thought, that they were being used. What made this work was no one was the loser in this ploy. My getting ahead was to everyone's advantage.

I felt little apprehension when it came to using people. In the back of my mind, I rationalized it by thinking that it was for everyone's good. They put themselves as your servant. These servants you don't even have to pay. It's similar to employing a prostitute, but having everybody else pick up the tab. However, this is even better than employing a woman of the night. You can make longtime friendships with these people, and you don't have to hide the fact that you used their services. What you get back has greater value than what you initially took, for them as well.

The more difficulties I've found have kept the fuel burning. The fire beneath me never extinguished. With the assistance of the many counselors I had throughout the years, it seemed as if each hurdle I surmounted gave me more confidence to attempt the next. It's ironic. I used one of my deficits to help another. I would've gotten lazy if not for the struggle, but I certainly would've gotten nowhere without a counselor.

None of my counselors, or anyone else for that matter, knew what I was capable of. This included me. My failed attempts prompted the push I needed. I needed my disabled condition. It opened many doors for me. The difficulties I've had with my education fed the rehabilitation process. If education would've been easy for me, then I'd have never discovered the rebound ability that I had.

I luckily never found the need to bellyache about my situation. What a good number of my fellow compatriots would do would be to simply dump on their counselors. I talked to other disabled persons, as I ventured through this winding path of disability, and I rarely heard anything good said about a counselor.

I never used my counselor as a punching bag. Actually, by using them like tools, it was better for all concerned. That would be like biting the hand that feeds you. I was wise enough not to do that. I used them like tools. Actually, I'd have to say that includes everyone.

My counselors were helpful in every aspect. I couldn't have made it this far without their assistance. Help is the key word. I had to put forth the effort in order for them to lend a helping hand. I used my counselors. However, I never used them as punching bags, as so many of my disabled brothers and sisters did. I used them more as a vehicle. A few sped me on the road to recovery, while others puttered me along. I was able to differentiate between the two, so as to use my time more efficiently.

Yes, there were one or two who did the whole rehabilitation thing as merely a task they had to complete. In other words, I felt as if I were only a paycheck to them. While there were those who were very concerned about my success/failure, and there were others who seemed rather distant.

My different counselors though the process of rehabilitation, academic, and work were all quite helpful. There were even a couple of remote ones who didn't do much for me, but they were helpful in the respect that they showed me who not to waste time with. I'm thankful that I worked with a couple of lemons. This gave me more confidence in the process.

With all the counselors I've had throughout the years, I've had only one or two whom I felt didn't help me at all. However, down the road a bit, I could see they certainly added something to the mix.

Amazingly, I seemed to follow persons who led me down the correct path. Whatever counselors told me had to run through my filter. I wasn't a robot. I was nonprogrammable. I had to let my counselor know me in order for anything to work. I found who I was and what I was capable of doing through the use of various aides throughout this journey.

I was in the right frame of mind when I first connected with the counselor. The first three or so counselors were transferred off my case after only a couple of weeks. I was frustrated; however, I kept my head up and was given to the right person at the right time. That person was Pam. Pam seemed to know what to do and, more importantly, how to get it done.

I feel I have used all my counselors very effectively. I sense their ego would build just as mine did as I improved. However, I didn't waste time concerning myself in how others would react pertaining to my performance. I merely kept pushing.

I felt that if I didn't use my counselors to my best advantage, then it would've been a waste of time for the both of us. I didn't initially have this feeling. It grew on me. My first thoughts of a counselor were them being a soft cushion in case I fell. However, because of my tenacity, I rarely fell. I found that working with my rehabilitation and academic counselors was best for all concerned. There's a right way and a wrong way to go about rehabilitation. Biting the hand that feeds you is a definite no-no. It works better, I have found, if you don't let anyone be your scapegoat.

I'm glad that I have always felt good about being disabled. I didn't need anyone, especially a counselor, to dump on. I needed my counselor to lead the way and open doors for me. The counselor tries to be your friend, lend a sympathetic ear, and use their expertise and many other things. It's easy to displace anger in their direction. This is easy because there are few times when a counselor is going to fight back. At times, a disabled person might project the blame for their disability onto the counselor's shoulders. This approach only slows, if not halts, the assistance that they can provide.

Counselors were really helpful in that they let me know about the many services that were available to me, as well as how to obtain them. They were also a great sounding board for bouncing my ideas off of. They let me know of the monies, services, and so forth that I could not find on my own.

There's no way I could have come this far without counselors. The majority of the time, I wasn't told what to do. Although, if I weren't as motivated as I was, then I'm sure they would've certainly lit a fire beneath me. However, the proper suggestions had to be made, and I chose the right ones. You have to realize that counselors don't have a crystal ball.

If this tool wasn't placed in front of me, who knows where I'd be now? It was to my advantage that I befriended the majority of my counselors. They, in return, did all that they could for me. We washed each other's backs.

I don't feel (even though I spent nine years after my head injury attending different schools) as though I'm any smarter than the next guy. However, with the blessings of this head injury, I've learned much more than I could have any other way.

Yes, I graduated from a community college in Cerritos, California, which took me four years. Then, I transferred to California State University, Dominguez Hills, which took three more years to complete. I then worked for a few months at a convalescent hospital and decided to attend another school to gain more education. I finished my certificate program at California State University, Long Beach, and graduated in two more years.

Attending school religiously (the only religious thing about me) mirrored the way that I feel about my disability. My formal education didn't seem, outwardly, to be a big help to me. Internally, though I realize that without having gone through the educational process, I would only be a shell of what I presently am. I needed both the formal and life education. They complement each other.

The majority of facts and such that I learned throughout school are no longer at my fingertips. Still, attending school for those nine years was the furthest thing from a waste of time. I was like the tin man, repeating the phrase, "If I only had a brain." I would've fallen on my face if I would've had any other concern dogging me. With this head injury, I didn't need more weight placed on my back.

I had very little to concern me while attending school. I had no love life, I was in good health, I had no conflicts with others, I had enough money, everything academic was paid for, instructors gave me the benefit of the doubt, and I was given all the time I needed. For me, this is the way it had to be done. Before my accident, I couldn't juggle a variety of things. With my head injury, significantly less could be kept in the air.

The important thing for me was to never take things too seriously. Everything that would happen to me was accepted as a part of the rehabilitation package. I found enjoyment in the process, not necessarily the outcome. However, through my tenacity, the outcome is normally in the positive genre. It's not so difficult for me because I know there's a cushion underneath me.

Essentially, all things are recreation for me. All things provide a bit of a challenge, whether they be mental or physical. Being able to surmount different obstacles, which is what recreation is all about, provides stimulation. The more I overcome, the better I feel. This provides the energy I need to take on the next challenge.

If I had not put forth the effort, then I would never have learned of all the doors that were open for me, simply because I am disabled. I needed this kick in the pants that was provided by my head kissing the pavement. It's a whole different ball of wax when you are attending school as a disabled person.

Having an education opened many doors for me. If I had never acquired this head injury, then I seriously doubt I would've pursued an education. When you are a "normal" person, you have to play on a level field. With a disability, everything is geared for your advancement. All you have to do is put forth effort. Whether you succeed or fail, it doesn't really matter. You are a winner if you're trying. When I was "normal," it seemed as if all the cards were stacked against me.

Rehabilitation is a process. I put my all into this process and stuck with it. It was not very hard. I was working with such a small portion of my brain that it wasn't very hard to know when I reached my limit. It's like remaining physically fit. You do have to put forth effort, but, after a while, it becomes part of you. It's just like if I had a woman constantly at my side. I would miss her if she left. It's conditioning.

Just as I lived very well without a counselor in the years prior to my first, I can function quite well. In fact, I can function better now than when I had to rely on a counselor. Conditioning, that's all it is. The more stringently you pursue this practice, the more you'll get out of it.

The trick was, for me, to never let my disability get the best of me. In regards to my many shortcomings, I consistently, as well as subconsciously, look the other way. The many challenges my disability has rendered have been ones, for the most part, that I can overcome.

In regards to what I do recreationally, my rehabilitation provides enough diversion. I've even had counselors, two or three, recommend diversion. I find this disability entertaining enough. It's not only challenging, it produces, good results with my continual positive attitude. There are many ways to skin a cat and just as many, if not more, to rehabilitate.

Working (as I've been doing since my move up north in the start of 1996), living alone (which I've done for about as long), and managing my finances fairly well are things that I'm proud of. I maintain excellent health, which is something I have practiced religiously throughout the rehabilitation process. Everyone is a lightweight friend. I don't get in over my head financially. I only owe my next month's rent. My social life is in limbo. However, that is something that will develop when I allow it. That would be as hard as falling off of a cliff when you're seriously drunk.

I have nothing to complain about. Things have been just about the same all throughout my rehabilitation—not too many highs and, just the same, not too many lows. I just keep the fire ignited and limp along.

10

In every segment of this society, you have your good and not so good. This differs little in relation to counselors. I had my share of good and bad counselors. The ones I could tell right off the bat who didn't give a hoot were ones I made quick work of. Counselors are only there to help you. I was fortunate to have the drive to maximize their utility.

I, in most cases, had to fend for myself. If I weren't getting too far as a result of a counselor, then it was I who had to make a quick work of him (or her). Fortunately, there were only a handful of various academic and rehabilitation counselors that I couldn't put to use. The more I used counselors, the happier they were to provide more and more.

Aside from helping me throughout my school years, counselors also aided me in my subsequent job searches. After about six months following my graduation from the final university I attended, I used the rehabilitation services to help find a job. At the time, a brand-new service was being created by Rosemary Clooney in honor of her deceased sister, who, if I'm correct, died of a massive head injury.

The counselor who put me in touch with the Betty Clooney Center (as it was named) and even the woman who interviewed me for the position were only trying to give me their best. Now that I think about it, the best things did result from not getting the position.

Honestly, very candidly, the Clooney Center is a bullshit (excuse the vernacular) operation. Their laid-back approach, as opposed to my confrontational, take-no-prisoners method of doing the best I could, wouldn't have been good in my situation.

Maybe this method was chosen because they had just started up and didn't want to scare off any clientele. It could be for any number of valid reasons, but their shoe didn't fit on this foot. Their method of rehabilitation was so much in contrast to mine that I simply threw my hands in the air. I can only imagine their rehabilitation was delayed by the soft approach that was administered here. I believe if the place is still standing, then an overhaul of sorts has to be made.

In my eyes, the participants at the center, for whatever reason, tended to be in a higher income tax bracket than I was from. I was in the lower echelon of brain-damaged individuals. It has been a long time since I have made connections with the Clooney Center, but I can still taste the sour residues they left in my mouth. I was going to draw up a list of what I thought to be their faults, but I drew a blank. I feel their deficits are ever so subtle.

I found places like the Clooney Center to be of not much help to me. As I look back on it, it seems that they were merely herding all the head-injured people into one locale for eventual slaughter. Like the cowboy, they would reap the majority of the reward.

Fortunately, I was then contacted by Westside Center for Independent Living (WCIL). They would do essentially anything to assist the disabled. They provided services that ran the spectrum of needs that the disabled might have. It was not that these were provided by WCIL, but they could effectively direct you to the right source.

I had, as well as others at WCIL, a comradeship. There were only about fifteen people working there and then a few volunteers. WCIL and the Clooney Center were like day and night. I feel good about myself. However, I can see that if I had stuck close to the Clooney Center at that time, in 1987, then it would've worn me down.

WCIL were merely interested in making life easier for the disabled. This whole place had a good concept. Everyone who worked there had some sort of disability. That is, everyone except Slate, Dr. Stan Greenburg's guide dog. Stan operated the place. The only impediment in Slate that I could note was that he had a "ruff" time singing the blues.

When I first became aware of what WCIL did, I could think of no better way than this to assist the disabled. I thought it to be very ingenious, the concept of highly educated disabled persons assisting other disabled persons down similar roads that they had been down.

I am continuously battling this disability. I push myself. I have this inner pride that keeps me going. I realize I have this innate drive that was brought forth by my disability. In the same breath, I can say that same drive might have been left dormant if I didn't have the right tools working for me. At WCIL, I have seen a few clients battle a lot of things I had to. However, realizing what a long, drawn-out and, most times, frustrating process it could be, I left well enough alone. I did not give advice.

The majority of the experiences I've had since this injury are neither seen as bad nor good. I simply do the best that I can. I'm thankful I've had the volunteer work experience such as the one at the Clooney Center. It wasn't a bad one, in the sense that it showed me I can last through the ups and downs (in a future book, which has already been written, I will explain my experience there and let the four-letter words fly) when it came to learning more about myself. If I would have been employed there, which I doubt seriously, then I would not have felt the gumption to write about being disabled. Fortunately, I only volunteered there for a few months.

My mental attitude and, secondarily, all the assistance I've received over the years have provided me with the ingredients to succeed. The Clooney experience, I feel, put one more feather in my cap.

Presently, I work at two locations in the field of gerontology. Because the activity director at one place had to have an operation, I've been covering her hours. In total, I put in close to fifty hours a week. I can do it because of my mental attitude. On a normal week, for the last couple of years, I have been putting in forty-five hours a week and have been simultaneously writing this book.

Once I was invited to attend a meeting of head-injured persons, but it didn't do a thing for me. It might have done others good, but I sensed it to be a mere licking of the wounds. To me, this gathering of head-injured persons served no helpful purpose at all. The blind leading the blind is a good analogy. I believe everyone at the meeting had a head injury. To me, very little was accomplished. The meeting of about fifteen other head-injured persons didn't do much for me. I felt that it was about these persons to get the feeling they were being listened to. I've been sent a few invitations to a few other meetings, but I'll have to pass on that bullshit (once again, please excuse the vernacular).

I suspect clubs for head-injured people will begin popping up all over. I don't feel that it produces much else but a false sense of security in numbers. This reminded me, to a large degree, of what the Betty Clooney Center was all about. It seemed as if people at the Clooney Center were merely denying their head injury and doing very little aside from tacit efforts to remedy it. We once had a Teflon president. I'm a Teflon disabled.

Let discouragement slide off your back. A person gains very little with discouragement. A disabled person gains even less. Discouragement rarely seeped into my consciousness. I was too busy doing things that I tended to succeed at. It was probably due to the fact that none of my close associates amounted to much—those who lived, anyway.

Essentially, everything that resulted from such a serious injury was a major limitation. However, I merely turned a blind eye to all my deficits, worked on things I could repair, and went on. I can't remember one thing about my disability that held me back. I can't remember ever feeling so bad about my condition that it stifled my efforts to overcome it.

11

Before my accident, I'd associate with anyone who'd get close to me. In the majority of cases, they tended to be people settled on the bottom of the barrel. Friends, or more correctly, the lack of friends, were an essential part of the rehabilitation puzzle. It gave me a lot more time to think independently.

As I give it more thought, friends are merely used to assure yourself that you're all right. I didn't need that. With all that I've been through over the years, making it this far gives me all the assurance I need. Ironically, or conversely, take that piece out, and everything else fits. Friends, or more correctly, my supposed need for friends, were what pulled me down in the past.

I had no close friends because that's the way I wanted it. I can't predict the future, but I don't think I ever will have that need again. I feel I know exactly who I am. However, I never imagined I'd do the things I did or be the person I am, so, possibly, I'll be the same old guy I was before this injury. Hopefully, I'll do all I want to beforehand.

The more I disregarded friendships, the less they meant to me. I subconsciously realized that friends helped me into the condition I was in. This disability gave me all the diversion I desired. This was something I was a continual victor at. I didn't find the need for friends. My family provided all the distraction and entertainment I needed.

The ups and downs of my family have provided a stimulating voyage through this disability. I'm always improving as long as I'm putting forth effort. The majority, if not all, of my former associates have done nothing with their lives. With all the diversions my family provided, such as marriage, divorce, financial ups and downs, estrangements, and so forth, who needs friends?

I didn't fall apart because I didn't have close friendships, either male or female. Now, I have many acquaintances, and I don't really see a need for anything more than that. I believe I could easily become a very good friend to anyone. It'll just be like when I jump into a loving relationship. These are merely primal instincts that I've held in check for many years. Having and building good relations isn't brain surgery. All one has to do is open up. I will open up when my time comes, no sooner. I'm thinking animal first. Before my injury, I realize now that part of me was being drowned out by the nonthinking me.

I now realize the reason I needed friends before my injury was because I had too many empty hours. With this head injury, there have been no empty hours, and I do most everything in a positive direction. In the past, close friends were my downfall. Lack of close friends cleared the way and has been my salvation.

I'm so happy that I was able to figure this out, even though it was not on a conscious level, as I embarked on the rehabilitation trip. I was fortunate that within my first few months after release from the hospital, back in 1972, I separated myself from my former friends. Even though I didn't have that many close friends before the accident, the ones I did have helped pave the way for me and primarily in the wrong direction. I needed this.

You have to think too much when you have people you dislike. I didn't need much more thinking than I already had. Since essentially everyone is my friend, I harbor no bad feelings for anyone, and I travel a less bumpy course. I found that by being friendly with everyone, it would open many doors.

Before the accident, I had to be concerned about who it was I was associating with. This was because when I hung out with my friends, it automatically excluded me from associating with another group, who then in turn automatically became rivals.

It has been a remarkably smoother voyage, in reference to relationships, having merely limited contact with everyone. This isn't to say I didn't have to work at it; it's merely that I didn't have any bad feelings toward anyone or them toward me. That eliminated much concern.

I know who I am and just what I can do. I don't need friends to justify my existence. Before my accident, I needed friends to reinforce who I was. To this day, all I can say is that I was a superficial punk.

While thinking about this, I would have to assume that it is my past experiences I had with close friends that color my view at this point. I've gotten along fairly well without close friends for many years now, and in my estimation, it has not been such a bad thing. I've accomplished in that time much more than I did in those years leading up to my head injury.

Lightweight friendships are all I need. Being friends with everyone throughout my rehabilitation has worked out swimmingly for all these years, and I don't want to tie any rocks to my leg. However, sometime in the near future, I will build a relationship with a woman that I'm sure will benefit from the lapse I've endured.

This is a refreshing change. I never suspected before my injury that I could be so fulfilled in this manner. Now, as opposed to before my injury, I can scrutinize who my friends will be. I no longer will take whatever comes. However, since everyone is a lightweight friend, I find no need for anything more. I don't need to begin thinking like anyone else and share the same values, likes, and dislikes. I'm my own man. This is something I wasn't before my head injury. Before my injury, friends were my downfall. Lack of friends, at this point, supplements my recuperation.

Since none of the people I know are that close, I have no responsibility. That's the way I like it. I no longer flow with the tide. I swim against it, with much assistance, and still grow stronger for it.

I didn't lose a thing by not having close friendships. A good number of the close friends I had before my accident are either dead, in jail, or floating around in the ozone. I don't have to make excuses for this, that, or the other. Having close friends takes time and energy. With everyone as a lightweight friend, you avoid all the crap of having to be a certain way and having to like and dislike things in accordance with your friends.

However, simply listening to and understanding other people's points of view doesn't sway me from mine; it merely helps me to understand other's points of view. Not closing oneself off to others opens up a lot of possibilities. With a head injury, you don't want to shut anyone out. It was ego building to realize that I could make rational choices, and the majority of these were good ones, when it came to associations.

I found that being disabled—this might be true for nondisabled people as well—if you're not friendly with everyone, then you unwittingly make enemies with at least one person. I can now see that if you don't make all people your friends, then you are limiting yourself. However, I never followed people or advice like a robot. All suggestions, ideas, or plans had to pass through a sieve. When I talk about making friends, I'm not talking about lasting relationships or throwing yourself in front of a speeding locomotive to save another's life. I'm speaking about being able to see the other side of things.

Never having enemies makes everyone your friend. I'm on an even keel with everyone. I don't feel as if I'm being shortchanged by anyone. In the back of my mind, I don't have to worry about a thing.

I never went out of my way to make friends. That consumes a lot less time and energy. By keeping an arm's distance from everyone, you ironically make better friends. It's like drugs. Needing close friends is merely a weakness. Things work out better this way. You never know when you're going to need someone else's help.

The more you depend on other people, the less you depend on yourself. What I did was use people and the services they provided. A good number, calculated by many scientific studies, of persons with head injuries are young persons who lack direction. It's ironic that with this injury I found all the direction I needed.

All throughout my rehabilitation, I found that what pushed me was myself. I didn't need any friends. I found that friends don't enhance my life; all they do is dilute it. I'm speaking now of close friends. Everyone I know is a friend. At this point, I have no need for close friends—those that you tell your deepest secrets to, lend money to (in excess of twenty bucks), or would be an organ donor to.

I found that when you don't make close friends, you make everyone your friend, and you don't alienate or exclude anyone. You don't need enemies when you're rehabilitating. Ironically, that's what close friendships do. They inherently exclude others, therefore causing enemies. I didn't need that. I didn't know this at the time, but, by keeping myself at an arm's length from everyone, I was giving myself the room I needed.

Since my injury, I've had light friendships with instructors, doctors, counselors, and all the way down to heroin addicts, as well as vendors of those commodities. When you don't allow anyone else to taint your rehabilitation, it's much easier.

Preinjury, probably like most of you, I always had one, two, or three close friendships who'd color my behavior. It takes energy to maintain close friendships. I spent the majority of my energy battling this disability.

You don't have to wear your hair a certain way, talk or walk in any manner, your beliefs can be whatever you want them to be, and you don't have to transform your behavior too much for anything. I don't have to change to be in accordance with anyone else's desires. I don't have to worry much about who's toes I might have to step on if I do this or that.

Being a loner, not confiding my deepest secrets to anyone, means I don't have to worry about what picture I portray. I'm free. That's what having no close friends does. It sets you free. If you think about all the crazy things you did in the past, solely because you were conforming to group behavior, then you might agree that it was a tremendous waste of time.

I'm one of only a few who have come from our gang who is proud to have gone through what he has. My former friends, half of whom are strenuously pushing up roses or taking extreme care not to drop their soap while in the shower, were a great example for me *not* to follow.

The majority of my friends, before the accident, were still around after my bout with death. However, it seemed as if after my release from the hospital, a good number of them started dropping like flies. It seems as if someone had scripted this beforehand. After my injury, I had all the right tools at my disposal, and all the bad influences were evaporating like stench in the wind.

After a two- or three-minute appraisal, I can say that friends are a give-and-take bonding. However, during my entire rehabilitation, the people I knew neither had no use for what I was giving nor did they have anything that I wanted to take.

I feel better at this point not having to rely or depend on friends for advice, comradeship, leadership, or anything else. There's a lot to be said about being your own man. This is something I could never do before my accident. I rarely did things on my own. I needed the reassurance of others to make me believe that I was doing the right thing.

Some of you people out there with close friends might be acting the way you're supposed to in order to conform to your group. It's subliminal. I found that the need for friends was merely a declaration that I didn't know where I was going and needed a guiding hand to assist me through all the ups and downs that this life provides. Friends, or what I called friends, are the bottom-line reason for my predicament today. However, by not having close friends at this point, I can enjoy the spoils.

The good feeling provided by my family made grappling with this monster called rehabilitation rather easy. As with everyone and everything else, there's never any conflict with my family. This was my base point. This is where everything for me began. It was an easy go not because my family had any expertise with rehabilitation, but mainly because they didn't provide any obstacles.

Before my accident, I never had any heavy squabbles with my folks or siblings. Your family is your roots. Like a tree, if those roots aren't fed, then that tree will wither. They all have a different belief system than I do, but that just adds spice to the mix.

Fighting wasn't my style—that is, fighting with someone who could fight back. However, I found that fighting this disability was easy because just as long as I never gave up, I always won, and my family tended to join in with me.

12

One day at work, a young lady named Cecilia (probably seven or eight years younger than me) put me in a strange situation. I had been flirting with this young lady for a couple of years prior to this date. Every time I'd see her in the hallway, medication room, kitchen or any other place, I'd approach her as if I were about to press my lips against hers. Playing along with my little folly, she'd merely brush me aside and reproach me verbally.

However, I sensed her heart wasn't in it and continued my little game. This went on for a couple of years for two or three days a week (we had different schedules and ended up only working together three days a week), when I cornered her in the medication room one day. A couple of times before this, she tried to ward me off by punching me in the belly, which had no effect at all. One time, she took a swing at me, and I stopped her fist midflight before it reached my pretty face.

However, this time, she grabbed my nuts. Actually, it was only one nut (I can't remember if it was the right or left; at the time, it didn't make much difference). At that moment, she was reprimanding me for my continual advances toward her. I would do this because it was safe. She was no ravishing beauty, though she did have a nice figure, and I wouldn't feel like such an ass if I were to be rejected by her.

Puerto Ricans have a quip that describes this situation to a T. It goes something like this, "Yo gusto el mango bajito." In other words, "I like easy pickin's." This phrase merely states that I don't like to put forth effort. This is only partially true. If I were to attempt to acquire a young beauty more equal to my good looks (so modesty stated), then I would've been more crushed. However, since I didn't fall off the tree very far, I just had to dust myself off.

Throughout my rehabilitation, I've never gotten so close to a woman that I couldn't pull out safely. I never let myself get emotionally entangled. I would consistently choose safe targets to play around with. I don't know what I can analogize it to, but it was a safe way to behave.

I remember once approaching Cecilia in the hallway and making a customary move to lay my lips on hers. It was almost as if she couldn't stop the words from coming out of her mouth when she said, in so many words, "Why are you attracted to me? You deserve someone much better than me."

She was obviously speaking about her plain-Jane facial characteristics and the fact that she was a mother of four from two previous marriages. I found myself somewhat speechless. Cecilia was a very nice young lady. If I would have met her before my accident, and before her marriages, then I would have felt good about being her friend.

It was safe to play around with her. She was attractive, in a carnal kind of way, but she was carrying too much baggage. This baggage provided a safety net for me. My back isn't strong enough to be a bellhop.

One day, I met Cecilia in the hallway, and instead of playfully trying to kiss her, as I would normally do, I expelled a lot of things that had been crossing my mind for a long time. I had never been this open to her before, and I guess I caught her off guard. At that moment, it was if my subconscious was speaking, and there was no way I could turn it off. I got everything that I had seemingly suppressed for a long time off of my chest.

I can faintly remember, but it went something like this, "Please look me straight in the eye as I talk to you. I want to tell you something that I don't want you to tell anyone else. Before you say anything, listen to my whole idea."

Very straightforwardly, I continued. "We've known each other for quite a while, and I've been physically attracted to you for as long as I've known you. I want to have sex with you—good sex, none of this five–ten-minute stuff. I have a lot of endurance, and I won't stop until you climax a few times. We can meet as many times as you like or as we can fit into our work schedule. Nobody will know except for the two of us. I have a nice apartment just seven miles away, just twenty minutes by freeway." I continued quite fluidly and without interruption.

I told her, "I will always wear protection so that neither of us will have to worry about sexually transmitted diseases or pregnancy. I don't want you to say anything right now; just think about it. But first off, just come to my apartment like a casual friend. There will be no commitments."

She was left speechless. I couldn't read anything on her face. She was as dumbfounded as me. Frankly, I could not understand what was coming out of my mouth, and it seemed as she understood even less. I could see by the blank stare in her face that she was processing the words that were flowing from my mouth. Both of us simply could not interpret what was going on.

A few days after this little episode elapsed, when she confronted me, I couldn't remember saying this to her. However, a week or two later, all the blanks were filled in. Something like this never happened to me before. At the time I was telling this to her, I was on autopilot. However, after she had essentially slapped my face a few days later, it all came into focus.

What I told her was nothing but the truth. Her reaction led me to believe that I could've stated something uttered by a popular actor of our time, "You can't handle the truth."

The day after I confronted her like this, she jumped down my throat. However, the last time I saw her, she was almost apologetic in her approach to me. However, I will remain like stone. The day following my carnal feelings for her, she chewed me up and spit me out. However, I knew her heart wasn't in it. The most apropos way I can describe it is that she chewed me without her dentures. She even left the door open by telling me, "That's not the way you're supposed to do it. You should have asked me out first." Then, not so convincingly, she followed with, "But, now I won't go out with you at all."

Now I know what it feels like to be gummed.

Since it was my subconscious that was talking to her the previous day, there was no defense I could put up against her tirade. I merely stood there like a sandbag. It was almost as if some kind of reprimand was in order after I had propositioned her the previous day. Frankly, I couldn't remember the incident. My approach to her was so unlike me that it must have been my subconscious talking. As time went by, I remembered more and more. Yes, as the days went by, bits and pieces came back to me. I was astounded. I had never approached a girl/woman like this before. In an odd sort of way, I was kind of proud of myself. I had always wanted to be able to speak my piece without concern about what might happen, and on the other hand, there was this other guy inside of me that couldn't comprehend what made me do this.

A couple of days later, Cecelia chewed me out, and she told me I talked to her like she was a whore. With the sternest look I'd ever seen on her face, and with the words coming out of her mouth like bullets, she put me in my place.

A whore is a woman who does things that essentially give pleasure to her. Cecilia seemingly does not give much thought to how she is perceived by others. Her immediate family will suffer the most from her actions, especially her children who seemingly don't matter at all. I'm not calling divorcees whores, but, surely, there must be an easier way.

Maybe I'm living in the dark ages, but I feel that parents owe the children that they bring into this world the two people that made them. I fathered a son and did not provide the stable upbringing for him that was necessary. I accept the responsibility for it. I scarred my son for life.

All the while Cecilia was reprimanding me, I sensed that her heart wasn't in it. I let her blow off all her steam without interruption. I did this so I could hear and understand all that she said, as well as to let her hear herself. I just let her blow off steam and didn't say a peep. This was a wise thing. As she listened to herself, she realized she was just spitting in the wind.

It took me a couple of years after merely playing around with her to draw up the nerve to confront her in the most honest fashion that I could. I wonder if she would have liked it better if I were to have spoken to her like her two previous husbands. Yeah, that's where I went wrong. She needs the assurance of a guy who's willing to promise everyone, including the Almighty God, that his union will last until the curtain closes on both of us.

She told me never to talk to her again. She told me that I spoke to her as if she were a prostitute. Hell, I was just trying to be frank. I had a combination of feelings when she confronted me with that tirade of admonition. Even though this was only a day prior, or it could have been a few days after I told her I wished to have sex with her, it seemed that I had suppressed that moment in time and forgotten what I had told her.

The subconscious mind is a tricky mechanism. Even at this point, it's all very sketchy to me. I do remember looking at her a few times and mentally undressing her.

As I now see it, it was a classic case of sexual harassment. Thank goodness for the statute of limitations. She could've, after reading this, taken me to court and had an open-and-shut case.

As I see it, I was speaking to her on a primary level. I have needs and desires, and she does as well. All I was doing was getting rid of the red tape. Tell me what is worse, children raised with their parents divorced and at each other's throat or an essentially victimless crime like prostitution? If you can't answer this question, ask your Lord.

Ask yourself if it more sinful to sexually satisfy a stranger when both parties can benefit and no one is the loser, or is it morally correct to get married, have a few of God's children, get divorced, and then have them being raised by a single parent?

I did the right thing by not verbally retaliating the moment that she confronted me with that outburst. I followed up nicely by giving her the cold shoulder the next few days. I let her stew in her own juices.

When she told me this, I was afraid she was sincere. She's a nice-looking young lady. I'd had fun playing with her and didn't want to stop. I longed to have that playful connection we once had, but I knew it would be the wrong thing to apologize.

I simply spoke the truth. It blew up in my face, at least for a moment. As a matter of fact, if she had accepted my proposal, then I would've lost respect for her. That is, of course, after I had rolled around in the bushes a few times with her.

Cecilia told me not to talk to her anymore, and she is no longer my friend. Did I do anything worse to her than her two previous husbands who left her collectively with four kids? She has to work two full-time jobs, which she has been doing for the last seven or eight years.

After a couple of days, she came to her senses. She almost appeared as if nothing had happened. Although I still behaved very cautiously toward her, I didn't want to press my luck. I sensed she realized that I didn't want to cause her any harm. I think that what she needed was a little truth back when she originally got married. If I remember correctly, there's a part in those vows that asks you to promise 'til death do you part.

In that respect, there's a lot more people out there who don't keep their word. I never apologized for the day I confronted her. Even though this was an unpolished method for telling her what I wanted to say, since it came directly from my subconscious, I didn't, and wouldn't, change a thing.

Today was the first time I'd seen Cecilia since I told her I wanted sex—perhaps she's not a liberated woman. She wants to talk the talk, but she won't walk the walk. She told me never to talk to her again. She said that she was no longer my friend. She told me that I had spoken to her like she was some kind of cheap whore. I wonder who was more "on the level" with her, me or her two ex-husbands.

It's almost as if she was a teenager, and I was asking for a first kiss. Maybe she wanted to be swept off her feet and ride off into the sunset. I was being as straight as I could with her. Perhaps, if her two previous husbands had been as straight, then she wouldn't have to work two full-time jobs as she has for the last seven years.

Today, a few days since I saw Cecilia last, she'd see me at work and cautiously send a word or two in my direction while we were around others. It was almost as if nothing ever happened. I made no effort to communicate with her when she spoke to me a couple of times. It fell on deaf ears.

She was essentially tiptoeing her way back into open communication with me. I held fast. I didn't give her the cold shoulder. I just didn't act toward her as I previously did. I wouldn't even make eye contact with her, as we usually would when we passed each other in the building. For a while, I let her stew in her own juices. I did this so she might see the errors of her way—and, moreover, because I have nothing more to say.

I had to mentally hold myself back so that she wouldn't think that it was I who was crawling back. It has a lot to do with the male ego. I'm not too accustomed to crawling.

Whoever said that love is a drug couldn't be more on target. After all, I still have a heartbeat, and I occasionally breathe. I could've easily made the same errors that she did if not for the accident. It's not too uncommon to hear of a woman who's been married multiple times with children from each marriage. I only wonder if the proliferation of divorces, escalating crime rate, and so forth has anything to do with the rising Senior populace.

It's great when you're on the highest level of hallucinogens; however, just as far down is the drop when the feeling dies. How do I know? The same way I know that falling out of an airplane from thirty thousand feet without a parachute will not add years to your life. I haven't yet stuck my hand in the fire, but I don't believe I can resist those flames forever.

The trouble with me is that I'm in search of the "mango bajito." I don't like to work very hard, and I have very little confidence. The fruit of my disability has been very easy to pick. Of course, more than likely, you might figure it must have been an easy go. You're right. It was an easy go. Still, it could've been harder than anyone could've imagined. It was all in how I approached it.

Throughout this disability, I've held the notion that it's much easier to confront it head on and suffer whatever may happen than to languish in my disability and gather sympathy from those around me. It has been the easier of the two choices.

I can't understand it because even after almost literally coming back from the dead and repairing myself both physically and mentally more than anyone could've ever expected still I have cold feet when it comes to stepping out on the dance floor. However, disability chose the right person to fall upon. It only required one thing from me, unwavering determination. As of now, I'm a loner. It has not been difficult at all. It's similar to this disability. I'm certain that the majority of you persons out there would never openly accept the many disabilities that have been laid on my doorstep. However, for me, this disability has certainly enriched me.

I don't know if I can say I've enjoyed this priestly lifestyle all these years of my rehabilitation, but I can certainly applaud myself for all I've accomplished in a positive vein, as well as having avoided the pitfalls that are encompassed in a relationship.

It's as though I've been stranded on this island for close to forty years, as I write this. Everything is provided for me—food, water, clothing, money (albeit a small amount), a good feeling of self, and a good education; however, all I would have to trade for this is sexual pleasure. If this were proposed to me before my accident, I would have laughed in your face. However, noting the outcome, I'd gladly hop aboard that vessel with Ginger and Mary Anne. I would, of course, have to kill Gilligan and the rest of the male crew members.

For every action, there's a reaction. I've met in the workforce several women, and it has left me a bit curious. Yes, would these same women, some who have multiple jobs because of the expense of having to raise a family singlehandedly, recommend this kind of life for their daughters? Is this what the liberation of women has done? It's like trading one set of evils for another. It seems as if women no longer concern themselves about the welfare of their children.

Call me whatever you want, but I'm ever so glad that my folks stayed together. I wouldn't have the self-confidence I now possess. My folks and Seniors in general would like to keep things going as they have been for the last decade or so. Naturally, Seniors would like to live a long, expense-paid life. However, they are doing this at the expense of our children. The breakup of the family, which can be correlated to the increased longevity of our Senior populace, is taking its toll on those who deserve the least amount of blame—the future generations. Of course, longevity is a good thing. However, I believe it should be maintained, on the most part, through natural means. This crap of keeping older people alive at the expense of the youth is something that will bite us back in the future.

13

I needed a stable environment. I'm sorry to burst your bubble. If you think it's not necessary for the family unit to remain whole, you are oh so wrong. As far as my rehabilitation was concerned, my parent's unity was a vital factor. The stable atmosphere my parents provided was paramount to my recovery. During my rehabilitation, my brother and sister, not too unlike our generation, were jumping in and out of marriages. However, my folks always stayed together with all the outside inconsistencies within our family, my mother and father were like a rock. I leaned on that rock to bring me this far.

It wasn't as if I could have done this alone. However, I was the star player. It's like a baseball pitcher; his win/loss record depends, to a large degree, on those playing in the field. My family provided the perfect infield, outfield, pinch hitters, and even a bat boy when I needed.

You will gain greater confidence in your abilities when how you feel about yourself doesn't hinge on others. It wasn't as if I brushed aside any compliments or congratulations for what I have achieved—I simply don't dwell in all that. I don't allow my future progress to hinge on the approval of others. I'm not sure how this was done exactly, but the biggest hand that patted me on the back was my own. Also, the largest thing kicking my behind had my own footprints.

It was a good thing; in fact, it was the best thing that I could've done. I made a conscious effort not to be close to anyone. I made everyone my friend. My identity had changed, and I had to make a total flip-flop in accordance with the way I was before my accident.

You aren't in the same world as your former friends, especially friends you make after your injury; you become uncertain whether people around you are merely being friendly because of your condition or if they truly want to associate with you. This was a lot truer when I first started to rehabilitate. However, I realize at this point that I have little reason to doubt the sincerity of anyone.

I don't concern myself with the problems of others. Everything else comes second. My concerns and problems come first. This has worked out quite well. While the lives of others around me were falling apart, I was putting mine together. I had enough problems. By not concerning myself with the things that were bringing down others, I had more time to devote to number one.

I had acquaintances, relatives, and others who had problems by the score. I had one more disability that proved to give me a helping hand all throughout my rehabilitation. I have a blind eye, and I turn it toward everyone else's problems. I used other people to deal with my problems. I didn't let other people's problems use me.

People put themselves in front of me to be used (not in a way that would be detrimental to them). I took the ball and ran with it. I know this sounds selfish and uncaring, but I also used my family, just as with all other things during my rehabilitation. In the end, they all reaped the benefits also.

Make no mistake, because we are all using each other. You are using me to dispense some of the information I received after I obtained this head injury. Likewise, it does me good to realize I have knowledge that could be of use to others. Throughout the many years of my rehabilitation, I put my concerns on the top of the list. I used many people, may have stepped on a few toes, and always placed myself and my concerns at the top of the heap.

This is arguable, but I feel I made the best with what I had to work with. It was the love and concern that my parents showed, not necessarily a didactic approach, that I fed off of during my rehabilitation. Even though there's never been a strong family unit, I don't feel as if I missed anything. In fact, I feel as though it would've hindered my comeback if I were immersed in a *Waltons* or *Father Knows Best* type of family life.

My understanding of the way my family is, the way they are, and why was one of those things that kept me going in the proper direction. I did not allow it to stifle me. I, luckily, was able to form my own rehabilitation around the type of family life that befell me. I realize, at this point, I have to give credit to what I went through as I was brought up, as well as to my heredity.

Yes, my desire to make a complete recovery actually superseded anything else. I feel my family life and the unique idiosyncrasies they provided me with were essential to my recovery. However different these qualities might be for the other persons who are also striving to make a comeback, what it took was determination.

I can't say for sure because I was not in any other situation, but I feel that my mental attitude would've assisted me and pulled me through in any situation. I would imagine that I would be able to survive and prosper in most any situation. My mental approach is what took precedence. Yes, it was my attitude that prevailed. In fact, I feel it was the failure my family was experiencing that promoted my comeback.

I used my family, but not in a bad way. They received as much, if not more, from my comeback. It was a two-way street. I never lashed back against my family, like so many of my compatriots do.

My family didn't have the proper skills to lead me through the rehabilitation process. However, they did provide the rich soil to help my rehabilitation germinate. The easiest targets to release my frustrations upon would've been my family. This would've thwarted or significantly slowed any progress I was making. This wasn't a conscious effort. Of course, we had our disagreements, but those were all worked out.

I believe it was in my makeup that never had me go against my parents. This would've been so easy to do, but it would have delayed much of my progress. Family can provide so much love, shelter, understanding, and advice—it makes little sense to bite the hand that nourishes you.

I had a positive force behind me. It would've been just as easy to allow the ever-present negative force to consume me, but I didn't allow it. I had power. No one could have survived what I did without having some kind of force behind them.

I am running a marathon right alongside everyone else. Even though I'm an extremely slow runner, I maintain a constant pace. Other average runners set up numerous road blocks in front of themselves (drugs, alcohol, relationships, family problems, and so forth). This tortoise will finish the race somewhere near the front.

Others around me were dismantling their lives. I was busy putting mine together. My brother's and sister's problems assisted in my recovery. I simply looked at myself as a success, while they, and others like them, were continually making mistakes.

My immediate as well as my extended family had its share of problems and concerns. With my disability, I was the nonstick family member. There were never any deep-seated family conflicts between me or anyone else in my family. The fact I was not playing with a full deck made everyone tread lightly.

My extended family (i.e., cousins, aunts, uncles, and in-laws) added to my successful rehabilitation. Once again, for the first time, it wasn't that they had a planned procedure. In fact, it worked out better because they didn't. However, as with everything else, it's the way I put myself forward. Just because they were family members didn't mean I could walk all over them.

I was down south, about four hundred miles this weekend, visiting my parents, when about twelve or so extended family members came by. My cousin then showed them a video she had recorded from a public TV broadcast. I had seen a portion of the show about a month prior. It was about the Puerto Rican culture. I believe it was made exclusively by Puerto Ricans.

Puerto Ricans have numerous funny quips that my mother had stored in her mental thesaurus, but she was stumped. When Puerto Ricans have a gathering, everyone and his uncle or, in this case, acquaintance will show up. I remember as a young kid whenever my folks had a party persons neither I nor my parents had ever seen before would make themselves at home. A quip that my mother had never heard before described Puerto Ricans to a T: "Just when we thought everyone was here, Grandma gives birth." When said in Spanish, this has a very humorous tone to it.

This hits the nail right on the head. Everybody and his brother are welcomed to a Puerto Rican gathering. No one questions it. I remember when I was a youngster my parents would throw a few parties that would always end up loud and raucous, mainly because of Grandma's children.

I realize this seems as if it is selfish and unconcerned statement, but, if not for the rough times my family was experiencing at the time, even at this point, I wouldn't have shown as brightly. In fact, I believe all the ups and downs my family went through helped me steer a straighter course.

I used the mistakes that others were making around me to pump up my self-confidence. I would tell myself, *With all the problems I have, I'm doing better than those around me.*

By not becoming overwhelmed by the ups and downs my family were going through, I cruised much easier through this disability. Divorces, illnesses, anger, and fights among family members were allowed to fly out the window. You don't know what straight is until you see those around you go a little haywire.

My folks were living in a quite adequate retirement home from 1996–1999 up in northern California. My aunt lived in the same facility. The two Quintero sisters were feeding off each other. My father never complained about my mother's mental lapses, but, when he was surrounded by stereo Alzheimer's, he and my mom moved south again.

My poor old man had a very perplexing decision to make at a very critical time in his life. At present, he is eight-six years old. He couldn't handle my mother's mental lapses. He moved down south with my mother to be closer to my sister, a registered nurse, so that she might be able to help if it were ever required. Yes, my father knew I wouldn't be able to handle all the things that would need to be taken care of after his passing. So, he wisely moved himself and my mom down south.

I still live up here in a nice studio apartment, work two jobs caring for the aged, and barely make enough money to keep my head above water. I work, on average, forty-eight hours a week. I plan on visiting down south in a few months to care for a couple of old folks (Mom and Dad) I know reasonably well.

The family environment made it an ideal environment for my comeback. My family was an essential part of my rehabilitation. However, it could've been just the opposite if I didn't use my situation. The adage, "When life gives you nothing but lemons, make lemonade," is a good way to describe how I made this comeback.

The phrase, rolling with the punches, almost describes the way I handle this disability to a T. However, I can add, when the bell was rung, I'd run behind this disability as it was walking back to its corner and deliver a few stiff punches to the back of its head. Sometimes, when the referee wasn't looking, I struck it with everything I had below the belt. All is fair in love and rehabilitation.

Although I am not the type who goes around tooting my horn, I've always had a sense of pride in what I've accomplished. Preinjury days were filled with insecurity about my concerns. I didn't know who I was, what I could do, or why I was here. I didn't have a clue. However, this time-out that has been provided by this head injury has given everything I needed to find myself.

Yes, to come back this far, I had to wear blinders. I could not look at others and be envious of what they had. I merely had to look at all that I could do, however limited, with the restrictions I had, but I feel this was easier because of my condition.

I consider myself one of God's illegitimate children. You have to consider that God has a lot of free time, and with all those beautiful angels floating around, God takes his share of liberty. "Thou and thy family" is something I have heard my mother say a few times in reference to my going to heaven. She has told me this a few times because I asked her, "How can you be happy in heaven knowing I'm burning down there in hell?"

On the other hand, the few times I have jokingly said to her that I am going to heaven without having to go through all the stuff that she does, she has quickly replied, "God does not have grandchildren."

I can't see the rationale of God taking one person to heaven and having that person's loved one having to suffer the ravages of hell. Hey, man, I'm a shoo-in. I don't have to do a thing to make it to heaven. I only have one thing to worry about, and that's the grandfather clause, that the jury is still out on.

Hell, I can do and say what I please. God wouldn't send me to hell. With my folks up there in heaven, it wouldn't be any fun for them looking down at me in the pit of fire. This is double talk. He sounds like a character on the Amos and Andy show many years ago. Yes, I am now talking about that show in the early 1950s, which was very politically incorrect. They might still have some copies of that program on videos you can rent. If you are at all curious about this, then I suggest you go to your neighborhood video store, and rent yourself a few episodes. This just might clear up some of what I have said.

My head injury was a piece of cake in comparison to the problems my family was having. Everything was on the up and up for me. The problems my family had to confront seemed worse than any I had to deal with.

The marriages that went down the drain in my immediate as well as extended family merely bolstered my self-image. *Look at those people over there destroying their lives, as well as their children's lives, and they're playing with a full deck*, I told myself.

My sister who's now married for the third time and my brother who's in his second go-round tested my folk's stamina after they were put through the ringer during my life-and-death ordeal. As it turned out, and my mother has confirmed this to me more than once, my surviving that ordeal made both of them stronger.

14

I don't mean to justify the wrong that I've done, but I don't feel alone. At present, this country has a divorce rate of a little over 50 percent in the first couple of years of marriage. This leaves millions of children being raised in single-parent homes. If I didn't have the accident in 1971, then I might have married, my son Ed's mom. By this time, we would've had a couple more kids and would've been divorced, thereby sealing the fate of everyone in the family. I and Oralia, Eddie's mom, would be at each other's throats. Our children's loyalty would be torn to shreds. You know the scenario. Hell, you're probably living it right now.

I'm not too much unlike you, in relation to the way our kids were brought up. It's simply the times we're living in. This doesn't mean we love our kids any less than previous generations; it's only that, in the past, they didn't have a steaming locomotive coming down the track about to barrel in on the younger generation.

There is no more that I honestly feel I could have done for Ed. I'm hoping that, in the future, I will have the financial means to reside with him and guide him along, as I was unable to do in his youth. He, and most everyone else, is unaware of all he has done for me. I realize this might sound selfish and ego driven, but he made me feel as if I was complete. I didn't have any more hills that needed climbing.

In retrospect, I honestly feel that I spared him a lot of strife from his mother and me constantly being at each other's throats, which might be the case for a good number of divorcees. "It's not over until the fat lady sings" is a quote taken directly from the Bible, I'm told. However, if it all turns out satisfactory in his future, then the bulk of the credit remains his mom's.

He lives some four hundred miles away, and though I wish I could be with him, I'm sure it would not help. With the influence of his mother's situation, and that of mine, this would leave him totally perplexed. Since her living situation with her children's concerns, as well as working full-time, differs from mine greatly, it would leave him perplexed, and like his nature (inherited from his old man), he would choose the easy way out.

I'm not where I'd like to be at this moment, and I realize I can't spare the energy it would require to put our lives back together. I strongly feel that once I have arrived at where I'd like to be, I could have Ed living with me, and I could help him along. I only hope that the fat lady is still warming up her vocal chords at this time.

The times I was with my son, very sporadically, I could see where I could've made a difference. His quiet, very sensitive nature would place tremendous guilt on my shoulders. He didn't ask for the situation he found himself in. I could sense his wanting me in his life in a more continual manner. However, I knew if I got derailed off this track I was on, it would be impossible for me to get back on.

Because of the connection he had with me, especially after his adolescence, I realize I could have made a big difference. I could have made a positive difference in his life. I noted quite a few of his traits that he obviously inherited from me. If he would've grown up with me, then I could have advised him on how he could've used those traits for his own good. However, giving up any of my strides to become rehabilitated in the best fashion would've been a detriment to both sides.

Currently, I have little contact with my son, since he lives some four hundred miles away, but I do what I can—which, admittedly, is very little. However, when I talk to him from time to time, I try to encourage him. At times, I send him a token amount of money, but I realize he needs more of me in his life.

It's a lukewarm feeling I have toward him. I know it would be entirely different if I ever had lived with him. The same is true with Oralia. If we were at one time married, then I wouldn't have appreciated her as much as I do at this moment. No matter how far away from each other we presently live, I'm sure I can influence him in the future. I'm different from the majority of other estranged fathers. I have no bad feelings toward his mother.

Conditions that might seem incorrect to most seem to me at this point to be merely a challenge. The situation that lies before me seems almost as challenging as I had with my disability. Like my disability, this challenge will never end. That's all right, because challenge merely seems to enrich my life. However, in reality, my condition dwarfs his. He has a good number of people in his age bracket that mirror his situation. However, to his benefit, and I hope it won't be too late, he'll have me in his corner. It's odd saying this, but I feel that before my accident, I had less than he has now. I had no ambition whatsoever.

Ed is a high school dropout, has spent a few months in jail, is unemployed, has two illegitimate daughters from two different women, and has very little ambition to do anything aside from a few pipe dreams now and then.

We are in the late rounds of this boxing match, and Ed is taking a beating, as he has all throughout this contest. I'm not ready to throw in the towel though. If I hadn't had the experience with my disability, then I would've lost hope long ago.

I'm glad I had the previous experiences that I had. They have certainly guided me to where I am at this point, and I'm very satisfied. It has given me the knowledge and, hopefully in the future, some of the tools I need. When Ed talks, it seems as if he's got some pretty good ideas. However, what he lacks is someone to show him how to walk the walk.

Hopefully, his criminal past won't hamper the rest of his life. It could be as my disability was to me. My disability has opened many doors for me. Ed has never had any doors opened for him. I feel that once he's had a few opened, with someone like me providing direction, he would find it rewarding to follow the straight and narrow.

A criminal past is a whole different ball of wax than the knock on the head I received. However, some of the tactics I've used during my rehabilitation are certainly interchangeable. My dream can be realized if I only have the resolve to see it through. I think, with the experience I've collected throughout this rehabilitation, I can see no man better suited to take the challenge.

I understand that what I hope for Ed might seem like a shot in the dark. However, you must realize that my past was not all that stellar either. Eddie simply needs to know the hows and whys behind the reasons why things happen and how easy it is to flow in the proper direction. Eddie needs accountability. I built accountability in myself. I had to do this because no one was going to push me. I had to push myself. Because Ed and I are cut from the same cloth, I think this can be easily engrained in him as well.

I chose to take on responsibility for my rehabilitation almost from the beginning. With all my disabilities, I essentially had carte blanche in regards to the way I rehabilitated. If I wanted to, then I could've done the least I could, and people would've attributed it to my disability. However, I use the same driving force that pulled me out of those sixty-seven days of sleep to wrestle with the harder and much more numerous challenges that face a disabled person. I have and will treat Ed as a disabled person. This isn't bad. It was my disability that helped me get this far.

I'm thankful that I had this comeback experience that I've had. It has allowed me to sit back and have a larger view of the entire situation. Through this large, panoramic view, I can make what I feel are the best choices.

With the proper guidance, Ed can turn his life around. I'm very willing, and hopefully, in the future, I will be quite able to turn his life around. If I never would have experienced my disability, and the dramatic comeback that I've made, then I too would've thrown in the towel concerning Ed's future.

My hope is that one day I will have a comfortable income, will have Ed come live with me, and start him off on the right foot. I could show Ed the proper way, in my narrow vision, to get around obstacles that present themselves. First, I will begin getting his health in the best shape possible. Then, if it's agreeable to him, he will get his GED. I will give him, like the millions like him, the things he has been cheated of.

Hopefully, I can encourage Ed to do something constructive with his life. I think with the one-on-one attention I could give him, plus the follow-up, he will certainly find his place. It's never too late. After I've done all that I wish to accomplish posthead injury, I will have the time, experience, and, hopefully, the money to do an effective job with the rest of his life.

I believe that the one-on-one approach from me, which he has had only a sprinkling of throughout the years, has certainly made a difference. It's not as though I feel that Ed is a piece of clay that can be shaped any which way I wish. However, I feel he could be like the Gumby toy, in that he could be pointed and shaped in the proper direction. However, I realize that it's all up in the air at this point. I'm thankful we had the relationship, sporadic as it was, that we did when he was growing.

I could picture Ed having a wonderful life, if only I would've known all that I now know before his conception. But, then would I have actually impregnated a woman? I realize at this point that you have to give up too much of yourself to raise a child effectively—that is, for him or her to reach a point where they can fend for themselves adequately as well as be content with where they're at in life. I'm merely a product of the "me" generation.

There are just so many variables that it would be impossible to see how things would've turned out if I had done this or that. It's similar to the time before I had the accident, if I had been asked what I would have accomplished with such an extensive head injury. Having such low self-esteem at that point in my life, I could never have guessed the outcome, much less an outcome so bright.

I now realize that it's a crapshoot. There are so many variables when deciding to bring a new life into this world that if you or I were genuinely concerned with the offspring's well-being, then mankind would eventually become extinct.

However, I don't believe that there is anything I could've done, considering all I had to deal with. I think I made the right choices. By being directly in the picture, as Ed was being raised, I would've made a mess of both his and my life. It would've genuinely thrown a monkey wrench into the machinery.

In relation to spending more time with Ed as he was growing, I feel that I've done the right thing. There's no sense in both of us going down the tubes. One has to play the cards that are dealt him. I feel as though I've effectively played those dealt to me. What Ed needs is someone who can guide him along the correct path. I can only hope that I can do this for him in the future. I wasn't able to do as much in the past. Having come back as far as I have since my injury, I don't see where I can justifiably lose hope.

Support, encouragement, and someone to stand behind him when times are rough are the things that I feel he needs. Hopefully, there will be a time in the future when I can turn his life around. I realize some of you are thinking that this is only a dream. However, if I weren't dreaming at the start of my rehabilitation, then I wouldn't have come this far.

It's not too late for anything. I had to build my own life over again at the age of nineteen. I had considerably less to work with than my son, who is now a young man. If I were to ask the referee to stop the fight at this point, then I'm assured of regret in the future.

Optimism, hope, or just plain blind faith is what pulled me along. The same tools can hopefully work in Ed's case. I had a very faint vision of where I wanted to be when I was through with all this rehabilitation stuff, and I have abundantly surpassed my dreams. I feel that all Ed needs is someone to stand behind him.

Over the years, I've concerned myself with Ed's well-being. I have worried about how he was doing in school and so forth, but never to an extent that it overshadowed my own needs. To be totally honest with you, I have never felt like a traditional father. Let me clarify that. I've never felt like my father.

If you have never lived with your children, then you naturally become more and more estranged. As the years went by, we seemed more and more distant, and we both accepted that. However, in the back of my mind, I knew Ed was continually being shortchanged. The fact that I lived with my parents for the first four years after my release from the hospital, as well as always keeping a close contact with them, I knew Ed was continually getting the short end of the stick.

Even though I've never lived with my son, I hope that someday, in the near future, I can help him put his life together. Realistically speaking, Ed's presence was essential in my rehabilitation. The fact that he was there, as opposed to his actual physical presence, kept me going. I owe him a great deal.

15

I consistently kept my eyes on the target. I have goals. Ed is in my future plans. If I were to pay too much attention to his plight at present, then it would dilute the energy I need to move forward. Hopefully, after I'm comfortable financially, I can help him learn from his experiences, as I certainly have from mine.

Ed has a lack of direction, and I take a good amount of blame for this. I'm hopeful that I can steer him in the proper direction. I'm sure that a lot of tactics I used in my own struggle could certainly help him in his.

Even though our times together while he was growing were quite limited, I'm sure the process that I had to employ to arrive at the level I am at could certainly help him. Even though Ed is now a young adult, I still don't believe he's a lost cause. If there's a chance in my future where I can offer him guidance, then I will certainly do so.

I haven't seen Ed since I left southern California in 1995. I've called him several times; however, my prolonged absence will take its toll. My father was always there, in the physical sense, which is something that was robbed from my son. My parent's stability was a greater gift than any other they could've given to me. I credit a lot of my recovery to my parent's marital stability, and it is partially my fault that Ed has none of this.

I know he lacks direction. While he was growing and we were spending time together, I always sensed that what he needed was a full-time father. I realize, by his actions as of late, that he needs direction. I'm not foolish enough to believe that I can provide him direction at this point in my life. So, I only hope the opportunity will present itself in the future.

It doesn't take a rocket scientist to figure out what's wrong with kids today. Quality supervision (of the parental type) has gone down the drain. I can understand my son's indiscretions with the law. If I had to grow up with the poor situation that he was entangled in, then I more than likely would be writing this book from the inside of a prison cell.

His overall lethargy about school is understandable. He is like a stray bullet. Because of the way this country's priorities are chosen, this condition will last until America wakes up and smells the dead bodies. Unless you're living in a cave, you realize that these dead bodies I speak of belong to our youth. My son is no different than his compatriots. Throwaway kids is only one of the phrases used to describe him and his counterparts.

You lose if you give up hope. Let me rephrase that. You'll never win if you stop trying. You can have all the hope in the world, but, if you don't make an effort to pull yourself up, then the odds are that you will stay where you are. It's my hope someday that I can give him what I failed to in the past, before he's too far gone. At present, he's incarcerated for violating his parole, but I haven't lost hope. Even though his life isn't as stellar as it could've been, it's not over until the fat lady sings. At last check, she was merely getting dressed.

If I can do all I have done battling a severe head injury, then it's quite possible that, with the proper direction, Ed too can get his motor running. It's never too late. Ed can be led down the right path. Hopefully, I can be the right person to lead him.

Ideally, I'd like to move out of state with my son and provide him with the things I couldn't while he was growing. I could walk him through his recovery. After all, he's also disabled. Living with and diminishing most things, my disabilities, leave me with the eagerness to help harness and redirect some of Eddie's powers to flow into the straight and narrow. He's got to rehabilitate. I feel that I can be the ideal tutor.

He has never lived with me before, so it will be a challenge, but I feel I'm up for the game. Lacking a father for all those years of his youth has left him with a void in his life. I feel I could fill this void because of the confidence I possess. If not for this injury, then I don't believe I would have all the things I presently possess. I'm not talking specifically of material things.

16

They're going to have to take me in heaven whether they want me or not. It's like Monopoly. I will not pass go, and I will not collect two hundred dollars, but I will go straight to heaven. My mother, a devout Christian, has told me that when they took me from the ambulance to enter the General Hospital in downtown LA, there was a priest there who gave me my last rights. So, if I die tomorrow, then I am absolved.

I vaguely recall, back in 1971, when all my sins were cleaned from my soul. I only wonder how that works. Does it carry over until today, or do I have to get washed and waxed as often as my car?

What gave the priest who gave me my last rites the right? I only wonder (actually, I don't care) what pull this priest has over the guy or gal who mops the floor in the hospital. In reality, those last rights are given more for the persons who surround the person dying than for the dying person himself.

It seems as if people, especially religious people, don't wish to accept what is and work to remedy it. Instead, they merely hope to wish it away. If we as a human race could accept occurrences at face value instead of trying to attribute the cause to heavenly intervention, then I think we would get off our behinds and solve a lot of problems. I feel that we will then realize how truly minuscule these problems are.

Everything happens for a reason. There are a cause and effect that go along with everything. I'm not going to waste my time analyzing why everything occur on this earth, and I am not going to take the easy road and give credit where credit is not due.

There is a certain power in thought. Your brain is capable of more than you realize. Instead of placing all the praise for all the good that occurs in your life or conversely accepting the blame as the wrath of God for something you did wrong, intellectualize. I'm thankful that with this injury I have gained the knowledge to understand from my personal point of view, which has been colored dramatically, ironically by that injury itself.

I did things primarily for myself, but not necessarily at the expense of others. My belief, or should I say nonbelief, system has pulled me through a lot. When you believe in something external, you're like a leaf blowing in the wind.

Of course, I could never have made it as far as I have without the assistance of others. However, I had to use what was available to me in the appropriate manner. I didn't follow, carte blanche, what people instructed me to do. I allowed everything to pass through a filter.

In retrospect, God saved me. If not for this Being to elevate myself in spite of, then I wouldn't have been able to give myself so many pats on the back. Yes, God saved me. With basically everyone pulling for me, I needed something to push against to propel myself. Like a runner in a race, I needed starting blocks.

Jesus kept that motor chugging. Praise the Lord. If not for this amorphous being, then I wouldn't have had the starting blocks I needed to push against. I needed something to subconsciously push against to keep up my motivation. This belief syndrome was a perfect foe. No matter how hard I pushed against it, it wasn't going to push back. Always in the back of my mind there was this person saying, "You're going to make it."

Yes. I believe—yes, and that's all it is—that the belief in a god is a total waste of time, but, for me, I'm glad to have this nonsense to push against. It's like if everyone in the world believed that if you step on a crack, you'll break your mother's back. How much time and energy would be wasted in the world if everyone was consuming time avoiding stepping on cracks?

Let me clarify one thing. Other people might need their gods for a whole array of things. I simply needed this god to push against. I needed something—something that wasn't going to push back—that I could propel myself against. In this sense, I did need God. It was perfect. It was something I could push against that wasn't going to push back. Yes, this is how God saved me.

Look how far I've come by not wasting time or energy believing in one of a multitude of gods. The world could do incredulous things with all the free time, energy, and money wasted on their gods. This is something that causes the greatest division on this planet. It's a hell of a lot easier to believe there is no God.

I don't have to put on a show for anyone else. I don't have to follow doctrines invented by who knows who. I can live my life as an essentially good person and not have to attribute it to anything but my genes. I don't have to spend my life second guessing whether what I'm doing is right.

There are no strings attached to my way of life. It would be like learning to walk for the first time; the first step is always the hardest. I felt much better not having to hold on to anything while I took that first step.

I realize this might sound trite, but why can't people believe in themselves? If there were no religion in this world, then I think humanity would need to create one. We seem to need justification to kill each other.

Religion isn't like hunger or the need to breathe. Man has conjured this up. Religion is what's destroying the world. If there truly were a God out there, do you think He would like all this death and destruction taking place in His name?

What religion does is simply separate us. In the same Christian belief, there are many divisions. If we didn't have religion in this world, would it be such a bad place? Would people kill each other arbitrarily? I think not. Religion, or belief in God, fosters this. A good number of the wars in this world stem from belief.

Divisiveness will be the destruction of this planet. This is what religion does; it separates us. What has the belief in a supreme being done in a productive way versus all the wars, hate, and so forth that such belief systems have brought to human kind? Wake up people! Belief is just one more form of division.

A token amount of goodness versus a much greater amount of division, in my eyes, doesn't make sense. My mother and other religious people like her have this new line. "I don't have religion. I have God." The only way I can reply to my mother is to quote one of her own quips, "Eso es mismo perro con differente collar." This simply states, "same mutt, with different fleas" or something to that effect. If you're a religious person, then you have unwittingly taken sides against all other who don't believe the way you do. Religion fosters division.

With so many religions throughout the world, you'd think we would live on a very peaceful planet. However, the opposite is true. Religion, belief, and oneness with God are all things that are destroying humanity. Religions haven't brought us together; they have driven us apart. It simply allows mankind to separate itself. I realize I have said this before, but it bears repeating. So much senseless destruction, in this world, takes place simply because of one belief or another.

Anyone who can think objectively and can abandon our archaic beliefs can see what the true peacemaker can be. We must begin to believe in ourselves. Objectively speaking, religion hasn't worked in the past to bring this world together. On the contrary, it has driven us further apart. How many more years will it take before this species has the courage to realize they are in control of a major part of their destiny?

My way is such an easy way of justifying my existence. There was a time when they thought the earth was flat. It was once thought the earth was the center of the universe.

With religion, you don't have to think—just believe. No mental exertion is required. I don't have to worry about what's going to happen if I do this or that. It's as if you don't even control your destiny when you believe in God. After all, you are the child of God. I say, grow up. It's simply a belief in God, and it wastes an enormous amount of time, energy, money, and lives.

I can't see why, because it just doesn't make sense. The belief in evolution as opposed to any other belief is simply more tangible. It's almost as if they want religious people to devise their own reason as to why they exist. Of course, there's a slight chance I might burn forever in hell, but I have weighed those options.

Persons who wish to prove to others that they have a handle on this life—fall in line. God is used in some way by his followers. The concept of God is used for our own insecurities. Belief in God, or gods, is merely a show. It's done so you can gain some respect from others.

It's comparable to having a brand-new bike when you're a kid; everyone seemingly likes and admires you. God-fearing persons have this need to be accepted. Yes, the need to be accepted is key, if not by people outside their religion then by their own cliques that they form.

People enter into religion to somehow gain the opinion they are in some way better. Let's face it; if others, by a large scale, would think worse of you, then I doubt if persons would swarm to such a belief. Religious people seem to have the belief that others might pay them a certain amount of homage simply because of their belief.

Religion doesn't end war, feed the hungry, shelter the homeless, stop crime, and the list goes on. However, with the millions, possibly billions, of dollars it has at its disposal, much more could be done.

I can't see why it's so difficult to believe we once lived in caves, made stone tools, and all the rest if others can believe in God without any tangible evidence. I chose to steer clear of that. God and the Wizard of Oz are, in essence, a parody. They each serve a purpose when needed. Think about it; all the characters in the movie can in some way be substituted by angels, disciples, the devil, and so forth.

When will man wake up, like Dorothy did in *The Wizard of Oz*? Man might then be able to appreciate all he has and see all he needs. I don't know everything, but it seems as if man has created God, and it seems as if these gods man has made will in the long run destroy him. If belief did more constructive things rather than things that tend to separate people, then I could see the usefulness of a god. Hopefully, when man emerges from that deep sleep, he will have enough left to rebuild this world.

We need each other. Some people have to use an intermediary, like a god, to admit to themselves that they're not complete. We need each other, and we are just letting "God" come in between. First, however, we must believe in ourselves. This confidence I have in myself isn't a solitary vehicle. I need others around me to make it work. How I approach others has certainly helped in my rehabilitation progress.

The god I have inside eliminates any need for any extraneous being. I feel good this way. Something I lacked before the accident I encountered in 1971—and grew to a great proportion in the sixty-seven days I lay in a continual dormant state—was the belief in myself. Something that never happened before my injury took place in the aftermath. I have a strong belief in self. This is something that's lacking in those who need God.

My disabilities have been my salvation. I, frankly, needed the attention of others around me who provided, essentially, a rooting section. Before my accident, I didn't know how to bring attention to myself. However, with this head injury, it was easy to bring positive attention to myself. I didn't need to be a member of any group, have any sort of beliefs, or whatever else to be special.

To borrow a phrase, "I was washed in the blood of disability." I believe that's how it goes. The blood was my own. With this disability, many doors have been opened for me. These doors could've been opened before without my disability. However, I was too lazy, insecure, afraid, or any combination of these feelings. I found I was strong enough to sideline the supernatural. Almost exactly what people are looking for, and then some, with religion, I have found with my disability.

Religion, belief in God, or whatever you want to call it has not relieved man of his problems. In fact, the opposite is true. It's incomprehensible to estimate the billions, possibly trillions, of dollars wasted on belief. What has religion produced in this world?

Religion not only diverts funds that could be used more productively, but it also promotes divisiveness. If you are religious in nature, then you are essentially saying, "If you don't believe like me, you're wrong."

Is the world a better place with all the time, energy, emotion, money, and so forth that have been squandered on religion? It's like buying a new car every year that breaks down as you drive it off the lot. However, you continue to buy that same model and make every year. Human kind keeps believing that one of these days, they'll get it right.

It's time to wake up. Ultimately, religion might have good intentions, but it's very divisive in nature. If looked at objectively, religion has done the population more harm than good. Religion is a waste of time, money, and people.

If we could start observing the whole picture instead of merely looking out for ourselves, then we would be much better off. Individuals turn into millions of people that need to latch onto something they feel will give them control, control they felt they never had, and it's destructive.

If you thought of the entire population and not only of your inert insecurities, then you would realize religion causes more harm than good. With all the time, money, dedication and energy wasted on this "God" charade, it's no wonder humanity will probably destroy itself.

The more I think about it, this belief in God is nothing more than a joke. However, the joke is on the true believer. There's still hope for all of you out there who have a smidgen of disbelief. Religious people must take off the blinders. With so many different religions out there today, someone has to be right, and the rest are dead wrong.

However, it's not funny when the masses are the butt of that joke. There are very few who can laugh at it. There have been a few times over many years I've had to laugh at myself. However, I have found this to be healthy.

In a few thousand years, if man is still on this planet, the present-day belief in God will seem as archaic as ancient Egyptian gods do to us today. However, if man awakens from his pie-in-the-sky mode of thought and begins to work on more tangible endeavors, then the joke will not be on man.

In the back of my mind, there's always this need to thwart God. "Without God, I would have nothing." This is a lyric from one of my mother's many Christian melodies. It couldn't be more correct for me.

In all reality, I can't say that "God" has not been a force in my rehabilitation. Without God, I'd have nothing to motivate me. I'm rehabilitating in spite of God. Maybe I'm making too broad a statement. I realize that the reason I'm on this continual trek has a lot to do with multiple factors. I shouldn't let disbelief in a God take center stage.

"God" is one of the reasons I kept on going. I continually pat myself on the back when I realize how far I've come without him in my corner. With God, I'd have no reason to pat myself on the back every now and then and tell myself, "You were able to come back this far in spite of …"

Religious people, as it seems, need a supernatural force to help them along. I give credit where credit is due. It would have been very hard to proceed if it were not for all the fine persons around me. This, of course, begins and ends with my parents. Everyone I touched or who touched me along the way was an important spice to the stew.

In anyone's life, there are going to be bumps in the road. Ability to surmount these hills, as well as to be able to acknowledge the tangible people and things that got you there, is much more satisfying than having to thank some amorphous being.

I realize I could've allowed any triviality to hold me down. However, like a train rolling down the track, I kept going. If I were to have depended upon any supernatural force, then I would've never learned of or utilized all that I had inside me.

Each individual is their own god. Instinctively, man does nothing against his will. Everyone has their own perception of what and who God is. It's similar to everyone's idea of what anything intangible is. For every individual, there's a separate idea for their idea of what good, bad, hot, cold, dumb, smart, and other things are.

There are and always will be a wide array of gods in this world. If you look at it with a clear head, then you can see that we are all our own gods. The belief in a god is a display of man's weakness. This god will fashion himself or herself into whatever need you have. The waste of time, energy, money, and emotion is as long as God's shadow.

An ideal god would make things better. An all-powerful God wouldn't allow all these bad things to be occurring to his children. Give a man a fish, and you feed him for one day. Teach him how to walk on water, and you've wasted his time. If he could make one blind man to see, why stop there? If I was one of the thousands who were left blind, then I'd feel slighted. As far as dividing one loaf of bread amongst many, bread alone doesn't provide a balanced meal.

If God were to present himself to me, walk on water, feed a million people with a single loaf of bread, allow me to touch his sacred hands or even dance the jig, I wouldn't be impressed. All that nonsense only serves to edify him. If he were to do something constructive, then that would merit my attention. Ask yourself, "Is there a need for a god?" If you answered yes, then that's why you believe.

With all the stuff man has to concern himself with at this point in time, God is merely excess weight on his shoulders. There is security in numbers. I suppose that is what prompts so many people to believe. I suppose I wouldn't be so antireligion if it caused more good in the world than it causes bad. Religion simply divides people.

So much time, energy, and money are wasted on religion that it's no wonder that we, as a people, find it hard to get out of the rut we're in. In the near future, I plan on flying to southern California to visit my folks. If there is a God, then let the plane fall out of the sky. I have no fear in God, of God, for God, on top of God, or anything else. What I have is fear of the masses of people who believe in God.

It was amazing; I gradually discovered the only god that I needed was myself. Successful belief in anything must begin with you. I'm not speaking about an overt belief in yourself, but, moreover, a covert belief in your abilities. There is this god inside of me that I refused to believe was there, until it took control of me through the effects of this head injury.

Before my accident, I didn't have a thing to believe in. However, after my head injury, I have accomplished so much. I have a great sense of self. It was tough, before my accident, to believe in myself. Actually, I had done nothing and would go whichever way the wind blew. Actually, I didn't know this person inside existed until he was magically let out of the bottle when this head injury rubbed it.

I feel better not having to give credit where credit is not due. There's no second guessing with my system of belief. I feel that I take full responsibility for my actions. It's easier that way. I don't need to invent a supreme being to ask forgiveness for when I do wrong things. I take responsibility for my actions, and if they turn out bad, then I try not to let it happen again. Since there's no God, I take total responsibility for the way things turn out.

If there is an all-forgiving God, then people will never take responsibility for their actions. Perhaps, this is why, no matter how many gods we have in this world, conditions always seem to get worse. It seems as if religious persons don't want to step up to the plate and take responsibility for their actions. They simply slip into Flip Wilson's shoes and declare, "The devil made me do it."

I'm no different than you. We all need something to believe in. I have my own belief (I believe in myself, not in a god), and like you, I believe that it's a true god. I'll believe it until something more believable comes along. Can you say the same, or are you locked into one belief?

If religion were government, then the masses would have overthrown it at the onset. Any number of realities could come along at any time. I simply don't want to lock myself into anyone as of yet. I believe in evolution, just as I believe the sun will rise tomorrow, but nothing is a sure thing.

My belief, and that's all it is, will do until something better and more credible comes along. I don't have to go to a building at regular intervals to congregate with others who have similar beliefs, and I do not have to line the pockets of the people who talk the talk but don't walk the walk.

Too much time was wasted in my life prior to this injury. I needed to find a way out. Others find alcohol, drugs, religion, and so forth. I found disability or, more correctly, I found rehabilitation. I'm thankful for this head injury. I don't sit on my hands. I'm constantly doing productive things. However, I could just as easily stick my finger where the sun don't shine and let disability consume me.

This head injury has given me more productive energy than I've ever possessed in my life. At the same time, I realize how easy it would've been to self-destruct. I'm currently on the move and have been on the move, since the acquisition of this injury.

It's a fine line between taking on a head injury such as mine and merely allowing it to swallow you. Over the years, I have witnessed those who feel a supernatural force is the answer. I didn't allow any extraneous being to swallow me.

This injury has really opened my eyes toward religion. What religion provides for most people, this head injury provided for me. Without this head injury, I don't feel I could've done all that I have. This head injury provided a hell of a lot of insight.

Dragging along a belief in God, or anything else for that matter, would have slowed me down. God bless this disability. It certainly has distanced me from any outside belief. Having this injury has allowed me to find myself.

In and of itself, this disability is its own religion. I am the one who is gradually coming back from the dead. In certain religions, a select few have visions from time to time. I too have had the opportunity to have a vision. Luckily, unlike others, I had the opportunity to see myself.

Religions have power. Religions in this country should speak out against guns. Religions should get their congregations fired up about the stupidity of gun ownership. However, they are lukewarm about taking opposition to things they fear will lessen their congregation. They, like the majority of politicians, take a middle-of-the-road stance. So, just like politicians, gun manufacturers and so forth, your pastors, priests, or other religious leaders have blood on their God-fearing hands.

I wonder if the church cares more about the safety of the parishioners or the fullness of their collection basket. I wonder what the church members would choose, gun ownership or their God. If all religions would take a stand against the NRA and the barbaric stupidity of gun ownership, then there would be a big positive light cast on the congregation.

Does God approve of gun ownership? Was Jesus, Buddha, and Mohammed a member of the NRA? If religion would take a stand against guns, then I wonder if people would turn against guns or against God.

17

When I eventually found a job working in a Senior citizen retirement complex, I worked among the disabled Senior populace in this facility. There was about seven or eight different buildings, housing about thirty or forty Seniors in each. I had the fortunate opportunity to work among the disabled Seniors. I enjoy working with Seniors and especially with Seniors who are confronting various disabilities. Among the group of Seniors I worked with, I met this elderly disabled man, Jim Wink, who brought joy to my heart. He and I seemed to click.

Jim, known in boxing circles as "Killer Wink", was a former professional fighter and fight promoter. He opened up to me a lot of things that I would've never been privy to if we had never crossed paths.

I have good luck. I always seem to find people like Jim to take the edge off of most work situations. Jim would truly open up to me. He pointed out things in the fight game that are quite believable but obscure to those wishing not to see. I would have to guess that it was as if Jim was in a confessional, and I was the priest. It was as if he needed to get that off his chest before his last round. I have given it considerable thought and have granted him absolution. I've also submitted his name for commissioner of boxing in heaven.

Jim told me the fight game was full of crooks. Well, imagine that. He would tell me coyly that he had taken a few "dives" from time to time. He told me, because a fight promoter's job was to bring in enough customers to make as much money as they could, they would build up a fighter's record by putting him up against a lot of stiffs. By doing this, when his record was big enough to draw swarms of people to watch him go against the champ, they would rake in the money for the fight hand over fist. Essentially, he was saying the promoter was raking in the dough from unsuspecting fight fans. Jim opened up my eyes. After he exited the ring, he too became a fight promoter/trainer. Wink was certainly a kick. He would be an added bonus to the day. He would tell me with a wink (he certainly was given the correct nickname) that he never threw a fight.

I'd continually implore Jim to get back into the ring. I'd tell him I'd be his manager. He laughed the whole thing off. There were times while we were in the activity room with twenty or so other disabled Seniors who were all sitting in a circular motif when I'd rise, pull down an imaginary microphone, and announce to the audience saying, "Tonight, you're in store for a history-making battle. Killer Wink has come out of retirement for the fight of his life." He then would rise from his chair, raise his arms with his fists clenched, and turn in a circle to greet the audience. We certainly had a kick, but I more than he.

Even though Jim and a multitude of other Seniors are good people, we must look at this entire quandary of the rapid growth of our Senior population in rational terms. If we care anything about future generations, then we have to stop allowing past generations to suffocate us. We are continually throwing money down the drain, while, at the same time, flushing our future down the toilet.

It seems that we care less about the expense to keep our older Americans alive. However, this all comes at the expense of our youth. Children need a family unit. Both a mother and a father need to be together for the children to have the optimum upbringing. I'm from the old school. The longer we continue throwing money down the drain, the deeper that drain will get.

If we invest in something that produces nothing, then the returns from the investment will be minimal, at best. The money for the comfort a good number of Seniors enjoy today doesn't come from a large pot that all of them contributed to while they were working. The money that was invested in their Social Security is depleted in a matter of few years after that person retires. It's the working public who currently pays taxes who must foot the bill. At the same time, taxpayers in this nation bend over as that foot makes contact with their posteriors.

It seems as if we must teach our older generation the value of money. Weren't they the ones who taught us to never spend money foolishly? In the ideal scheme of things, it would be kids first, then parents, and, lastly, Seniors.

We have to start somewhere. If you are now middle aged, there will be a good chance that there will be no more money in the bucket when you retire. With a high rate of divorce, dilapidated schools, high crime among juveniles (which can be traced back in some way or another to our growing Senior populace) and a long list of other invariables, the middle-aged people today can't expect to retire half as well as their parents did. The persons at the lowest end of the totem pole will feed off of scraps.

The emphasis on the kids is being depleted by the emphasis on our older generation. After a person reaches age seventy-two or so, freebies should be curtailed. Let them live off what they have saved. The more money that is saved, the more money banks have to loan businesses and such, and this will make the economy stronger and stronger.

I am no different. If I were given something for nothing and others around me were receiving the same, then I too would turn a blind eye to the destruction it was causing. Let's face it; they're productive years are gone. It's like never putting a horse out to pasture but instead, continually providing these old horses with the best feed, stables, veterinary care, and so forth at the expense of the up-and-coming generation of young horses. This is horse manure!

Concerning the elderly, why prolong the inevitable? It doesn't make any sense. We are born to die. It's what we do in between that's significant. If there is a Senior out there who's reading this, ask yourself, "Is this what I want to leave as my legacy?" The way we are proceeding at this point, after a baby is born and the doctor slaps him on the rump, it's like the baby is taken to the next room where they are slapped in the face by Seniors who care merely about themselves.

A rising aging populace has to account for a lot of bad things in this society. Can you name a few of the benefits they provide in this culture? I feel that divorce is an indirect result of our aging population. Divorce has a great, if not the greatest, effect on the children of the couple. Our aging population didn't have to wade through all the crap the younger generation must confront today.

Divorce is a big deal. I've never been married, but I've been told, or read somewhere, it's like taking a piece from you. This effect only multiplies when it concerns our children. Divorce is not only a single problem because it blossoms and gives fruit to a chain reaction of maladies. Realistically speaking, in relation to prolonging the Senior's life, the bad outweighs the good.

Who do you think is the preliminary cause of the family breakup? You guessed right; it's our beloved Senior populace. Do you think it's a coincidence the rate of divorce has escalated at almost the same rate as the Senior population in the last couple of decades? There has to be some sort of correlation.

Let's be realistic. It's the workers today who pay for the majority of the benefits these Seniors acquire. Long ago, there wasn't this rising population of Seniors. Long ago, marriage used to last longer. Is there a correlation? I don't know, but I smell a fish, a somewhat aged fish.

If families continue to dissolve, then this nation will begin to fragment. I'm not a statistician, but I believe the divorce rate must correlate somewhat to the rise in juvenile crime. It's as if we are placing more value on a person who gives back statistically less than a person who can potentially render unthinkable assets in the future. However, with the current escalating family breakup statistic, we are only ensuring the need for more people in the future who can add to the tax base that finances this older population.

In my view, the family unit is the most important intangible, concerning the development of our future generations. Read the tea leaves. The family unit will inevitably strengthen when Seniors rank below kids. With Seniors merely allowed to live their natural life spans, they would be less of a burden. It's like keeping every old pair of shoes you've ever owned merely lying in the closet.

You would see the divorce statistic decline. You would begin to see less and less crime among our kids. Wake up America! There's a reason for everything that happens. We have to take our heads out of the sand and smell the roses, and we have to turn our noses away from other more pungent aromas. It's as if the family has lung cancer, and instead of curtailing our smoking, we go out and purchase an endless supply of smokes.

All of us Americans are going to drown in a sea of age. We should encourage financial responsibility. What we're doing now is simply saying, "Live past a certain age, and Uncle Sam will take care of all your needs." This is child abuse of the highest form. Everyone merely looks the other way.

The well will eventually run dry, if we keep throwing buckets of money down a bottomless pit. Certain things that could've been avoided caused the downfall of the Roman Empire years ago. Will the Seniors be the cause of ending our current empire? If people want to live long, healthy lives with monetary security, fine. This will only encourage savings and good health practices when people are young.

It's mob mentality. Seniors know what they're doing. They realize they're taking out more than they ever put in. However, they don't want to rock the boat. Anyone with half a brain, or even a severe head injury, can tell you the entire nation will suffer with the amount of money we waste. Let me reiterate, the money we waste on our Senior population.

It merely depends on what you'd like to see. In the United States, we are the most prosperous nation. However, if we continue to throw our money down the pit of old age, then we can say good-bye to our prosperity. If you are a Senior citizen, leave as your legacy care and concern for our future generations. Vote for individuals that place the up-and-coming generations first.

It's not too late to rectify the mistakes of the past. Seniors should have to pull their own weight. We should eliminate the free ride status they now enjoy. Eliminate all freebies for Seniors. I'm sure that this would make the majority of people take better care of themselves when they are young, put away more money for their retirement, and take better care of their children, for it's they who will care for them in their waning years.

It's like financing our own destruction. As it stands currently, every time a Senior farts, they can see a gastroenterologist at our expense to find the culprit.

If we don't do something about our rising Senior populace, then it will only eat us up down the road. It doesn't take a rocket scientist to figure this out. Increased livelihood of our Senior populace equals decreased livelihood for our younger generation. In essence, increased longevity of our Seniors means depletion of what's left for our younger generation.

The only legacy the Seniors of today will leave is reduction of our economic status. Let's be pragmatic and not frivolous. We can pay now, or we can pay later. Cutting back on all the services (financial and otherwise) for our Senior segment of the population will only benefit our future generation. If you are a Senior, then you can either stick your head in the sand and say, "It's not my problem," or you can stand up and be part of the solution. I might have said this in other terms before, but it holds true. We can either pay now or definitely pay in the future.

In time, Seniors will begin to realize this is for everyone's benefit. At a time in our past, this country could afford to pay a person until he or she dies. We no longer have that luxury.

I have a proposal. Let's say, when a person reaches the ripe old age of seventy-two, all medical freebies go out the window. The money they receive will be given at a flat rate of just a comfortable amount (just about subsistence). No extraordinary, expensive treatments will be issued to our Senior population. Take, for instance, a person who has abused alcohol, drugs, food, sex, or what have you, and have them pay for their own up keep after a certain age; let's say, again, seventy-two.

I would like to think the Seniors would take responsibility, but it's almost as if Seniors can't see the forest for the trees. However, it's understandable. If you continually give a person something for nothing, then they're going to begin to believe they're entitled to it.

Foresight, and not an endless supply of benefits for our Seniors, is what we need. If we keep extending the lives of our Seniors, then all we're going to need in this country is doctors and nurses aides to change soiled diapers. The only high-tech jobs in the country will be people who care for and prolong the lives of our Senior populace. We're short changing our youth.

We must be more pragmatic and not so shortsighted. It would be wonderful if we had endless resources, time, energy, and space to make life an endless journey, but that's not the case. This will inevitably make the family unit stronger. A person will take greater care in the way they raise their children when it's realized that they must count on their family, not Uncle Sam, to see them through their final days.

Things that are thought of as free that we give away to our Senior populace are, in reality, not free at all. It's our younger generation who has to foot the bill. We should begin investing more in our youth, who are our future, and show less concern for the people of our past. At present, we have birth control. Let's institute life control before it kills us all.

Let's pay more attention and fund more projects for our youth. They have a future ahead of them. More concern must be shown to our budding youth, and Seniors should, at the ripe age of seventy-two or so begin to have services curtailed.

It's time for a change. We are spending vast amounts of money to improve things for our aged, primarily because they vote. We are shortchanging our up-and-coming generations because they can't vote. Is that the American way?

I guarantee the largest block of people who will object to this will be the people who will want to continue their free ride status. The current system makes no sense at all. If we want to make this country strong in the long run, then we must nurture our youth.

There's a current slogan on TV that states, "We must put children first." If older people are smart and want to leave a positive legacy, then they will begin to ask for a change in the way things are conducted in this country. Are simple greed and unconcern about our future what today's Seniors want to leave as their legacy?

However, this is not to blame our Seniors for their actions or inactions. It's like a spoiled child who gets everything they want. The child will not care if you lose everything you have, just as long as they get what they want.

18

Roberto Quintero, my maternal grandfather, was the O. J. Simpson of his time. Everyone knew who he was. He killed (allegedly) a few people, but everyone looked the other way. I wonder if he could play football.

He was a very generous guy. A lot of people owed him money, but he didn't care. However, if you rubbed him the wrong way in one of his soft spots, then you'd soon see the other side of him. My grandfather had a temper, and a few have seen his wrath. However, those who did couldn't speak about it.

I have no objection, deep down, to the defense that O. J. had. When you're drowning, you'll pull the person next to you under waster so that you can take a gasp of air. In the same manner that population as a whole excused that football star, we are allowing the Seniors to do essentially the same to our youth.

The adults must teach their young stronger values. If we get rid of guns, then we can teach morality to our youth in a more effective manner. How the heck can you teach youth strong values when you give sanction to something that brings such destruction?

We can begin by ridding this country of guns. Then, we can work on other killers. We, as a people, could spend more time, energy, and money on important concerns—ones that aren't so easily remedied. With kids getting less and less parental supervision, brought about by both parents having to work and with the proliferation of a single-parent household, the results are inevitable. With the elimination of guns, a major element of crime, we could spend more time, energy, and money in more productive venues.

How brave does it make you to shoot down a poor, defenseless animal? The NRA has the need to kill other living organisms for sport. These people are sick. Are we going to allow people with Neanderthal intellects to lead this country by the nose? We, the silent majority, greatly outnumber these primates. All we would have to do is let these people know how we feel at the ballot box. A congressperson who has any guts should write a law, send it to congress, and see what happens. Disregard the gun lobby. All the money in the world means very little if the people won't vote for you.

When it comes to heart attacks, strokes, cancer and other diseases, do we merely shrug our shoulders and say, "Nothing can be done?"

The other day, I went to LA to visit my folks. On the news was a crazy man who randomly fired a shotgun, mowing down innocent people. On that same day, a person was involved in a robbery where he shot down people who were merely in the wrong place at the wrong time.

Do gun ownership rights in this country outweigh the right for peaceful citizens, like you and me, to walk the streets without having to worry about some disgruntled person inclined to blow someone away?

I've never found the need for a gun. It's my guess that a vast number of citizens in this nation can say the same. News coverage of the shootings at Littleton, Colorado, in 1999 showed how stupid we are. Why do we need guns?

Somebody's paying for all this. Who could that be? If you think the NRA is footing the bill for this, then you are right. Yes, however, they are not paying as much as you and I are paying for it. We all seem to watch the news like zombies and feel like we can do nothing. However, this is America. We have all the power.

The news media are merely saying to you, as they report gun violence, "Look how stupid you are." However, they're not so stupid, because you are watching, reading, and listening to *them*. Those school children being escorted out of their classrooms, across the street, with their arms raised are all of our children. Until we stop looking at the problems guns cause as someone else's problem, we will slowly allow this to eat us up.

Somewhere in Georgia, another high school student came to school and mowed down another six innocent people. God bless the NRA. If guns are out there, then they're going to be used. We could end all of this. If you do nothing, then it's as if you had your finger on the trigger at any crime committed in this country utilizing guns.

We should be thankful for organizations in this country whose sole concern is for our well-being. Just do the math. Do the benefits that gun ownership provide compensate for the death and destruction that this right levies on the majority of the population? It's so easy to commit acts like this in this day and age. At no time in our history did we have such a high stress environment.

The big question is why? Cars and other vehicles are a cause of much death and disability in this country, but you would have to weigh that against the benefits that they provide. I have a number of former friends who are now dead—Jack, Conejo, Bear, Weasel, Ruben, Robert, and the list goes on. Some of these deaths were the direct result of firearms, and the rest were indirect.

Perhaps, you might say that my friends wouldn't have amounted to much anyway. However, we will never know. Think of all the wasted lives that might have lived many rich and fulfilling years if they hadn't stood in the way of a bullet—the lives of hardworking people, like gas station operators, liquor store attendants, and the list is as long as a high-powered rifle. Now, more and more, the future generations are being wasted.

A couple of centuries ago, there was no way they could've comprehended what we have today. Why live by all the same laws that they had then? Back then, as well as now, it was difficult for some to look down the road. The constitution stipulates that it's everyone's right to own a gun, but the framers of that bill neglected to stipulate just who was going to pick up the tab for all the expenses guns have created. Could it be that our forefathers simply had no foresight?

Whereas society back in the 1700s was moving at a snail's pace, it's now moving along at a much swifter flow. Guns can no longer serve a purpose, as they once did. A horse and buggy served a purpose a hundred years ago. However, at this point, it would cause more disruption, even in the slow lane of the freeway, than it's worth.

The times are a changin'. Years ago, when a youth had a disagreement with someone, a black eye would result, but this is just a memory. Now, it's a good chance that a person would have to get out of the way of a bullet instead of a fist.

The laws are changing. There was a time when your wife and children were your property if you were the man in the house, and beating either one was your right. Life, at this time, doesn't have the same values, for various reasons, as it once did. Yes, old-time laws have to change with the times, and these archaic laws are hitting you right in the pocketbook.

Who do you think pays for all the hospital stays and follow-up treatment given to gunshot victims? It's like shooting ourselves in the foot. With the pace of society rapidly accelerating, ways to settle one's disputes must also. There's no question as to why today's youth are so violent.

The youth in this nation are currently taking a back seat to the Seniors' concerns. From that same back seat, they're conducting various drive-by shootings that everyone pays for. The youth have to be heard in some manner, and this seems to be the easiest way.

I simply can't understand why there's a need for anyone aside from law enforcement, guards, and military to posses guns. I heard something very stupid on the news this morning. They're proposing a law that would make it mandatory for every person to have a trigger lock on every gun they own. That's as stupid as having a Breathalyzer installed in every car to determine if a person is drunk before he can start his car. How stupid can we be? If guns were merely possessed to thwart a potential burglary or assault, then I'm sure the average criminal will allow you enough time to get your key to unlock your gun. It wouldn't be any more effective than the health warning on cigarette packages.

The second amendment to the constitution should go by the wayside. There was a time when your wife was your property. Also, women weren't allowed to vote. Let's not forget there was once a time when blacks were slaves. These are only a few of the archaic practices that have gone by the wayside. The late Charlton Heston was an archaic thinker. He came on TV and tried to talk his way out of responsibility for the massacre of Columbine, Colorado. I don't know what it would have taken to show him that guns were the direct cause of this senseless act, but may he rest in peace.

In the twenty-first century, let's allow future generations to prosper. Perhaps gun ownership, child labor, and witch burning were okay in the past, but times are changing.

Let's have the NRA be a tad more responsible. There are consequences to having certain freedoms. NRA members should be required to attend funerals for those who have been killed by firearms. Members should be required to make regular hospital visits to those who have been injured. Also, they should be required to counsel persons who are victims of armed robbery. It's easy to sit back with your eyes closed. Let's have the current president of the NRA make visits to the families and loved ones of those who have been killed by firearms. I'm sure all those people would appreciate the NRA's warm and sincere consolation. Eulogies should be given by NRA members to those who have been killed by guns. For each person killed by gunfire …

As a taxpaying citizen, I obviously pay my share of the costs that guns bring upon this nation. I would like to hear a pro–con debate and then make an informed decision. This is a democracy; let's put it to a vote. Both sides could then inform the public of the reasoning behind each tenant. This is America. Let the people decide.

Write your police department. Ask them why they want guns to be legal. The police chief in your city would be a good place to start. Ask him or her why, if they do, want guns to be legal. Ask if it's worth it to suffer all the tragedy we suffer simply in the name of the right for a minority of persons to own guns. My guess is that the police wouldn't even know why the public has such a primitive right. Supposedly, it is *our* police department. There is just so much that can be abused if these things are overlooked.

Who polices the police? Is there an outside objective body? The phrase fox guarding the henhouse rings in my ear. One day, I was at the airport with my buddy. At the airport, my friend met a fellow officer. I was introduced to this guy who must have weighed at least three hundred and fifty pounds. His uniform appeared as though it was painted on. This would be like hiring a blind person to drive a school bus. He must've had Seniority. There's no way he could've been hired in the shape he was in.

It's like a brotherhood, I suppose. You wouldn't disown your brother or sister if they were on the portly side. You might say a few things, try to help, or a number of other things, but, in most cases, you wouldn't turn your back on your sibling. If this were a professional sports team, then this person wouldn't even be sitting on the bench, for fear it might break.

Supply and demand are what takes place here. The more crime that takes place, the more police are needed, and higher salaries are needed to thwart this epidemic. I'm sure police want to stop crime, killings, robberies, and so forth that involve the use of guns. So the public should think of their safety.

Wake up America. Police need crime. That's their business. Do you think your auto mechanic hopes your car never breaks down? Police are the major cause of crime, or maybe they just instigate it.

I have a close and personal friend whom I've known for many years. This person used to hang out, in the late 1960s with the same group of incorrigibles that I associated with. He was similar to me, in regards to illegal behaviors, but a bit more tentative. A dramatic transformation has been made in this individual. He is now a cop. All the things he's doing at this point have always been there. However, he needed a sturdy platform to stand on.

I have known Jerry for years. It's only at this point that he displays such self-confidence. Are we merely giving cops balls? Over the years, posthead injury, I have built self-confidence. Jerry has found his after becoming an officer. I suppose that you must get in where you can.

I only wonder if the salary of the police commissioner, or other higher-up, is equal to what is produced. The reason they pay a college graduate who becomes a cop a higher salary than the mere high school graduate is because its hush money. Jerry, my friend, a college graduate doesn't do a significantly better job than his cohorts. The department merely figures he has no better way to make as much.

It also gives law enforcement more credibility. Higher education is desirable in most professions. However, the extra money should be commensurate with what is provided.

The police are doing the same thing as my beloved godfather. They are stealing from the rich (and poor) and giving it to themselves. These are legal scam artists. There has to be a better way. As man keeps improving his life situation in one area, we must find a way that we can also assist lesser individuals, aside from merely giving them a badge and a gun.

Police keep the people in fear. Like you and me, we get away with what we can. If any business or organization were to ever do something so blatantly destructive to the public as law enforcement, then it would be splashed all over the news. How else could they justify their salaries? However, police are just people. If we keep doing things this way, then we will all lose in the long run.

Producers, writers, and advertisers are very shortsighted. It seems as if they can't see beyond their noses. Why don't the TV stations show a program about how crime should be halted? They just want to make a quick buck. Programs on TV, the movies, and, to a lesser extent, the radio could air an equal amount of time devoted to programs that show things we could do to make this a better nation. Instead, it seems as if the solutions are beyond their noses.

It could be said that people don't want anything but violence, destruction, or murders on the news. Has anything else been tried? The majority of stations merely care about what will make them money. However, to make everything work to its optimum, this whole idea has to be a voluntary effort made by the media. For a while, they'll have to put on their glasses to look beyond the bottom line.

What we're doing is buying more and more Band-Aids as we continue to hemorrhage to death. These Band-Aids become less effective as time goes on. It's not working as it is. It's almost as if the public is afraid criminals will take to the streets and shoot up the town. We are, to employ an overused phrase, putting the cart before the horse.

Let's begin educating and caring more about our future generations than merely feathering the pillows of persons who do less and less to give hope to the future. The police do very little to dampen the surging crime statistics. Like the media, they find a way to feather their own pillows. It seems as if everyone is merely out for theirs.

In my slanted view, I have a close relative whose actions mirror, somewhat, those of a cop. My uncle Pete is similar to a cop. They both take advantage of the situation they find themselves in. They are both on the right side of the law. However, they both twist it to their own advantage. This close relative uses the law to essentially bend it. However, with the law on both of their sides, they come out smelling like roses. In essence, you wash my back—I'll screw the guy next to you.

This close relative has made his riches from all of us who pay insurance premiums. However, the cops have a larger pool to drain. I will mention this relative in future writings, but I just couldn't pass up this analogy. Besides, the news media is sleeping in the same bed.

It seems as if the news media can't see further than the end of their microphones or ballpoint pens. If I would've exhausted all my time worrying about all my disabilities, then I wouldn't have gotten anywhere. What a waste of time. How can you use in a productive nature all the bad news that reaches your senses? Reporting murders, robberies, assaults, and so forth doesn't help society.

I wonder what effect it would have if news reporters would spend a majority of their time reporting on all the good things happening in this world, in our nation, and your community and only lightly, if at all, cover the bad news. The news media must take blame for this explosion of crime. They and police officers feed off this tragedy. It's natural that they do this because it's the bottom line—but for how long?

This quick-buck mentality will destroy all of us in the long run. I wonder if the longing to hear such barbaric killings would subside if the public were also notified of how much this is costing each and every one of us. The news media can also jump into the same bed as the NRA, cops, and gun manufacturers. These groups are the only ones that seem to profit from the use of guns, aside from funeral directors.

I only wonder if the money that was saved from the senseless carnage that is produced by gun violence were to be channeled into more productive venues for our youth, would this be a better place? I believe, speaking very facetiously, there was once, a very long time ago, an association quite similar to the group that now keeps firearms available. This group was called the NCA. However, as man became more and more civilized, he found there wasn't as much need for a club to kill his food. I believe even the caveman would see the rationality of my point.

The news media is responsible for the majority of this destruction. The news media fuels the fire. They are the ones chanting to the distraught person standing on the bridge, "Jump! Jump!"

We all watch it on TV, hear it on the radio, and read it in the papers, but nothing gets done. The majority, the ones who pay for the costs run up by firearms, has got to speak up, preferably at the ballot box. The news media seems as if they are merely fanning the flames for their short-term profits. If the news media has any sense, then they would realize that if this nation goes down in the tubes, so do their jobs. They have us like zombies witnessing the destruction and feeling that there is no remedy.

Let's look at it realistically. If you worked at a plant that made toxic substances, these products would kill hundreds of people each year, and they also would produce fringe maladies too high to enumerate, but, you and your fellow workers could end all this senseless waste by refusing to produce this product, would you? Also, you would be convincing the people that there's realistically little need for this, but would you open your mouth? You probably wouldn't—that is, if you were paid ridiculously high salaries for making these foul substances.

The other day, on the news, I saw these cops on TV almost crying. They were describing how they were trying to apprehend the killers in this one incident. Those law enforcement officers are the ones to blame for this, and those same individuals, when caught, will be sent to a place that you and I foot the bill for. I'm sure that that money could be better spent. Do cops wish there was no crime? I believe cops, as a whole, want things just the way they are.

The news media could have a dramatic part in the reduction of crime, if only they wouldn't revel in the crimes. The news media merely applauds all the crime, instead of talking of ways it could be curtailed. The news media is similar to a person standing next to a burning house that hasn't been fully engulfed. Instead of grabbing the garden hose in the front lawn and beginning to douse the flames, they merely fan the flames to make a better story.

Apparently, the news media can't see further than its nose. If the country falls apart because of the high crime and violence, which is consequently fueled by the method they use to report it, then they go down the drain as well. If the news media would take a stand against all this gun violence this country suffers instead of merely capitalizing on it, then changes would surely be made.

I realize newscasters are merely doing their jobs. They are similar to the tobacco farmer. However, consider for a moment, if the farmer could add fertilizer to their field that would merely avert all the cancer, heart disease and so forth, and all these farmers didn't use this fertilizer, because it would eliminate the addicting quality of the tobacco, would you consider them smart or just killers? Essentially, this is what the news media is doing to us all.

They look so stoned faced and concerned while reporting this violence. Those newscasters merely care about the bottom line. I suggest all print, radio, TV, or any other medium take a week moratorium and provide no coverage on violent crimes. See what happens.

If you think about it for a while, newscasters are similar to that crazed person in a crowded theater who yells "FIRE!!" That same person has the option of calmly escorting the moviegoers out of the theater row by row, but, in essence, it wouldn't have such a great effect.

TV station after TV station each makes a few bucks off this slaughter, such as local newscasts, *48 Hours*, *20/20*, *60 Minutes*, and the list goes on. Do you suppose if the news media had to pay for all the death and destruction caused by firearms instead of merely cashing in on it, then they would find ways to avert this waste?

It wouldn't make sense for the networks to oppose the gun industry. Your favorite newscaster has blood on his hands. It's not a case where you kill the messenger. The messenger is killing you. The last time you heard of a senseless shooting, did the newscaster seem as if they wanted this to stop? ... That's their bread and butter.

The way to stop this proliferation of senseless deaths, robberies, and other crimes is to end the profits these persons who report them make.

Newscasters aren't the only people with blood on their hands. Religious leaders must share in the blame. I've never heard religion take a stand on gun control. "Praise the Lord, and pass the ammunition." If religious persons and their religion had the balls ... Do you suppose that if this Jesus person were on earth today, he would be in favor of the proliferation of guns as it is?

Let's not kid ourselves. Religion could take a stand against gun ownership, and even ardent gun owners would begin to see what they're essentially doing. Religion could end these senseless killings and other crimes perpetrated by the mere fact that guns are so readily available. Do you suppose churches/religions prosper also because of the fear these weapons generate?

What is religion afraid of? Is religion for or against gun control? Is religion afraid of the NRA? Does God sanction the killing of defenseless animals for sport? I suppose religion, like the majority of Americans, doesn't want to rock the boat.

Religious leaders want to play it safe. Although guns and killing God's creatures for sport are diametrically opposed to their beliefs, not a word is whispered.

Religious leaders are so very quiet about something that could curtail the slaughter of God's creation. It makes you wonder, is God a member of the NRA?

Why don't religions say something about gun control? I suppose they know which side their bread is buttered on. Religion is afraid. I'm sure, if there were any way they could stand to profit with their stance on gun control, then they'd cast the NRA to hell in a heartbeat. The NRA is most likely made up of a good number of God-fearing churchgoers. The fear of the collection plate drying up is more threatening than a few murders or robberies.

If the clergy is really all that concerned about you and me, then they would stand vigilantly for gun control. With so many followers, they could do it. Ask you pastor, priest, minister, or whoever bounces the word of God against your ear drums how they feel about guns. It's not too farfetched to believe that these NRA members put a little something in the coffer from time to time.

Religion displays no ethics. Religion stays on the safe side of the street. The clergy of any denomination has a controlling influence on their followers. Do you just carry around a thirty-eight caliber gun for protection? Ask your preacher, priest, evangelist, or witch doctor where they stand on gun control. I'm sure that if all the clergy took a stand against guns, then it would definitely have an impact.

In reality, by sitting on our hands, we must accept some of the blame. There's a simple explanation for all the killings, armed robberies, and so forth—the availability of firearms. Legalize hand grenades, and they too will be used.

The answer is right in front of our faces. However, the majority of us are afraid to do anything. The reason it's fearful is because it's the NRA holding the symbolic gun to our heads.

If guns were no longer in such great supply, then the incidences of gun violence would dramatically decline. Guns instigate crime. There are a multitude of crimes that could get more attention, and possibly greater resolution and eventual decline, if police didn't have to use up their time in gun-related crimes.

Think of all the other crimes that could be slowed if we made guns illegal. The percentage of times a gun is used to thwart crime is significantly less than those where it is used to commit a crime. If you have a gun in the house, then there's a much greater chance that it will be used against someone in the home than against an intruder.

The money that would be saved, merely from the elimination of firearms in the society, would be phenomenal.

19

I don't have any problems with my many disabilities. This has been the case over the years. I never looked at them as something I wanted to rid myself of. They were just there. Instead of denying their existence, I used them. Even though I've rarely felt uncomfortable about my situation, places like the Westside Center for Independent Living (WCIL), who fight for the rights of the disabled, are like an oasis in the desert.

WCIL helped give me the confidence to push forward and realize there were people around me who could help. Even though I felt I could handle it on my own, there's always been this safety net beneath me. I can certainly see where the WCIL, a place I was employed in the early 1990s, would play an important role in a disabled person's life.

Project Re-Entry and WCIL were two of the institutions, among all of them that I used, that seemed to be on the correct path when it came to assisting head–injured people. This is not to say I didn't receive benefits from other organizations; it was only that they seemed in tune with where I was at during that time. These two operations were in their infancy at the time, and that's how I liked it. However, even though the WCIL had been in operation for some years before I got there, the idea was relatively new to me. That is, the disabled people were banding together to make their existence easier.

Project Re-Entry was a no-nonsense, cut-straight-to-the-chase type of organization that would help disabled persons find work, but I nevertheless played them like a fiddle. I wasn't too crazy about finding work. School, nine years of it, was very hard work. I needed a vacation. However, Jim and then Tom, my two job coaches, saw through me like a pane of glass. However correct they might have been, I used them in a way I felt more proficient.

Since Project Re-Entry was a new organization, I proceeded to form it into something I felt suited my needs. Still, in the back of my mind, I realized I was only stifling myself. At the time, I had another agenda. However, I didn't know what it was. I had all this stuff inside of me just begging to be expelled.

I dragged my feet. At the time, I was living with my parents. I had no bills and no obligations. Project Re-Entry took a no-bullshit approach to getting me out in the workforce. However, at the time I used their services, back in 1988, I had my first book burning a hole in the back of my head.

Yes, I had other things that I wanted at the time. I didn't know what these were except for the aforementioned book, but I knew that finding a job would merely impede the voyage. Little did I suspect that I needed to get into the workforce to put the whip cream on top of my rehabilitation trophy. These books would be a subsequent cherry.

I'm self-motivated. Everything I do is for the benefit of yours truly. We are all like this. No one does anything that doesn't in some way benefit himself. Shoot for the stars, go for the gold, or any other similar analogy describes my effort. Once you put yourself on this track, it's quite easy to stay on it. As I think about it, it was as easy to originally get on this conveyor belt.

Work and rehabilitation are very similar to me, for I wish to do my best. This isn't for anyone's sake but my own. If others benefit from it, then so be it. In this respect, it's not bad to be selfish. Everyone comes out a winner in this respect. I have found that it's not so hard to do one's best when one is severely disabled.

Before my head injury, I was lost in this twisted maze of life. Yes, this disability gave me purpose. Before my disability, I was like a leaf in the wind. I didn't know who I was or where I was going. I realize this might sound a bit over dramatic, but I found myself with the aid of this disability. I realize I must have said this a few times before, but please bear with me.

The reason work isn't as hard for me as it is for others is that I found it ever so debilitating while I was collecting dust. I've been, and still am, going through that road. When I look at the disabled Senior (the population I generally work amongst), I say, "There for the grace of rehabilitation go I."

Work isn't difficult for me because it has a lot to do with my choice of study while in school. I can see where working with the old might turn some people off, but, for me, it fits like a glove (an old, worn, and beat-up glove).

I think the reason why many of the young are turned off by the aged is because they fear that that is them down the road. I have the luxury of having been there, and it's not such a horrible place to be. You have to conform; that's all. If you don't, the same with disability, then it can swallow you.

For me, I can identify with the aged. They are continually losing more and more as time goes on. I too have lost a lot. I too have had to conform to my many disabilities. However, at this point, and from here on in, I'll be continually recovering. However, the aged have to conform to more and more loss.

I can recall when my head felt as if it were filled with nothing but air. Now, I'm able to do a task and, at the same time, have someone pay me to do it. It's a very remarkable change of events. Being able to work for a salary is a reward in itself. The thought of someone who's willing to pay me for doing a specific task is a feather in my cap.

Work is very rewarding. The monetary gain is secondary. The ability to be able to do something, and then have someone willing to pay me to do this, is reward enough. I also get the feeling that I make a positive difference.

To think that I can still do something after sustaining this massive head injury is just one more feather in my cap. My cap is getting so heavy because of all the things I can do. My neck is having a hard time supporting the weight. I should be busy taking bows at this moment. However, at this present time, I work two part-time jobs, and exercise daily, and scribbling on this paper, along with other things, doesn't give me the time.

There's a limit to what I can do. Let me clarify that. If not gone about the right way, I can certainly burn out. With my first job, after my head injury, in 1983, I pushed myself too hard. I burnt myself out quickly. I'm glad that I had that short experience.

In that first work experience since my injury, I lit the fuse, continued to fan the flame, and burned myself out. I didn't pace myself. Pacing myself, I found, was the key.

While in school, I went whole hog. I maintained that same stature while on that first job, and that hog took a crap on me. While at school, even though it was difficult, I had cushions. I quickly learned while in the work arena that you have to make your own pillows.

I have found through my knowledge, experience, and education that I don't need to play any games. I conduct myself the same way as I do in any other circumstance. At the beginning of my rehabilitation, I felt as if I was on stage, and I had to put on a show. However, at this point, there's no longer a performance, and I'm virtually the same individual.

It's much easier to work in this fashion, rather than always trying to put on a façade as super handicapped. There's no change as to the way I conduct my affairs outside the work environment from the way that I do in any other circumstance. It's a relaxing feeling. All throughout school and my previous jobs, it seemed as if I were on a stage. As of this moment, I don't make any compromises because of my disability. As Flip Wilson, or was that Bill Clinton, said, "What you see is what you get."

I never realized this, but work, for me, is less debilitating than my time in school. Even though I work two jobs at two different locations, my mental approach to the whole situation makes it a piece of cake. However, this is only due to the fact that I've never stopped pursuing that goal. I've been on this treadmill for so long. I've forgotten what the hell the goal is.

It's not necessarily that I like what I'm doing. I like the fact that I *can* do something that they are willing to pay me for. Being on this treadmill has been good for me. I know I wouldn't be able to do this if I hadn't put myself through a strict regimen of health practices, school work, lack of meaningful relationships, and so forth. I keep the ball rolling. I never stop to catch my breath. This is mainly because I never lose my breath.

I will be continually rehabilitating, and that's something I like. There's no loser in the process of rehabilitation. Before my accident, I was overweight and in need of a lot of exercise in the sense that I was getting fat by the process of doing nothing.

Work is just another section of this treadmill I'm on. This treadmill is not tiresome or something I wish to get off of. I now realize that this is something that I needed. The process of rehabilitation has conditioned me to work with little wear and tear.

I'm on a never-ending road to overcoming this disability, at least until my time on earth is done. As long as I stay in the fight, I will never lose. I realize that might sound trite, but I can't think of another axiom that can pinpoint it as well. There'll be a few more treadmills that I will have to get on before this ride is over. That's if it ever ends. However, as long as I keep myself physically, emotionally and socially fit, I welcome the next treadmill with open arms.

It was a long and tedious road that brought me here, but I wouldn't change a thing. I'm glad that I have the sustenance. For the past nearly five years, I've been working what might be considered a little excessive. It's amazing, I don't get tired. I could see where it might tire someone who had a multitude of other concerns. However, I keep it simple.

Amazingly, when I'm at work, I remember that I am at the type of job I always felt well suited for and the type of job that I can handle. I don't know if it was I who conformed to the job, or if the job simply fit like a glove, or maybe a bit of both. I look at it as, "This isn't work; this is a walk in the park." However, I realize this wouldn't be so if I didn't have this other outlet of writing.

This accident certainly brought out the better side of me. I can work, exercise (however limited it might be), and write this book, among other things. Before my accident, it was a chore to wash my face.

Work is good for me. I don't tire, feel bad, or have any other negative feelings. It was the same while I was going to school. I believe it's because I'm reaching for that carrot at the end of the stick. Before my accident, there was no carrot, and the only stick was the one being shoved up a delicate crevice of mine.

The continual fight that I had to fight over the many years has strengthened me. I can only attribute my endurance to the continual effort I've had to make throughout my rehabilitation.

I feel I've chosen the best career path. Gerontology, in my eyes, is a make-work career option, and I'm a make-work kind of person. There's nothing I do that requires a superior intellect. However, what it does require is lots of patience and understanding, I, fortunately, have both.

There's nothing that has to be completed by such and such a time. The product doesn't need to meet any specifications. There's no one looking over my shoulder, and there's no complaint department. This occupation merely promotes the idea of longevity. I have nothing against long life. However, I feel this long life must have a price, and persons must be willing to work for it. They also must give something back.

At this point, I'm much more relaxed at my current positions. I don't overextend myself, like I did in my first position when I was first out of college in 1983. I can recall that, at my first position after I spent seven hard years at school, work was harder than school. Now, I'm more relaxed, which makes me more capable to handle whatever comes up.

I took it too literally. I mistakenly got the impression that I was not supposed to enjoy it—otherwise, why where they paying me to come to work day in and day out? I was very fortunate to have had that job after I finished at the Dominguez Hills University in 1983. That first position taught me quite a lot. I looked at that first position as a test. Even though it blew up in my face, it taught me more about the need to pace myself.

I'm more casual and relaxed, and I work more efficiently. This isn't work for me. Back in 1983, that was work. Now, I'm doing the same things, in a relative sense, and I'm breezing right through them.

Once I attended a party given by the Senior Day Care, where I work. It was given by the higher-ups to show appreciation for all the fine work we did with the patrons. I thought it was rather nice. I find appreciation for what I do within. However, I thought it was rather nice to be thanked.

It's a very good organization that I work for. The services we provide are a big help to the community and, likewise, for our growing Senior populace. At a lot of other work sites, little recognition is given to the persons who have to do the menial labor. However, when the board members come and rub elbows with the common folk, that displays true commitment.

It seems as if everything at work goes a bit better because of the good relations between all the staff and the board members. At this work site, there's no hidden animosity toward the big boss. It seems as if all there are working for more than a paycheck. For me, however, quite subconsciously, there's a good feeling. This is a good feeling that I'm sure wouldn't come if I were a bricklayer.

I believe essentially in other people. I would never have come as far as I have without others. However, the credit I can take is the ability I have found in just how I can use everyone. You must realize that we all use each other. Essentially, I don't believe in myself. After all, who the hell am I? However, I feel I can use other people and things effectively for my own benefit.

Without the things I have derived from others, I would be nothing. However, it's not a one-way street, so I don't lose any sleep. I believe in the positive things that could happen if I travel in a certain direction. I'm the same old insecure guy that I was before my accident. However, at this point, I have a wide array of old tools I can use for my own benefit. I'm able, with a clear conscience, to use people for our own good. You must realize, the more I rehabilitate, the better it is for everyone in this country.

It's a continuum. Everything works for the best as long as I'm on this road. My physical as well as mental abilities continue to improve as I push myself forward. It's relatively easy for me to maintain a proper weight. What I'm doing at this moment, writing, is good exercise also. Keeping active and even writing this book have kept me in top shape.

It's extremely easy to stay in shape. I hadn't weighed myself in a couple of years. When I did, I tipped the scales at 165 pounds. Knowing this was ten pounds heavier than when I was routinely working out with weights, I started calisthenics and limited junk food, and in less than a week, I took off five pounds. For my height and medium frame, I can handle that. Work and the way I function while engaged in it have kept my weight right where I want it.

I have no reservations. I'm proud of how I've come back. In fact, I'm kind of proud of my condition. It would be different if I had been born with a disability. For some reason, I never would have strove as diligently as I have. As long as I continue my upward movement, it's a win–win situation.

I'm open to people around me at work considering my shortcomings. Of course, I always try my best; people around me notice this, and in most cases, they will bend over backward to accommodate me. It's no big deal. If others at work are going to do this or that for me so they can feel good about themselves, more power to them. It's much easier this way. People, on the whole, will bend over backwards for me.

My disability doesn't hamper my affiliation with others. I work around it and use it. I feel that I'm very proficient. I feel in no way does this disability hamper my relations with others. In some respects, it enhances them. Getting along with others is much easier now with this head injury than it ever was before I had it. I don't have to play games. That game-playing nonsense wastes a lot of time.

It's quite similar to the way I was before my accident. However, at this point, it's a lot easier, and I'm second guessing myself a lot less than I ever did. To me, getting along with others is only moderately difficult. At this point, I can sense who I can eventually derive help from, and I do my best to get on their good sides.

It seems as if, because of my disability, I would fall short amongst my fellow employees. However, in my particular field, my disability enhances my work performance. At present, I'm no longer mentally consumed by my performance. I'm able to do just about what any fellow employee can do. I have a multitude of true life experiences that I can draw upon.

I use my physical as well as mental abilities to add spice to my work performance. In my field, gerontology, my disability provides an understanding that none of my nondisabled co-workers possess. I have to qualify this statement. I can do most anything my fellow worker can do. However, everything is done at my own pace. My fellow workers seemingly understand this, because nothing in regards to my performance has been said to me. In fact, I've been told by a few of my fellow workers over the years, "I wish I could get on the same level with Seniors as you do."

I remember seeing a poster a number of years back that read something like this, "When the world gives you nothin' but lemons, open a lemonade stand." I have done just that. Even more than that, I've created a dairy. Yes, I'm also milking this disability for all it's worth. You are presently drinking some of its fruits. My ability to work with the Seniors, like very few of my compatriots, has definitely been assisted through the use of this head injury.

Also, I don't have any extraneous things in my life that could hamper my upward movement. I don't drink, smoke, chase women, overeat, neglect my health, and so forth, because all of these things are vices in and of themselves. All these idiosyncrasies would have certainly tainted my progression. I was fortunate. I didn't have to deal with a lot of the stuff that others in the work environment have had to. These skills I've developed over the years, to deal with the incongruities of my head injury, have certainly helped me in the workplace.

Getting along with others, which is a priority in my profession, is a piece of cake. These jobs fell out of the sky. Perhaps, it's only my perception and my ability to make things work my way, but I feel as though this whole disability has been a piece of cake—that is, now that I am where I am.

In a way, work is a grand accomplishment for me. There is more effort given to not working and then having to justify my existence to myself. There's just no time to waste time.

As I have previously stated, a few months ago, the activity director at my night job, where I work three nights a week for a total of twelve hours, took a vacation. My hours were increased to twenty-two. I was already working thirty-six hours a week at my day job, but, for a two-week period, I did this. It didn't even tire me. Of course, I had to refrain from taking notes for this book as I had been for a while.

I'm conditioned. All those years I put into school paid off. In fact, it was much harder work being in school and not being paid. Work is a breeze for me. For the last week or so, as I've stated before, I've been working fifty plus hours a week, but it's considerably easier than when I was attending school.

School was considerably more difficult for me. I believe it was because I felt more at a loss because of my condition. However, now I feel as though I'm one up on my cohorts working in the same field. At school, there was always this thing awaiting. It was always deep in the recesses of my mind. I was fearful I would fail. By not making any close friends with anyone aside from teachers, counselors and so forth, I cut right through the crap that can result from close connections at the work site.

I let my current employer read my first book. Amazingly, to me, upon returning it, she requested I go to the police station to get fingerprinted. It makes no difference if I'm a well-mannered, courteous, and intelligent person. After she read my first book, she had me go to the police department and get fingerprinted like a common criminal. I'm presently allowing another of my superiors, in the same workplace, to also read the first book I produced. I'm going to have to tell her to check the records, because the woman who held the position before her placed my police printout in a file, and incidentally, I'm clean as a whistle.

It's a good thing that police records are destroyed for crimes committed when you were a juvenile. The last time I got busted, it was only a few weeks away from my eighteenth birthday. So, technically, I'm as clean as the Pope.

It's hard to imagine what kind of meager person I'd be if not for the traumatic blow I suffered to my head. The jobs I have at present fit me to a T. As I was attending school all those years, nine in total, in the back of my mind, this is what I visualized as the perfect work scenario. Once I shared some of my glee with one of the young Latin gentlemen who works in the kitchen, I simply told him, "Yo puedo hacer este trabajo dormido." In translation, "I could do this job in a coma." He replied with a grimace.

Having the ability to write about my circumstance is just one more plus. This adds frosting to the cake. If I were only able to rehabilitate, then this wouldn't give me the good feeling I possess at this moment. It's not that I'm lacking at any part of this job; it's only that I feel it fits me like a glove. I could perform it blindfolded. I would have to assume still that it has a lot to do with the point in time of my rehabilitation.

At work, I'm friends with everyone, though some more than others. I don't dislike anyone. Having animosity toward anyone only rebounds back to you. This is such an easy and, most of all, productive way to do things. I realize now that I was crippled before the accident.

It's easy to be friendly with most everyone. You don't have to remember if you should be friendly to this person or that person. Everyone is your friend. One of the benefits is you don't have different people out to get you.

Conflicts with others are produced, on the most part, by my own. I never made deep friendships with anyone, and at the same time, I don't have any deep conflicts. The fact that I'm disabled helped considerably. I only found a few people, less than the number of fingers on my hand, who would not bend over backwards to help me. I don't ask if I don't feel the inclination on their part to render assistance.

I try to have a good relationship with everyone because I realize that bad feelings toward others will only rebound back to myself. Ever since I could remember, I've gone out of my way not to ruffle anyone's feathers. In my preinjury years, it always made me feel like such a wimp. However, with this injury, being nonconfrontational has bestowed upon me quite a number of benefits.

I feel that I am liked rather than pitied. I realize this can be a fine line. Perhaps, I am pitied. However, I don't think that way. If I would ever have thought that way, however true it might have been, then I would never have come this far.

Co-workers and bosses alike are treated with good humor. I'm on good terms with all of my co-workers. This is especially important for those who might feel less intelligent than a person who has been through school or, should I say, less educated. In fact, the less educated, the better. I can joke around on that level like a champ.

It helps that I come from where I come from. I can relate with various types of people. I don't have to put forth such a pretense. If you were trying to get down to such a level with common folk, I'm as common as they get, yet I can still hold court with higher-ups.

I have a good time with the majority of working folks who don't have degrees in this or that. I am there at present. It's good to be where I am, on both sides of the fence at the same time. I'm glad to have had the experience on both levels, so as to have this well-versed sense.

It's a tremendous relief of tensions. I can do the job I'm appointed to do on a most professional level and still be able to clown around with the worker bees. I make it a fun place for me to be. Having the combination of work and playfulness makes it very tolerable.

Here's an example. One evening, I heard a Mexican comedian on television use the term whey, pronounced "way" in English. I did not know what this term meant. However, on the show, it was taken as an insult/comic term.

At work, one of my fellow employees was kind enough to set me straight. After a bit of stalling and acting as if it were a compliment to be referred to as whey, a term I had heard from another source, he laughingly let me in on the connotation. At first, while grinning underneath his explanation, he implied it was an honor to be labeled as a whey. However, I detected the howling laugh beneath the stern look he displayed.

Whey, pronounced "way," is a bull. However, it's a bull that just stands by and watches all the other bulls in the field screw his cow. One of my other Latin co-workers explained this to me. Not being of the Mexican persuasion, I wasn't in on the connotation. If you are a man with any self-respect, then this is one of the lowest blows you can sustain. I have a good relationship with the majority, if not all, of my co-workers.

Here's an example of what I mean, which might clear it up a bit. Yesterday, I went to a mandatory seminar given by my place of employment. In the class of about thirty students, we were given instructions on how to best care for the Alzheimer's patient. The majority of the students in class were nurse's aides. They are the people with the bulk of the contact with patients. It was like I was in high school again.—lots of laughter, the instructor having to clown around to keep the attention of the students, and so forth.

I'm very glad to have all the education and practical experience that I have at this point. Even though this class was given as if it were less meaningful than it was, I knew the opposite was true. Being in such a relaxed atmosphere did nothing to change the way I did things. It was as if I were back in grade school again.

One day I along with the other activity director were out on the grounds of the facility taking about ten Seniors for a walk. Jim, the former pro boxer, and I were in the back of the pack bullshitting. Jim would find joy when we talked about the old days. Then, jokingly, I challenged him. Taking it in stride, grinning from ear to ear, Jim put up his fists and feigned a right cross to my jaw. It was like we were in slow motion. I moved out of the way of his half-opened fist. By this time, we were both laughing quite heartily. Because of his condition, however, Jim lost his balance. I quickly noticed this and reached over to him. I grabbed both of his arms and tried to keep him erect. Jim, about five feet seven inches and about 160 pounds, was more than I could handle. I also felt stupid by fooling around like this because he could have easily gotten hurt.

I probably could have held him up if we were face to face, but he was approaching me from the side. As Jim was reaching for me, he was falling to the ground quite swiftly. I was a bit off to his side, and I grabbed his arms tightly. I thought I could easily hold him up, but, because of the angle he was in and my poor balance, we slowly headed for the grass. Even though I was out of control, I was able to slow Wink's fall a bit. We both went down for the count. I helped him up, we dusted ourselves off, and we were no worse for the wear.

Among the primary reasons why things have gone so good for me has got to be my good health. I'm very happy I got on the road to good health at the outset of my road to rehabilitation. Good health was and is the force that allows me the power to fight this large beast that is a head injury.

My eating habits haven't changed significantly. I still eat a good portion of fruits and vegetables, rarely any meat. I chew my food very well, and I still drink a good supply of water. With the several practices I adopted over the years, if I let one go by the wayside for a period of time, then I can quickly amend this. One hundred and sixty pounds is very comfortable weight. I have a medium frame, and I hold it very well. Even though I must have stated this at least once, or twice, I owe a great deal to my good health. Hopefully, one of the reasons you are reading this book is to some way be able to help a brain-injured person.

To marvel at my accomplishments would be a waste of time. It would be the same as wasting time grieving about my losses. Both actions would be fruitless. I have noticed in the past, when I stop to catch my breath, I merely slide backward. At this point, I don't marvel at my accomplishments. There's always something to do. As far as work goes, I feel comfortable.

Work, at this point, seems as if I'm coasting. Nothing that comes up is too grandiose that I can't handle it. There's an endless litany of things I've yet to accomplish. I'm afraid I will merely become complacent with what I have, and this might incline me to end my push. I never applaud myself, no matter what I've accomplished in the past, because others do that for me. If I were the one to do all the clapping, then that would just tire me.

Work isn't the same for me as it might be for another. Work isn't work. It's an accomplishment. It's just one more feather in my cap. The years that I spent in school have merely been something I've experienced. Even though it was probably the most difficult period of my rehabilitation, I liked the structure of it. Work provides similar structure.

In fact, I feel it's a bit easier because I know I'm in the big leagues now, and I'm getting paid for it. I have an incentive to work. It's not only the money it provides, but I get a good feeling just knowing how much I've been through and have the ability to come back, in many ways, better than I was when I went in.

People are the same, whether you're getting paid for what you do or not. The only difference is in the people who are paying you. However, I did and still do my best in both situations. I'm very grateful for having the opportunity to have given those hundreds of hours of volunteer work that I did.

It's as if I'm still in the volunteer mode, and I'm getting paid for it. Paid employment, to me, is no different than all the volunteer positions I held while I was attending school, as well as after I graduated. Even how I spend my money hasn't changed. I'm still very frugal, not tight, in regards to how I spend my money.

To me, in the depth of my heart, I realize there's very little produced, tangibly speaking, in a profession such as this. It's a continual cycle, and some leaves have to fall off the trees in order to make room for new life. I feel my off-the-cuff attitude around Seniors might tend to make their passage a bit easier.

To me, it's very simple. You merely play around until the grim reaper pays a visit. However, it seems as though, through the advancement of medical science, we are simply disabling the grim reaper. More and more, he is simply dragging his feet.

I'm not a production kind of person. Gerontology doesn't qualify the final product. After all, the final product is death. In this profession, there's not going to be anyone to complain. I don't have to worry if there's a problem with the steering or the brakes, because there's not going to be a recall. In fact, I feel that this is the perfect scenario. I work in an unproductive field, and yet I feel I have the ability to write and give hope to millions.

Before entering the workforce, I always had a fear that it would be too much for me. However, work is much easier than it was attending school for all those years. In fact, while at work, I'd catch myself saying, "This is a breeze," or something to that effect.

In fact, I felt school was supposedly the easy part, and I would crumble when I entered the real world. I felt this way even before my head injury. I remember, while in high school, realizing even that was a load to carry. I didn't feel I could ever work day in and day out.

Even while attending the universities, I didn't gain the confidence that told me I could go out and work for a living.

I don't make anything tangible, like say, a person in the auto industry bolting fenders to a car. I can't say, "I did that," as the car comes off the line. However, I can breathe easier because of my rehabilitation, and that's more tangible in my eyes. Once you learn the easy dance steps, it's a breeze. It's unlike school where you always had the dance instructor breathing down your neck.

At this point in my short work history, I'm comfortable. I no longer try to be super handicapped. The areas I fall short in at the job site, I make up for by creatively displaying the good feeling I have toward my disability. I stayed on my toes while enduring all those years of school. It has engendered a level of enjoyment, as well as relaxation, while in the work environment at present. However, the first job I had, back in 1983, after graduating from the first university, I tried to assume the same posture as I did while in school, and I fell flat on my face.

In my field, gerontology, there isn't much I can't do when it comes to placating the crowd as they await the final bus out of the station. Everyone at both jobs I presently hold is aware of the magnitude of my disability and tries to treat me as normal, but I realize I'm being treated with a pair of kid gloves. That's all right. I can live with it. I enjoy myself at work. It's less difficult than rehabilitation.

Work is a goal as well as an obstacle that I'm hurdling over every day. This adds fuel to the fire each and every day. No matter how things turn out, I'm a winner simply by remaining in the fight. At present, I don't involve myself in any recreation, per se. I enjoy my work, and I don't feel as if I'm shortchanging myself. I could classify my work as my recreation.

I enjoy what I'm doing. I'm not sure if it's that I enjoy what I'm doing, or if it's just that I can do something. I get along with everyone. I make no enemies. Recreation for me, for the sake of using my empty time, is taken up by pushing this pen against the paper. Being able to function at this level provides as much entertainment as I need. As compared with the negative way I approached things before my head injury, beating this disability is an enjoyable diversion.

I can work! I have found that I can do something that is worthwhile to someone else, and they will pay me for it. There was a time when I thought I would always be on the receiving end. I get along with people, and they get along with me. I don't feel my disability hampers my relationship with anyone. In fact, I feel my disability enhances my relationship with my co-workers as well as with those that I work for.

It feels good to work. I have gone full circle. Maybe I'm jumping the gun a bit. I guess I will have gone full circle when the mortician pounds the final nail in my coffin. However, that's not how I wish to go. I prefer to be cremated. I'll go off in a puff of smoke. Besides, I want to get used to the heat.

The frosting on this rehabilitation cake is that there's now someone who is willing to pay me for the task I can perform. While I was growing, I never pictured myself in a work environment. I was continually in that blah existence. I never looked further than the end of my nose.

The work at rehabilitating, traditional work, and enjoying myself have become intertwined. In a sense, the ability to work is a recreational venue. I don't much find the need for recreation. This struggle I've been engaged in over the years has been entertaining enough.

I have enjoyed this voyage I've been on since emerging from the coma back in 1971. I enjoy it to a much greater extent than I did the time before my head injury. Having the ability to work gives me more satisfaction than if I had never suffered this injury. It's like a badge I wear. With this disability, I find a whole array of different things entertaining. I couldn't pay for a better diversion. Everything I do, or attempt to do, results in a positive outcome. Everything about this disability has been a challenge. However, the challenges were nothing that I could not surmount.

I'm very comfortable with my disability. I've been this way since the outset of my rehabilitation. Having the ability to work and getting paid for it are giant pats on the back. Disability agrees with me. Living a clean lifestyle for a number of years has certainly rendered a large amount of dividends.

Working is merely a different part of my rehabilitation. I look at it as an accomplishment. Thus, working and rehabilitation complement each other. However, this is only because I view it in this fashion. The work I do isn't physically tiring. The mental part of the job is even less exhausting. I do very little paperwork at both jobs, which I feel is important.

At present, due to the illness of my supervisor, I'm working many more hours than I would normally. However, this is not difficult. If I were not able to work at all because of my disability, then that would have been hard. I can remember studying for exams, attending classes each day, maintaining a high level of health, and remaining aloof toward any kind of relationship. That was work.

Working at a job is much easier for me than it was attending school. I seemed to fit in better at each job I had. I adjust to the routine a lot quicker at each job. I don't step on anyone's toes. Likewise, no one at work wants to scuff my shoes. I'm disabled and giving an honest effort.

With my disability, people aren't going to expect me to mesh in at a rapid pace. So, I step back and look over the surroundings before I make a move. For the most part, I can dance to their tune. I'm not rigid. I can stand back, view the landscape, and judge how I will have to perform to get the most from my condition. However, I will always do my best.

I retain my inert qualities. However, I hone them to each situation. Before my injury, I never considered myself a people person. However, at this point, relations with others are a breeze.

It's wondrous how perceptions change when you're wearing a different pair of shoes. Before I had this brush with death and subsequent rehabilitation, just looking at the disabled would tend to turn my stomach. Before my accident, I used to be put off by the disabled. Now, I consider myself fortunate to be disabled and to have used my disability constructively.

It's similar to the way boys view girls as creepy, but, down the road, a young man's mind turns to other things. That's the way I had to look at it. I accept my disability. I worked with it to get the most

I could from it. I didn't do this consciously, but subconsciously I was reveling in the fact that I was disabled.

Because of my disability, I'm distinct. However, because of the way I've used it, I'm different in a good way. It's been and continues to be my ace in the hole.

20

Without their love, tolerance and a vast quantity of other things, I surely wouldn't have rehabilitated as well as I have without my parents. Yes, I give a great deal of credit to my folks for my recovery. It has nothing to do with any didactic plan they employed. It was simply them being there that helped me.

I could feel the gratitude for my survival in their hearts, and it was almost as if I didn't want to let them down. I pushed for their sake. I inertly realized what I had to put them through, and I needed to rehabilitate for their sake as well as my own. My mother once told me that my accident brought her and my father closer together. It was that family unit that my rehabilitation fed off of.

I feel it was very important that I never laughed at myself. It would've taken the wind out of my sails. I needed all the momentum I could muster. Yes, I can't say I ever actually laughed at myself. However, I did see the humor in things concerning my disability. I never felt good about laughing at myself. It would seem as if what I was doing was a joke. This would take the seriousness from the whole venture. I laughed at things around me and some things concerning my disability, but never, or hardly ever, at myself.

I found what worked best was the positive attitude I maintained throughout the whole rehabilitation process and likewise the push that I enlisted. My counselors guided me along and provided many other essentials. Counselors are like the fuel. The disabled person is the engine.

I worked well with my counselors, whether rehabilitation, academic, or whatever. Of course, over the long stretch that I've been rehabilitating, I've had a few, very few, lemons. The majority of my counselors have been good, but, just like the manual lawn mower, it will do very little unless you push it.

Yes, I don't believe anything would've happened without that initial push. I had to have some kind of drive or nothing would've happened. Anyone who has lived through an incident such as the one I did has that innate drive. However, with medical science reaching new heights every day, less and less of that drive are required. I would assume that more of an outside push needs to be given. Yes, I had to draw that inner strength that I believe everyone must have in order to bring me this far. However, with all the new procedures, medicine, and other stuff, less and less inner drive was needed.

My sense of self and self-confidence have increased to a level that could have never been expected. Before the accident, I was such a flake. This accident, head trauma, and subsequent disability gave me a foundation I could build upon. This disability provided me with the building blocks I needed.

I needed the ladder this disability provided. There was a lot of climbing to do, but there were always people around me to help me along. With others around me, ironically, I had a greater sense of self.

I'd be nothing without this disability. I owe a great deal to the vision I was awarded through this disability. My self-confidence began to grow as I surmounted obstacle after obstacle. I learned how to sidestep other road blocks. After a while, I began to use these obstacles for my own benefit.

I think we should believe, primarily, in ourselves. Then, we should look to the larger picture, humanity itself, then the environment, and down the line. If looked at rationally, we don't seem to have our priorities in the correct order. We have our priorities mixed up. We must think rationally. This isn't so hard to do if you throw emotions out the window.

As human beings, we all want and need the same things. If we all worked together and stopped arbitrarily putting obstacles in our way, then we could all survive a little better on this earth. For some reason, we have allowed our emotions to control the course of our ship will take instead of sound reasoning.

There were several different ways I could've looked at my disability. I could've felt sorry for myself. I could've used it as a reason to simply give up. I could have tried to make others feel responsible for my plight. The list of unproductive things I could've done is endless. However, it was remarkably easy, in fact easier, to go down the other road.

I worked to the best of my ability the counselors, teachers, and others who I knew could be of use. So much help was thrown in my direction. I merely had to distinguish which I could use effectively. Remarkably, over the years, there have only been a few, I can count them on one hand, people throughout this disability that I could not use for my own good. Amazingly, even those who were of no service to me gave me great confidence. This was simply because I could distinguish one from another. This was a great confidence builder.

My disability is something that is and always will be there. My poor memory, even though it is loads better than in the past, will surface from time to time. This will happen when I unintentionally forget to make a note of something. I have done numerous things over the years to compensate for my poor memory. These methods are numerous. They are so numerous, in fact, that I forget what they are.

However, I know when I forget something, that it's only that I didn't try hard enough to remember it. I've conditioned myself over the years to be a bit wary. I've always been very fortunate. Still, my ever-present disability will manage to show its face. If I don't remain on my toes, something I've had to do all throughout my rehabilitation, then I would've fallen into a pit of disability, and it would have used me instead of vice versa.

I currently have a female doctor because my former doctor no longer accepts the medical coverage I now use. My new doctor is a very pleasant woman. The only thing that is wrong with me is that I carry the Hepatitis C virus in my blood.

My new doctor couldn't be much older than me, if that. I now have only one concern. That is getting rid of this virus I have. I only have one more shot to go. I don't realize what these shots are for, but apparently they aren't for this Hepatitis C virus. I still have to have my blood checked every several months in order for the doctor to determine whether it's strong enough for the medication.

I realize, I must have stated this at least once before, but it bears repeating. So much time, money, and emotions are given to the belief in a god. I'm sorry if my repetitious nature puts you to sleep; however, this is so important to me. In fact, I feel my nonbelief deserves the majority of the credit for my recovery. I currently believe in nothing else but myself. I never used to be this way. I always felt that I should be like other religious people who surrounded me. In my opinion, evangelists are merely suckering other followers. If one belief is right, does that make the other belief wrong? It would make religion seem trivial if one would begin bad mouthing the other.

I wonder what ratio of time is devoted to preaching the gospel and doing good deeds as opposed to the time exhausted in raising capital. This is such an easy way to make money. The perpetrator fails to see that if they are right, then that makes all the other beliefs wrong. I am only a single voice in this vast array of opinions in this world, but, hopefully, I can be heard. Once again, I realize I must have said this in one form, or another, but it must be said.

This book is now about to end. I frankly don't know how to do this. I will always be rehabilitating. It's a very fulfilling journey. About six years ago, I finished another book that detailed my life, in which I left few stones unturned. It was all encompassing. It took me close to five years of daily work to complete my books. It was originally one book, but because of its length (2,100 plus pages), I broke it into four palatable size books. I, hopefully, can get those books published after this one.

In those other books, I detail succinctly what makes me tick. I don't hold back a thing in those books. I talk and write as if I were a young man from the neighborhood. I don't cater to anyone's objections. I feel my clarity throughout those four books allows the reader to jump into my shoes.

I wrote to over one hundred different publishers and agents. I had no luck in either case. Believing this was due to the strong approach I had taken toward my situation, I decided to show you the softer side of myself with this book. Both sides tell an accurate side of my disability. However, I take off the gloves in those first four books. This book was written to show the reader, and myself, that I don't have to resort to dipping in the gutter to get my message across.

Now that this book has reached its conclusion, I will reiterate some of the points I have found to be very relevant to my recovery. Forgive me if I bore you, but these things were, as I look back on them, some of the most relevant positions I took during my rehabilitation. To reach the point that I have at this juncture in my life, I had to gradually eliminate God. It was this Almighty God that most everyone was attributing my rehabilitation to. I suppose it was easy for others to assume that it was God who did this. There was also a time when human beings worshipped the stars, sun, and moon. I searched for more tangible things.

I will now repeat several things I found very important for me, while writing this book. It will seem repetitious to most—but it was these things that meant the most to me while I was rehabilitating.

Yes, there was a time when the majority of people believed the world was flat. When man begins to see that all can be done by the elimination of an innate need for a father figure, I believe we will see a more sane society. When man can objectively view the negatives versus the positives without letting emotions get in the way, people will begin to see the senseless futility of belief.

The belief in a god is amazingly similar to carrying around a rabbit's foot, although I don't believe wars were ever waged because of rabbit's feet. Just think of all the expenditures that would be saved. It wouldn't only mean the direct cost of religion, but all the extraneous costs as well. If the belief in God was at all productive, let's say more productive than divisive, then I could then see the validity of such a thing.

Religion, like any other business, needs cash to stay afloat. Let's take our heads out of the clouds. If religion continues to persist, then tax it and ministers like a business. God doesn't rain down money for churches from the sky. The money collected should be taxed. While we're on the subject, prostitution should be legalized and taxed. Both things will go on, so why not let the government prosper a bit?

It makes money from people who prosper solely because they live and work here in the United States. Why not tax them? Have these churches opened their books? What do they have to hide? Why are churches so shy about opening their books? They, of all institutions, should be on the up-and-up. What have they got to hide? These are supposedly the most honest people in the world. They should set the standard.

Let's kill the virus that's slowly killing us. The more benefits you give, the longer people are going to live. The more money and benefits you throw at Seniors, the less there will be for the up-and-coming generations. What kind of legacy will today's Seniors leave?

If Seniors want to live longer and longer, then that's something they should've thought of when they were younger. They shouldn't think that now they've reached a certain age, taxpayers should foot the bill for every sniffle or cough they present to their doctor. The more we pay this age group to survive, the more they will simply accommodate us.

I realize this sounds quaint, but I believe we should celebrate our differences. As much as this might be dismissed by believers, religion simply divides us. We are people first and different people second. This disability has rounded me out. I can now appreciate different points of view. Everyone has a valid reason, in their own mind, for anything they might do.

Variety is the spice of life; you can quote me. If we're all the same, then this would be a boring place. However, we must find constructive ways to celebrate our differences. I'm sure that my beliefs don't coincide exactly with anyone else's on this planet. However, we don't need to kill each other because of that.

It's good to have everyone's perspectives a tad different from the next guy's. Some people are as different from one another as night is to day. However, this is good also. If we all end up somewhere in the middle, then all will be fine.

Individuality is nonsense. Anyone who tried to live on this planet without any help of some kind or another wouldn't make it very long. We all need each other. I needed much assistance to get where I am today. I would've never made it this far without the help of others. Likewise, I've washed someone's back also in this process.

We must end the thinking that says, "I'm better off than the next guy." No one is better off unless we are all better off. Individuality is senseless. We're all aboard a large sea vessel. If that boat sinks, then we all drown.

The Marlboro man is now probably living in a hospital hooked up to a respirator with the doctors and nurses and a host of others keeping him alive. What happened to that rugged individual? Imagine all the good that could be done if we worked together. I realize I sound like an idealist; however, I think I'm much more of a pragmatist. Good won't happen until we come down to earth.

We should improve things for the family. I believe if the family crumbles, so goes the country. We should stop throwing money, services, and so forth down the drain. If this country would devote more time, money and resources to the family, imagine the improvements that would come about.

The two-parent family could once again be the norm. This country should provide incentives to keep the family alive. The country should devote more time, money, and services to the up-and-coming generations. I implore the government to put youth and the family first. The Seniors should be allotted no extra funds to keep them going. It's a bottomless pit.

Did justice get a fair shake with the O. J. Simpson trial? In my opinion, the public got screwed twice. They were screwed once by letting a person with that much evidence against him "walk" and then a second time with the cost of the trial to us taxpayers. With all the money we spend on the legal system, do we have anything to show for it? People in the legal profession make a living, but law and order don't prosper.

The media should have to foot some of the bill. They certainly made some loose change by telecasting it. This is taking justice to extremes. If some of the money wasted on these high-profile cases was spent on eliminating some of the causes of these crimes in the first place, then crime might be reduced. Who exactly is better off for the length and expenditures of these high-profile cases? We spend too much time with trials. Do all the money, coverage, debates, and so forth lead to greater justice?

The media makes tons of money reporting crime; tax them as this rate rises. With the inordinate amount of money they're making off crime, why would newscasters want crime to stop? They are sleeping in the same bed as the law enforcement officials we employ to curtail crime.

It's not working the way things stand at this point. It's time we curtail the reporting of all senseless crimes. These persons who commit these crimes just appear to need a stage. I think we should try anything we can. These people in the news media continually go to bed with blood on their hands. It's time we change their bed sheets. I realize I must have said this before—but if it wasn't important, I wouldn't have said it to begin with.

I realize we have freedom of the press in this country, and it would be unheard of to restrict the press, but we also have freedom of speech in this country. Yet, isn't it illegal for a person to yell "FIRE!" in a crowded theatre? An old analogy comes to mind, "What if the man on the moon laid a fart and there was no one around to hear it? Would it make a sound?"

This country should legalize prostitution. We should control the spread of disease and other crimes connected to prostitution, but "moral" people don't want this. God wants us all to continue the way it has been for years. Cigarette smoking does more harm. Why doesn't the church question the morality of tobacco growers?

Think of all the tax revenues that could be collected if we made the employees of the oldest profession in the world fill out a W-2 form. I get my hair cut every so often, and I do this because it's a bodily need. Prostitutes and barbers fill a need in this society. Let's throw all those immoral barbers in jail also. Then, you'd need a pimp to get your hair styled. Hopefully, all or most of these archaic fears will dwindle in time, and we can concentrate on the here and now, not the hereafter.

This country is throwing money down a bottomless pit. There will be very little return on investments made on Seniors. I realize

I'm biting the hand that feeds me (I presently hold two separate jobs caring for the elderly). However, if we would just invest more in productive ventures, then we would see the fruits of our labor. There has been a public service message being aired on TV that states that we should put children first. I'm in total agreement. However, this means we're going to have to nudge these old people off the pedestal they're now seated on. I realize I have said this before, and that I'm also taking on a very powerful group, but if I don't do it, who will?

We are spending enormous amounts of money to repair ripped upholstery, retread worn tires, have new paint jobs, fix engines, and repair exhaust systems, and for what? At the same time, we're neglecting to invest in the production of new innovative vehicles. It doesn't make sense. I'm not talking about throwing money into the wind. We certainly can scrutinize very judiciously how to allocate the money in the proper direction. We simply have to put more money into children. It doesn't make sense to keep throwing money at Seniors and shortchanging our youth. If you want to know why kids are going down the drain at this point, as opposed to my generation, contrast the number of old people you see on the street today with the number you might have seen forty or fifty years ago.

Another way we can better this country is by eliminating guns. It would have a snowball effect. This country, by no means, is any safer, more prosperous, or more judicious simply because guns are legal. Would this country be any less safe if only police and other law enforcement officers were the only ones to possessed firearms? I think not.

This is a wakeup call for all people with a head on their shoulders. When was the last time freedom of gun ownership helped you? We are being railroaded by a group (the NRA) that needs to hang onto their security blanket. Imagine all the money saved. Of course, the police force says nothing about gun control. They need to keep the public in fear to keep their salaries soaring through the roof. Who do you think pays their salaries?

We should cut police salaries. The more money they make, the more they are going to want crime to flourish. One of the big problems in this society is that we fail to see the nose in front of our face. The more the crime rate escalates, the higher the salaries are for those we employ to curtail it. A while back, American cars were seen as superior to Japanese, but then this country began to see the value and economy of the Japanese car. For a decade or so, imports flooded the markets. American car manufacturers realized what had to be done; they had to start making better cars. Do you think the American auto industry would've changed if not given a wakeup call from our friends overseas?

Let's be realistic; do you think police want to see an end to crime? It would be like prostitutes wishing men to have no sex drive. Don't get me wrong. The police are doing a job, and they are getting paid a very good salary for doing it. It would be hard, even for the police officers who know what they are doing, to say a thing. It would be like the tobacco farmer, years ago before all the health dangers were discovered, refusing to go out and farm the tobacco field, believing it was morally wrong.

With priorities given to the family unit, this will build stronger family bonds. The reason the family isn't a unit as it was in the past has a lot to do with both parents having to go out and work.

Consumption of tobacco products and alcohol would soon find its place among the dinosaurs. The benefits that would be supplied by the elimination of just these two things would be enormous. Then, one by one, other needless things in this society could be toppled. However, this will require a new train of thought.

With the many millions of dollars saved by eliminating guns, religions and other unproductive vices from our midst, can you imagine the wealth of more productive things that could be born to this country? Let's get the country's priorities straight. At the top of the list, good health must stand much before anything else. Without good health, you can produce only things of less value.

Can you imagine the things this country could produce if everyone was in tip-top shape? Of course, there'd still be sickness and disease but at a diminishing scale.

I am much more than I ever thought I was. I had to make my own scenes and write my own script as I went along. I tried my best to conform to the situation handed to me and thus be able to extract what I needed from others I was trying my best to conform to.

For me, there was a large safety net on this island. It was hard to fail as long as I gave it a forthright attempt. I tried my best to conform to the situation handed to me and, thus, be able to extract what I needed from the others I was trying my best to conform to. Just as the professor's creations seldom failed, I too found success as long as I was putting forth a genuine effort. Failing was the hard part.

I've tended to manipulate this disability. In fact, it's been an enjoyable experience. I've had to give up a lot throughout this rehabilitation process, but, if I had to, I sense I'd be able to give up more. I found the trick to this was to sense what was expendable. I feel, at this point, better than I ever have, and this includes every minute prior to the head injury. Disability is neither an end in itself nor is rehabilitation; they are both a process.

I had to grin and bear all the stupid things in my makeup, just as the Skipper had to overlook the majority of incongruities that resulted from Gilligan's behavior. I had to silently cheer for myself. I fortunately didn't allow my disabilities to devour me. It was essential for me to constructively utilize the situation placed before me. Oddly enough, this disability gave me more than it has taken away. I found everything I needed to rehabilitate with this head injury (the use of the word disability would be a misuse of the term), just as the shipwrecked crew found everything they needed to coexist successfully on that island.

If I would have ever sat down and scrutinized the severity of my condition instead of viewing it like slap-stick comedy, then I would have digressed even further. Just as Mr. Howell, the wealthy entrepreneur, talked through his hat the majority of the time, so were a minority of the persons who were assigned to help me. I waded through all that refuge. Some amenities that were doled out through this rehabilitation process were delivered by people who essentially did not know what they were doing. I dubbed them the Mrs. Howell's of my rehabilitation. However, there is use in virtually everyone.

If you know someone with a severe head injury, give them a silent cheer. They have displayed a portion of themselves, proving they have the power to survive. However, that was the easy part. They must now realize how to direct that power to guide them through rehabilitation; it is a different path for everyone. I found everything I needed with this head injury. I used the majority of facilities rendered me just as the shipwrecked crew did on that island. This was very important to understand when "the weather started getting rough."

Postscript

Today is sometime in May of 2004. I was watching a TV program. I believe it was *Headliners and Legends* on cable MSNBC. I was astounded when they revealed that George Bush Jr., current president of the United States, had once been arrested for drunk driving. He could have easily killed or maimed someone accidentally. I only wonder if in his drinking days, Bush Jr., ever morally sunk so low and relieved himself outdoors—maybe behind an oil rig.

As of this point, spring of 2004, I have yet to see justice levied on me for my indiscretion behind that bus stop bench. It's been about six months since my immoral behavior. Whoever coined the phrase, "The wheels of justice turn slowly," was right on the mark. I'll explain just what happened in one of the forthcoming books. That would be the appropriate place for it because in those books, I use an abundance of "thous" to drive my point across.

Yes, after about four or five visits, I made to court for my immoral behavior, my public defender urged me to plea to a lesser charge. He told me he had a discussion with the judge and showed him my resume and letters of recommendation from my past work as well as volunteer assignments, and even though I was given a different public defender at each appearance, the same judge must have realized that I couldn't be all that bad. So, I eventually pled guilty to a lesser charge and was sentenced to do eighty hours of community service at the place of my choosing.

After my eighty hours were complete, I continued volunteering at this same place for a year and a half for five days a week, six and a half hours a day. It was during this volunteer work that I felt I should go out and find a "real" job and not waste all the education I have accumulated over the years. So, I contacted a rehabilitation counselor, and she connected me with an agency that works with head-injured people. I attended this agency for a few months and made a good impression, but I decided to go back to my volunteer position. I did this because my volunteer position was working with Senior citizens in an athletic gym, and it was within walking distance from my apartment. After a few months, the agency that gives services for brain-injured people called me up and told me they had a position they felt I could fill. I have held that position for the last couple years and currently. At the start of my next book, I will let the reader know how well this job fits me. Since this job is part time, it allows me the time to try and get this book out, as well as the next four—I wrote these from 1989 to 1994—which will try to slow the numbers who will join my ranks.

From 1989 to 1994, after I had lost my first job and after I had received my certificate in gerontology from Long Beach State University, I began collecting notes for a book that I needed to write. This book contains everything that makes me, me. I didn't hold a thing back. Before I began writing this book, I spoke to an instructor at Cerritos College. The reason I had to speak to this English teacher was because, after a few days of collecting notes for this book, I realized that I would have to trample on a few toes to get my point across. I also realized I would offend some people, both by a lot of the words I would have to use, as well as a lot of the people I'd refer to. However, this professor told me everything I needed to set me free.

Yes, this professor, who has his doctorate in English, told me all I would have to do would be to pretend that everyone who I wrote about was dead. This was the best advice I could have gotten. After collecting notes for a year and a half, I bought a computer and began writing about dead people. I finished four years later, of almost daily work, and I finished a book that contained more than one thousand single-spaced pages. I wisely broke it up into four digestible sized books. The dead played an important part in my life.

After only a few years of married life . . .
Marriage really takes its toll

(Actually, a few years after their 50th aniversary --
My father's laughing in his grave)

My folks on a cruise in the Bahamas for their 50th Anniversary.

Made in the USA
San Bernardino, CA
10 January 2013